76

ADVANCED STATISTICAL METHODS
IN THE SOCIAL SCIENCES

Advanced Statistical Methods in the Social Sciences

Norman Schofield
Monojit Chatterji *and* Stephen Satchell
University of Essex

Paul Whiteley
University of Bristol

PRAEGER SPECIAL STUDIES • PRAEGER SCIENTIFIC

New York • Philadelphia • Eastbourne, UK
Toronto • Hong Kong • Tokyo • Sydney

Dedicated to the memory of Neil Gordon Schofield

**Published and Distributed by the
Praeger Publishers Division
(ISBN Prefix 0-275)
of Greenwood Press, Inc.,
Westport, Connecticut**

Published in 1986 by Praeger Publishers
CBS Educational and Professional Publishing
A Division of CBS, Inc.
521 Fifth Avenue, New York, New York 10175, USA

Library of Congress Cataloging-in-Publication Data

Main entry under title:
Advanced statistical methods in the social sciences.
   Bibliography: p.
   Includes index.
   1. Social sciences — Statistical methods.
2. Econometric models. I. Schofield, Norman, 1944–
HA29.A358   1986   300′.1′5195   85-28173

ISBN 0-03-007502-5

Photoset and printed in Malta
by Interprint Limited

Last digit is print no: 9 8 7 6 5 4 3 2 1

Foreword

The intention in writing this book was to make available a text that could be used by students following a series of courses in statistical methods in social science and economics that would start at quite an elementary level and progress to a fairly advanced undergraduate or graduate level in econometrics, with detailed applications in both economics and political economy.

The first part of the book develops the fundamentals of probability theory and bivariate regression. After the introductory Chapter 1 on sampling, Chapter 2 presents a self-contained development of the topics of matrix algebra and quadratic forms, which are important in setting up the general regression model. Chapter 3 is suitable for a final-year student of econometrics and introduces the general linear regression model and generalised least squares, etc.

The second part makes use of the statistical methodology developed in Part I to discuss a number of theoretical and substantive problems in estimation in economics. In particular, Chapter 5 is devoted to a careful econometric analysis of labour supply and unemployment, based on a classical paper by Lucas and Rapping (1969). Chapters 4 and 5 both contain extensive exercises for the students. The motivation underlining these two chapters is to help the student become aware of the theoretical problems in econometric estimation, and then to use this awareness in following through in detail how econometric theory and economic theory can be combined.

In the third part of the book, time series analysis is developed and applied to two examples: the relationship between money supply and the national income, and also the estimation of a 'political' popularity function in Britain.

Most of Part I of this volume has been taught by Norman Schofield or Paul Whiteley at the summer school on data analysis organised by the European Consortium for Political Research at Essex University over a number of years. Part II is based on a graduate course in econometrics taught by Monojit Chatterji and Stephen Satchell at Essex University.

The manuscript was prepared while Norman Schofield was the Sherman Fairchild

v

Distinguished Scholar at the California Institute of Technology. He is happy to acknowledge the generosity of the Fairchild programme and to express his appreciation of a grant from the Nuffield Foundation. We are all grateful to Linda Benjamin who worked so carefully on typing the manuscript at Caltech.

Norman Schofield
Monojit Chatterji
Stephen Satchell
Paul Whiteley

November 1985

About the Authors

Norman Schofield: Reader in Economics, University of Essex. Previously he has been Visiting Lecturer in Political Science (1973) at Yale University, and Associate Professor of Government, University of Texas at Austin (1976–1979). During 1982–1983 he was Hallsworth Fellow in Political Economy at Manchester University and in 1983–1985 was the Sherman Fairchild Distinguished Scholar and then Visiting Professor at California Institute of Technology. His fields of research include game theory, social choice, optimisation theory and political economy and he has published in these areas in a number of academic journals. He has recently published *Mathematical Methods in Economics* (New York University Press, 1984) and *Social Choice and Democracy* (Springer Verlag, 1985) and has edited books on international political economy and on data analysis.

Stephen Satchell: Lecturer in Economics, University of Essex. He took his undergraduate degree at the University of New South Wales, Australia, and his Ph.D. in Economics at LSE. He has worked in both economics and statistics departments at LSE and Essex University. His research interests and publications cover econometric theory, applied economics, economic demography and economic history. He has published articles in *Econometrica* and *Economic Theory*.

Monojit Chatterji: Lecturer in economics at the University of Essex. He has a B.A. in Economics from Bombay and B.A., M.A. and Ph.D. in Economics from Cambridge. He has been Visiting Associate Professor in Economics at the University of California, Davis. His fields of interest are macro-economics and applied econometrics, and he has published in these areas in *The Economic Journal, Economica, Journal of Public Economics, Journal of Macroeconomics,* and *Applied Economics.* He has taught undergraduate and graduate courses in macro-economics, econometrics and mathematical economics both at Essex and at Davis.

Paul Whiteley: Lecturer in Politics at Bristol University. He obtained his Ph.D. in Government from Essex. He has been Visiting Associate Professor at the University of Kentucky, Lexington and at the Virginia Polytechnic Institute and State University. He has edited *Models of Political Economy* (Sage, 1980), and is the author of *The Labour Party in Crisis* (Methuen, 1983) and has published various articles in the *British Journal of Political Science, Political Studies, Electoral Studies* and other academic journals.

Contents

Part I

Statistical Methods

Chapter 1

Sampling and Distribution Theory

In many experimental situations, the act of performing an experiment is equivalent to bringing into being, or selecting, an event from a population of events whose properties, in terms of probabilities etc., are unknown. The purpose of the experiment, or series of experiments, is to obtain information from the samples so obtained in order to infer some of the features that the population itself displays. In many cases the information that the experiment provides is in the form of a distribution of numbers associated with a variable that in some sense characterises the population under examination. For example, a set of responses to questions on political preferences from a subset of an electorate can give an indication of the actual distribution of political preferences in the electorate. However, to be able to make any inference about the population from the sample, we do have to suppose that there is some relationship between the two. The art of inference essentially depends on the assumption that the variable under question in the population obeys some statistical regularity, and further depends on the use of an indicator, derived from the information in the sample, to characterise this statistical regularity. The task is relatively easy when the 'statistical' structure of the population is well understood. In this chapter we consider the situation where the population under examination is known to have a statistical structure, but where the parameters of this structure are not known. In this case the purpose of sampling is to use information from the sample to obtain estimates of the population parameters.

1.1 INDEPENDENT TRIALS AND RANDOM VARIABLES

One way of setting up an experiment is to list, in exhaustive fashion, the set of all possible results of the experiment, in terms if possible of elementary events

$\{O_1, \ldots, O_N\}$ say. The most convenient situation that can occur is when we have reason to believe that each elementary event is as probable as another. In this case we may suppose that the probability of the occurrence of the elementary event O_i is

$$P(O_i) = \frac{1}{N} = p, \text{ say. The } \textit{probability } \text{associated with a more complex event, } C, \text{ is then}$$

$$P(C) = \frac{\#(C)}{N}, \text{ where } \#(C) \text{ is the number of elementary events in } C. \text{ Of course even in a}$$

simple coin-tossing experiment, it is an act of faith to suppose that the probability of heads is one-half. One of our intentions here is to show how experimental observations can assist in indicating the nature of the true probability of an event. Since we are emphasising the act of sampling here, we shall call the set of possible experimental events $\{O_1, \ldots, O_N\}$ the *sample space*, $\mathscr{S}$.

Suppose now that we form a compound experiment by performing the experiment twice. An elementary event for this experiment is of the form (O_i, O_j) where $O_i \in \mathscr{S}$ and $O_j \in \mathscr{S}$. Thus the sample space is

$$\mathscr{S} \times \mathscr{S} = \{(O_i, O_j): O_i \in \mathscr{S}, O_j \in \mathscr{S}\}$$

Another way of writing (O_i, O_j) is $(O_i, \mathscr{S}) \cap (\mathscr{S}, O_j)$ where this is the *intersection* (written $\cap$) of two events $(O_i, \mathscr{S})$ and $(\mathscr{S}, O_j)$. For the first event we know only that O_i occurred in the first experiment, and for the second event we know only that O_j occurred in the second experiment. Clearly $P((O_i, \mathscr{S})) = P(O_i)$ and $P((\mathscr{S}, O_j)) = P(O_j)$. Suppose now that for each O_i, O_j in $\mathscr{S}$, the result of the first experiment in no way affects the result of the second. In other words, suppose the two events $(O_i, \mathscr{S})$ and $(\mathscr{S}, O_j)$ are *independent*. Then

$$P((O_i, \mathscr{S}) \cap (\mathscr{S}, O_j)) = P((O_i, \mathscr{S})) P((\mathscr{S}, O_j))$$
$$= P(O_i) P(O_j)$$

In this case we say that the *trials* O_i and O_j are independent. Now consider an experiment where a coin is tossed *once*. Let H stand for the event when a head shows, and T stand for the event when a tail shows. If we let '$\rightharpoondown$' stand for negation, then clearly $\rightharpoondown H = T$ and $\rightharpoondown T = H$. Then in the experiment of a single toss of the coin the probability $P(H)$ of obtaining a head may be written $P(H) = p$. Since we may further assume that either a head or a tail occurs with probability 1, then

$$P(H) + P(\rightharpoondown H) = 1$$

and so

$$P(H) = p, \ P(\rightharpoondown H) = P(T) = (1 - p)$$

A compound event in the experiment of tossing a coin twice is then of the form (O_1, O_2) where O_1 and O_2 can be either H or T. Since we further assume the experiments are independent it is evident that

$$P((O_1, O_2)) = P((O_1, \mathscr{S}) \cap (\mathscr{S}, O_2))$$
$$= P((O_1, \mathscr{S})) P(\mathscr{S}, O_2)$$
$$= P(O_1) P(O_2)$$

In the case where there are but two possible independent results, O_1 and O_2, from the experiment with $P(O_1) = p$ and $P(O_2) = (1 - p)$, then the trial is called a *Bernoulli trial*. Obviously the single coin tossing experiment is a Bernoulli trial. If we toss the coin *twice* then there are four possible results (H, H), (H, T), (T, H), (T, T). Here (H, T) means for example that a head results from the first toss and a tail from the second. These four compound events have the obvious probabilities:

$$P((H, H)) = P(H)P(H) = p^2$$
$$P((H, T)) = P(H)P(T) = p(1 - p)$$
$$P((T, H)) = P(T)P(H) = (1 - p)p$$
$$P((T, T)) = P(T)P(T) = (1 - p)^2$$

More generally, if one of the events $\{O_1, \dots, O_N\}$ must occur, and each of these events is *disjoint*, or distinct, then we call $\{O_1, \dots, O_N\}$ a (disjoint) *partition* of $\mathscr{S}$. In this case it is evident that

$$\sum_{i=1}^{N} P(O_i) = 1$$

In the compound (two experiments) case it is evident that

$$\{(H, H), (H, T), (T, H), (T, T)\}$$

is a partition of $\mathscr{S} \times \mathscr{S}$, and thus

$$p^2 + 2p(1 - p) + (1 - p)^2 = 1$$

Suppose that we know that in the compound experiment the trials are indeed independent. Let C_1, C_2, both in $\mathscr{S}$, be complex trials made up in each case of a set of elementary events from $\mathscr{S}$. Let E_1 be the event in $\mathscr{S} \times \mathscr{S}$ in which we know that C_1 occurred in the first trial, and let E_2 be the event in $\mathscr{S} \times \mathscr{S}$ in which we know C_2 occurred in the second trial. The compound event $C_1 \times C_2$ belongs to $\mathscr{S} \times \mathscr{S}$ and $P(E_1 \cap E_2) = P(C_1 \times C_2)$. Moreover if O_i and O_k belong to C_1, and O_j belongs to C_2, then we know that (O_i, O_j) and (O_k, O_j) are disjoint compound events.

Thus $P(C_1 \times C_2) = \sum P(O_i, O_j)$ where the summation is over all O_i in C_1, and O_j in C_2. Moreover $P(O_i, O_j) = P(O_i)P(O_j)$, since the trials are independent.

Thus

$$P(C_1 \times C_2) = \sum_{i,j} P(O_i)P(O_j)$$

$$= \sum_i \left(\sum_j P(O_j) \right) P(O_i)$$

But since the elementary events must be disjoint

$$P(C_1) = \sum_i P(O_i) \text{ and } P(C_2) = \sum_j P(O_j)$$

where the summation over i means for all O_i in C_1, and similarly the summation over j means for all O_j in C_2.

Thus $\qquad P(C_1 \times C_2) = P(C_1)P(C_2)$

However $P(E_1) = P(C_1 \times \mathcal{S}) = P(C_1)$

and $P(E_2) = P(\mathcal{S} \times C_2) = P(C_2)$

Thus $P(E_1 \cap E_2) = P(C_1 \times C_2) = P(C_1)P(C_2)$
$$= P(E_1)P(E_2)$$

Thus the events E_1 and E_2 are *independent*. We also say that the trials C_1 and C_2 are independent. Note that the events E_1 and E_2 are defined in terms of the first and second experiments respectively, and that, as a result of the independence of the trials, the events themselves are independent. Below we shall consider events which are defined in terms of results from more than one trial, and in this case compound events need not be independent.

Suppose now that, to each elementary event that occurs as the result of an experiment, we may measure some aspect of the event. That is to say we may obtain a reading of a real number x_j, say, from each elementary event O_i in $\mathcal{S}$. This defines a function, or *random variable*,

$$X: \mathcal{S} \to \mathbf{R}$$

For each value x_j in $\mathbf{R}$, let

$$\mathcal{S}_j = \{O_i \in \mathcal{S} : X(O_i) = x_j\}$$

Suppose for example that $\{x_1, \ldots, x_r\}$ are the possible values that the random variable may take.

Clearly $\{\mathcal{S}_1, \ldots, \mathcal{S}_r\}$ forms a disjoint partition of the sample space $\mathcal{S}$, since we suppose that for each $O_i \in \mathcal{S}_j$, we obtain only one reading. Now define $P(X = x_j)$ to be probability associated with the set $\mathcal{S}_j$, that is

$$P(X = x_j) = P(\{O_i \in \mathcal{S}_j\}) = \sum_{O_i \in \mathcal{S}_j} P(O_i)$$

This probability we write as $f(x_j)$. The function $f: \mathbf{R} \to [0, 1]$ is called the *probability distribution* (pd) of the *random variable X*.

Since $\{\mathcal{S}_1, \ldots, \mathcal{S}_r\}$ is a disjoint partition

$$1 = \sum_{j=1}^{r} P(\mathcal{S}_j) = \sum_{j=1}^{r} f(x_j)$$

Suppose now that two random variables X, Y are defined on the same sample space $\mathcal{S}$. For each value x_j of X and y_k of Y let

$$\mathcal{S}_j = \{O_i : X(O_i) = x_j\} \text{ and } \mathcal{T}_k = \{O_i : Y(O_i) = y_k\}.$$

Clearly $\{..\mathcal{S}_j..\}$ and $\{..\mathcal{T}_k..\}$ form disjoint partitions of $\mathcal{S}$. Let f and g be the probability distributions for X and Y, i.e., for each j, k, $f(x_j) = P(\mathcal{S}_j)$ and $g(y_k) = P(\mathcal{T}_k)$.

Define the *joint probability distribution* of X and Y to be $h: R \times R \to [0, 1]$ given by $h(x_j, y_k) = P(X = x_j, Y = y_k) = P(\mathcal{S}_j \cap \mathcal{T}_k)$. Suppose for example that X, Y may take a finite number of values $x_1, \ldots, x_r$ and $y_1, \ldots, y_m$ respectively.

Then
$$\sum_{k=1}^{m} h(x_j, y_k) = \sum_{k=1}^{m} P(\mathcal{S}_j \cap \mathcal{T}_k)$$

Now $\{\mathcal{T}_1, \ldots, \mathcal{T}_m\}$ forms a disjoint partition of $\mathcal{S}$ and so $\{\mathcal{S}_j \cap \mathcal{T}_1, \ldots, \mathcal{S}_j \cap \mathcal{T}_m\}$ is a disjoint partition of $\mathcal{S}_j$. Thus

$$P(\mathcal{S}_j) = \sum_{k=1}^{m} P(\mathcal{S}_j \cap \mathcal{T}_k)$$

and
$$\sum_{k=1}^{m} h(x_j, y_k) = P(\mathcal{S}_j) = f(x_j).$$

In the same way $\sum_{j=1}^{r} h(x_j, y_k) = P(\mathcal{T}_k) = g(y_k).$

If it is the case that

$$h(x_j, y_k) = f(x_j) g(y_k)$$

for all $j = 1, \ldots, r$ and all $k = 1, \ldots, m$ then the two random variables X and Y are said to be *independent*.

More generally the sample space under consideration may be generated by a series of experiments. For example, suppose $\mathcal{S}$ is the sample space associated with one experiment. If the experiment is performed n times, so that no one experiment affects the population being examined, then the sample space for the compound experiment is

$$\mathcal{S}^n = \mathcal{S} \times \cdots \times \mathcal{S}$$

A random variable $X : \mathcal{S}^n \to \mathbf{R}$ can then be defined, just as before, on the compound sample space $\mathcal{S}^n$. Very often the compound sample space consists of sequences of Bernoulli trials, and the random variable is defined as a sum of random variables defined on the single sample space.

For example consider an experiment consisting of n Bernoulli trials. For each trial there are two outcomes O_+, O_-, called *success* and *failure* with probabilities p, $(1 - p)$ respectively. On the ith trial let X_i be the random variable which has value $+1$ if event O_+ occurs, and 0 if event O_- occurs. Clearly X_i has probability distribution given by

$$f_i(0) = (1 - p)$$
$$f_i(1) = p$$

Now let Y be the random variable defined on $\mathcal{S}^n$ by

$$Y(O_1, \ldots, O_n) = \sum_{i=1}^{n} X_i(O_i)$$

That is to say the value of Y on the compound elementary event $(O_1, \ldots, O_n)$ is simply the number of successes out of the n trials. Suppose then that we choose a value r between 0 and n. Let g be the probability distribution of Y. By definition $g(r) = P(Y = r) = P\left(\sum_{i=1}^{n} X_i = r\right)$. Since all of the trials are independent, the probability $P(X_i = 1)$ is independent of i. It should be clear that the probability $P(Y = r)$

is simply the product of the probability of obtaining exactly r successes out of n in a particular sequence [i.e., $p^r(1-p)^{n-r}$] times $C(n,r)$. Here $C(n,r)$ is the number of ways of picking r successes exactly (i.e., with $(n-r)$ failures) out of n attempts. This number is sometimes written $\binom{n}{r}$. Thus $g(r) = P(Y = r) = C(n,r)\ p^r(1-p)^{n-r}$.

To see how to compute $C(n,r)$, the number of *combinations* of r from n, we first introduce perm (n,r), the number of *permutations* of r objects from n. Clearly perm $(n,n) = n(n-1)(n-2)\ldots 1$ since we may pick the first object in n ways, the second in $(n-1)$ ways, etc. (perm (n,n) is generally written $n!$ and called factorial n.) In the same way

$$\text{perm}(n,\ r) = n(n-1)\ldots(n-r+1)$$

$$= \frac{n!}{(n-r)!}$$

$C(n,r)$ is different from perm(n,r) since in the former we are uninterested in the order in which the successes occurred, but only interested in the occurrence of exactly r of them. Since there are perm$(r,r) = r!$ ways of ordering r events, clearly

$$C(n,r) = \frac{\text{perm}(n,r)}{\text{perm}(r,r)} = \frac{n!}{(n-r)!r!}$$

If we let $\mathscr{S}_r$ be the subset of $\mathscr{S}^n$ such that $Y = r$, then clearly $\{\mathscr{S}_0,\ldots,\mathscr{S}_n\}$ forms a disjoint partition of $\mathscr{S}^n$. Thus we require

$$\sum_{r=0}^{n} C(n,r)\ p^r(1-p)^{n-r} = 1$$

Suppose we now define a second random variable Y say on the same sample space $\mathscr{S}^n$, with probability distribution g, where Y can take values $\{0,\ldots,y\}$. Then as before we can define the joint probability distribution of X and Y to be $h(x,y) = P(X = x, Y = y)$ and determine whether X and Y are independent.

Example 1.1

Consider the compound experiment of tossing a *fair* coin (i.e., $p = \frac{1}{2}$) three times. Let Y be the random variable, whose values are the number of heads obtained in the three trials, and whose probability distribution is g. Let X be the random variable which has value 1 if the first toss shows a head and 0 if the first toss shows a tail. The sample space for each trial is $\{T, H\}$ so the sample space for the compound experiment is $\mathscr{S} = \{T, H\}^3$. Since X is defined on the first experiment only we expect

$$f(0) = P(X = 0) = \tfrac{1}{2}$$
$$f(1) = P(X = 1) = \tfrac{1}{2}$$

since the coin is fair. We obtain the following array.

$$
\begin{array}{c|c|c|c}
TTT & Y=0 & g(0)=\frac18 & X=0\\
TTH & & & X=0\\
THT & \}\,Y=1 & g(1)=\frac38 & X=0\\
HTT & & & X=1\\
THH & & & X=0\\
HTH & \}\,Y=2 & g(2)=\frac38 & X=1\\
HHT & & & X=1\\
HHH & Y=3 & g(3)=\frac18 & X=1
\end{array}
$$

Note that in four of the eight cases we obtain $X=1$ and so $f(1)=\frac12$ as expected. The joint probability distribution is given by Table 1.1.

Table 1.1

x \ y	0	1	2	3	$P(X=x)$
0	$\frac18$	$\frac14$	$\frac18$	0	$\frac12$
1	0	$\frac18$	$\frac14$	$\frac18$	$\frac12$
$P(Y=y)$	$\frac18$	$\frac38$	$\frac38$	$\frac18$	1

Note that $h(1,1)=P(X=1,Y=1)$
$$=\frac18$$

but

$$P(X=1)P(Y=1)=f(1)g(1)=\frac12\cdot\frac38=\frac{3}{16}$$

Thus the two random variables are not independent.

1.2 THE EXPECTATION AND VARIANCE OPERATORS

Let $\mathscr{S}$ be a sample space and suppose that X is a random variable which can take a finite number of different values $\{x_1,\ldots,x_j,\ldots\}$ say. If X has a probability distribution f, then the *expected value*, or mean, of the random variable X is written $E(X)$ and defined by

$$E(X)=\sum_j x_j f(x_j)$$

Suppose now that Y is a random variable, defined on the same sample space $\mathscr{S}$, which again can take a finite number of values $\{y_1,\ldots,y_k,\ldots\}$, and which has probability distribution g. Again the expected value of Y is

$$E(Y)=\sum_k y_k g(y_k)$$

We may now define a new random variable Z on $\mathscr{S}$ by defining the value of Z on any elementary event O, say, in $\mathscr{S}$ to be

$$Z(O) = X(O) + Y(O)$$

Clearly Z can then take on a finite number of values

$$\{x_1 + y_1, x_1 + y_2, \ldots, x_j + y_k, \ldots\}$$

Moreover the probability distribution r of Z is given by

$$r(z_i) = P(Z = z_i) = P(X = x_j, \ Y = y_k \text{ and } x_j + y_k = z_i)$$

But $P(X = x_j, \ Y = y_k) = h(x_j, y_k)$ where h is the joint probability distribution of X and Y. Thus

$$r(z_i) = \sum_{x_j + y_k = z_i} h(x_j, y_k)$$

The expected value of Z is then

$$E(Z) = \sum_{\text{all } i} z_i r(z_i)$$

$$= \sum_{\text{all } i} \left(\sum_{x_j + y_k = z_i} (x_j + y_k) h(x_j, y_k) \right)$$

Now consider

$$\sum_i \sum_{x_j + y_k = z_i} z_i h(x_j, y_k) = \sum_i \sum_{x_j + y_k = z_i} x_j h(x_j, y_k) + \sum_i \sum_{x_j + y_k = z_i} y_k h(x_j, y_k)$$

$$= \sum_{j,k} x_j h(x_j, y_k) + \sum_{j,k} y_k h(x_j, y_k)$$

But

$$\sum_k h(x_j, y_k) = f(x_j) \text{ and } \sum_j h(x_j, y_k) = g(y_j)$$

Thus

$$E(Z) = \sum_j x_j f(x_j) + \sum_k y_k g(y_k)$$

$$= E(X) + E(Y)$$

Given two random variables X, Y on a sample space $\mathscr{S}$ we may define a new random variable by combining the variables X, Y in any way we choose, or by functions such as $\exp X$ or $\log_e X$ of one or the other. For example, if we choose $Z = XY$ then the probability distribution, r, for Z is simply

$$r(z_i) = \sum_{x_j y_k = z_i} h(x_j, y_k)$$

In general the expectation operator E is *linear* in the sense that

$$E(X + Y) = E(X) + E(Y)$$

for any random variables X, Y. However, it is generally the case that

$$E(XY) \neq E(X)E(X)$$

as the following example illustrates.

Example 1.2

Consider Example 1.1 again of the experiment of tossing a coin three times. Y is the number of heads obtained, and X is 1 or 0 depending on whether a head or tail is obtained in the first toss. As we have already shown the random variables X, Y are not independent. The probability distributions f, g for X, Y respectively and the joint probability distribution, h, are given, as before, by Table 1.2.

Table 1.2

y	0	1	2	3	$P(X = x)$
x					
0	$\frac{1}{8}$	$\frac{1}{4}$	$\frac{1}{8}$	0	$\frac{1}{2}$
1	0	$\frac{1}{8}$	$\frac{1}{4}$	$\frac{1}{8}$	$\frac{1}{2}$
$P(Y = y)$	$\frac{1}{8}$	$\frac{3}{8}$	$\frac{3}{8}$	$\frac{1}{8}$	1

Let

$$Z = X + Y$$

Then

$$P(Z = 0) = P(X = 0, Y = 0) = \tfrac{1}{8}$$
$$P(Z = 1) = P(X = 0, Y = 1) + P(X = 1, Y = 0) = \tfrac{1}{4}$$
$$P(Z = 2) = P(X = 0, Y = 2) + P(X = 1, Y = 1) = \tfrac{1}{8} + \tfrac{1}{8} = \tfrac{1}{4}$$
$$P(Z = 3) = P(X = 0, Y = 3) + P(X = 1, Y = 2) = 0 + \tfrac{1}{4} = \tfrac{1}{4}$$
$$P(Z = 4) = P(X = 1, Y = 3) = \tfrac{1}{8}$$

Thus

$$E(Z) = 0 \cdot \tfrac{1}{8} + 1 \cdot \tfrac{1}{4} + 2 \cdot \tfrac{1}{4} + 3 \cdot \tfrac{1}{4} + 4 \cdot \tfrac{1}{8} = 2$$

Now

$$E(X) = \tfrac{1}{2} \cdot 0 + \tfrac{1}{2} \cdot 1 = \tfrac{1}{2}$$
$$E(Y) = \tfrac{1}{8} \cdot 0 + \tfrac{3}{8} \cdot 1 + \tfrac{3}{8} \cdot 2 + \tfrac{1}{8} \cdot 3 = \tfrac{12}{8} = \tfrac{3}{2}$$

Thus

$$E(Z) = E(X) + E(Y)$$

Suppose now we define $Z = XY$.

$$P(Z = 0) = P(X = 0, Y = 0, 1, 2, 3) + P(X = 1, Y = 0)$$
$$= \tfrac{1}{2} + 0$$
$$P(Z = 1) = P(X = 1, Y = 1) = \tfrac{1}{8}$$
$$P(Z = 2) = P(X = 1, Y = 2) = \tfrac{1}{4}$$
$$P(Z = 3) = P(X = 1, Y = 3) = \tfrac{1}{8}$$

Hence

$$E(XY) = 0 \cdot \tfrac{1}{2} + 1 \cdot \tfrac{1}{8} + 2 \cdot \tfrac{1}{4} + 3 \cdot \tfrac{1}{8}$$
$$= 0 + \tfrac{1}{8} + \tfrac{1}{2} + \tfrac{3}{8} = 1$$

But

$$E(X)E(Y) = \tfrac{1}{2} \cdot \tfrac{3}{2} = \tfrac{3}{4}$$

Hence

$$E(XY) \neq E(X)E(Y) \text{ in general.}$$

We can show that the expectation operator is linear, in the following way. First of all, for any real constant a, and random variable X on the sample space $\mathscr{S}$, define the new random variable $Z = X + a$ in the obvious way by defining $Z(O_i)$, for any elementary event O_i in $\mathscr{S}$, to be $X(O_i) + a$.

Then

$$E(Z) = E(X + a) = \sum_{j=1} (x_j f(x_j) + af(x_j))$$

$$= a \sum_{j=1} f(x_j) + \sum_{j=1}^{M} x_j f(x_j)$$

$$= a + E(X) \qquad \text{as} \quad \sum f(x_j) = 1.$$

If we define $Z = aX$, by $Z(O_i) = aX(O_i)$, then

$$E(Z) = E(aX) = \sum_{j=1} ax_j f(x_j)$$

$$= a \sum_{j=1} x_j f(x_j)$$

$$= aE(X)$$

In general then

1. $E(X + Y) = E(X) + E(Y)$

2. $E(X + a) = E(X) + a$

3. $E(aX) = aE(X)$

More briefly we can write $E(aX + bY) = aE(X) + bE(Y)$. Because of this property, E is known as a *linear operator*. Suppose we define $Z = XY$. Then

$$E(Z) = \sum_{\text{all } z_i} \sum_{x_j + y_k = z_i} (x_j y_k) h(x_j, y_k)$$

$$= \sum_{j, k} (x_j y_k) h(x_j, y_k)$$

Suppose that X and Y are independent. Then $h(x_j, y_k) = f(x_j)g(y_k)$, so

$$E(Z) = \sum_{j, k} x_j y_k f(x_j) g(y_k)$$

$$= \left(\sum_j x_j f(x_j) \right) \left(\sum_k y_k f(y_k) \right)$$

$$= E(X)E(Y)$$

Thus if X, Y are independent $E(XY) = E(X)E(Y)$.

Now define the *covariance* between the random variables X, Y to be

$$\text{cov}(X, Y) = E(XY) - E(X)E(Y)$$

Another way of expressing this is

$$\text{cov}(X, Y) = E[(X - E(X))(Y - E(Y))]$$

To see this note that

$$E[(X - E(X))(Y - E(Y))]$$

$$= E[(XY - YE(X) - XE(Y) + E(X)E(Y)]$$

But $E(X), E(Y)$ are real numbers. Since E is linear the expression reduces to:

$$E(XY) - E(X)E(Y) - E(X)E(Y) + E(X)E(Y)$$

$$= E(XY) - E(X)E(Y) = \text{cov}(X, Y)$$

Clearly when X and Y are independent, then $\text{cov}(X, Y) = 0$.

To illustrate, in Example 1.2, we showed that $E(XY) = 1$ although $E(X)E(Y) = \frac{3}{4}$. Thus $\text{cov}(X, Y) = 1 - \frac{3}{4} = \frac{1}{4}$. This corroborates our previous observation that the two random variables are not independent. Note also that the covariance between X and Y is positive. To see what this implies, consider the probability that $Y = 1, 2$ or 3 given that $X = 1$. Now if $X = 1$ then there are four possibilities, namely $Y = 0$ with probability 0, $Y = 1$ with probability $\frac{1}{8}$, $Y = 2$ with probability $\frac{1}{4}$ and $Y = 3$ with probability $\frac{1}{8}$. Thus the probability that $Y = 1$ *given* that $X = 1$ is

$$\frac{\frac{1}{8}}{\frac{1}{8} + \frac{1}{4} + \frac{1}{8}} = \frac{\frac{1}{8}}{\frac{1}{2}} = \frac{1}{4}$$

This *conditional probability* that $Y = 1$ given that $X = 1$ is also written

$$P(Y = 1/X = 1)$$

It is evident that $P(X = 1) = 0 + \frac{1}{8} + \frac{1}{4} + \frac{1}{8}$ in this example, and so we see that

$$P(Y = 1/X = 1) = \frac{P(Y = 1 \text{ and } X = 1)}{P(X = 1)}$$

We elaborate this in section 1.4 below. Thus the conditional probabilities for Y given that $X = 1$ are as follows.

$$P(Y = 1/X = 1) = \frac{P(Y = 1, X = 1)}{P(X = 1)} = \frac{\frac{1}{8}}{\frac{1}{2}} = \frac{1}{4}$$

which is less than $P(Y = 1)$.

$$P(Y = 2/X = 1) = \frac{P(Y = 2, X = 1)}{P(X = 1)} = \frac{\frac{1}{4}}{\frac{1}{2}} = \frac{1}{2}$$

which is greater than $P(Y = 2)$.

$$P(Y = 3/X = 1) = \frac{P(Y = 3, X = 1)}{P(X = 1)} = \frac{\frac{1}{8}}{\frac{1}{2}} = \frac{1}{4}$$

which is greater than $P(Y = 3)$.

In other words the conditional probabilities, that Y takes on the higher values (2 or 3) given that X has a high value (i.e., 1), are greater than the unconditonal probabilities for Y. That is to say, as X increases, Y has a tendency to increase as well, and so X and Y are positively related, or *correlated*. Clearly if $X = Y$ then they are not simply dependent, but positively dependent. Suppose on the other hand that X and Y are *dependent* in the sense that for each x_j there is only one y_k with $h(x_j, y_k) \neq 0$, and all other $h(x_i, y)$ are zero. Then we should expect $\text{cov}(X, Y)$ to be a 'maximum' in some sense. If X and Y tend to increase together, then we expect $\text{cov}(x, y)$ to be positive, and if X decreases as Y increases then we expect $\text{cov}(X, Y)$ to be negative.

Example 1.3

Consider Example 1.2 again and let Y be the number of heads again, but this time let X be the number of tails. In this case we obtain the *frequency* distribution shown in Table 1.3.

Table 1.3

	Y	X
TTT	0	3
TTH	1	2
THT	1	2
HTT	1	2
THH	2	1
HTH	2	1
HHT	2	1
HHH	3	0

The joint probability function is then given by Table 1.4.

Table 1.4

x \ y	0	1	2	3	$f(x)$
0	0	0	0	$\frac{1}{8}$	$\frac{1}{8}$
1	0	0	$\frac{3}{8}$	0	$\frac{3}{8}$
2	0	$\frac{3}{8}$	0	0	$\frac{3}{8}$
3	$\frac{1}{8}$	0	0	0	$\frac{1}{8}$
$g(y)$	$\frac{1}{8}$	$\frac{3}{8}$	$\frac{3}{8}$	$\frac{1}{8}$	

In other words

$$h(0,3) = \tfrac{1}{8} \text{ and } h(0,1) = h(0,2) = h(0,0) = 0$$
$$h(1,2) = \tfrac{3}{8} \text{ and } h(1,0) = h(1,1) = h(1,3) = 0$$
$$h(2,1) = \tfrac{3}{8} \text{ and } h(2,0) = h(2,2) = h(2,3) = 0$$
$$h(3,0) = \tfrac{1}{8} \text{ and } h(3,1) = h(3,2) = h(3,3) = 0$$

Here we see that $h(x_j, y_k) = f(x_j) = g(y_k)$ if $x_j + y_k = 3$, and zero otherwise. In this example clearly

$$E(X) = E(Y) = \tfrac{3}{2}$$

However,

$$E(XY) = \sum (xy)h(xy)$$
$$= (0 \cdot 3)\tfrac{1}{8} + (1 \cdot 2)\tfrac{3}{8} + (2 \cdot 1)\tfrac{3}{8} + (3 \cdot 0)\tfrac{1}{8}$$
$$= \tfrac{3}{2}$$

Thus

$$\text{cov}(X,Y) = E(XY) - E(X)E(Y)$$
$$= \tfrac{3}{2} - \tfrac{3}{2} \cdot \tfrac{3}{2} = \tfrac{6}{4} - \tfrac{9}{4} = -\tfrac{3}{4}$$

Note that cov $(Y,Y) = E(Y^2) - E(Y)^2$.

Since

$$E(Y^2) = (0)\tfrac{1}{8} + (1 \cdot 1)\tfrac{3}{8} + (2 \cdot 2)\tfrac{3}{8} + (3 \cdot 3)\tfrac{1}{8}$$
$$= 3$$

and

$$E(Y) = \tfrac{3}{2} \text{ as in Example 1.2,}$$

we find that $\text{cov}(Y, Y) = 3 - \tfrac{9}{4} = \tfrac{3}{4}$.

Thus if the two random variables are not only dependent but positively dependent then the covariance has a maximum value, which in this case is $\tfrac{3}{4}$. This value of $\text{cov}(Y,Y)$ is also known as the *variance* of Y. On the other hand the variable X in our example is perfectly, but negatively, dependent on Y, and in this case

$$\text{cov}(X,Y) = -\tfrac{3}{4} = -\text{cov}(X,X)$$

The *variance* of a random variable X is defined to be

$$\text{var}(X) = E((X - E(X))^2) = \sum_{j=1} (x_j - E(X))^2 f(x_j)$$

Now

$$(x_j - E(X))^2 = x_j^2 + E(X)^2 - 2x_j E(X)$$

Let us write

$$E(X) = \mu_x$$

Then

$$\begin{aligned}
\text{var}(X) &= E((X - \mu_x)^2) \\
&= \sum (x_j^2 + \mu_x^2 - 2x_j\mu_x) f(x_j) \\
&= E(X^2) + \mu_x^2 - 2\mu_x \sum x_j f(x_j) \\
&= E(X^2) - \mu_x^2
\end{aligned}$$

We defined

$$\text{cov}(X, Y) = E(XY) - E(X)E(Y)$$

so

$$\text{cov}(X, X) = E(X^2) - \mu_x^2 = \text{var}(X)$$

For example suppose $Z = X + Y$. Then

$$\text{var}(X + Y) = E(((X + Y) - E(X + Y))^2)$$

But

$$E(X + Y) = E(X) + E(Y)$$

so

$$\begin{aligned}
\text{var}(X + Y) &= E((X + Y - \mu_x - \mu_y)^2) \\
&= E(((X - \mu_x) + (Y - \mu_y))^2) \\
&= E((X - \mu_x)^2 + (Y - \mu_x)^2 + 2(X - \mu_x)(Y - \mu_y)) \\
&= \text{var}(X) + \text{var}(Y) + 2\text{cov}(X, Y)
\end{aligned}$$

If X,Y are independent, then $\text{cov}(X,Y) = 0$. In this case $\text{var}(X + Y) = \text{var}(X) + \text{var}(Y)$.

Now let $Z = aX$, for some constant a. Then

$$\begin{aligned}
\text{var}(aX) &= E((aX - E(aX))^2) \\
&= E((aX - a\mu_x)^2) \\
&= E(a^2(X - \mu_x)^2) \\
&= a^2 E((X - \mu_x)^2) = a^2\text{var}(X).
\end{aligned}$$

Generally if $Z = aX + bY$, then

$$\text{var}(Z) = a^2 \, \text{var}(X) + b^2 \, \text{var}(Y) + 2ab \, \text{cov}(X, Y)$$

Example 1.4

Consider the example of the three coin-tossing trials again. The relationship between the random variable Y (number of heads) and X (number of tails) is $Y + X = 3$. That is to say, for any elementary event $O_i \in \mathcal{S}$ it is the case that $Y(O_i) + X(O_i) = 3$. Now consider $E(XY)$. Since $Y + X = 3$ we may write $X = 3 - Y$ and so

$$E(XY) = E[(3 - Y)Y] = E[3Y - Y^2]$$
$$= 3E(Y) - E(Y^2)$$

since E is linear.

But
$$\text{cov}(X, Y) = E(XY) - E(X)E(Y)$$
$$= 3E(Y) - E(Y^2) - E(3 - Y)E(Y)$$
$$= 3E(Y) - E(Y^2) - 3E(Y) + E(Y)^2,$$

since E is linear and $E(3) = 3$.
Thus

$$\text{cov}(X, Y) = E(Y)^2 - E(Y^2)$$

However, as we have seen

$$\text{var}(Y) = \text{cov}(Y, Y) = E(Y^2) - E(Y)^2$$

Thus

$$\text{cov}(X, Y) = - \text{var}(Y)$$

Another way of showing this more generally is to note that for any constant a, it is the case that $E(a) = a$. Thus $\text{var}(a) = E[(a - E(a))^2] = E(0) = 0$. Suppose that X is a random variable defined so that $X + Y = a$. By definition

$$\text{cov}(a, Y) = E(aY) - E(a)E(Y)$$

Since E is linear, $E(aY) = aE(Y)$ and so $\text{cov}(a, Y) = 0$. Moreover, since $X = a - Y$,

$$\text{var}(X) = \text{var}(a - Y) = \text{var}(a) + \text{var}(-Y) + 2\text{cov}(a, -Y)$$

However, $\text{var}(-Y) = E(Y^2) - E(-Y)^2 = \text{var}(Y)$ and $\text{cov}(a, -Y) = 0$. Thus $\text{var}(X) = \text{var}(a - Y) = 0 + \text{var}(-Y) = \text{var}(Y)$.
  Finally we have established that

$$\text{var}(X + Y) = \text{var}(a) = 0$$
$$= \text{var}(X) + \text{var}(Y) + 2\text{cov}(X, Y)$$
$$= 2\text{var}(Y) + 2\text{cov}(X, Y)$$

Thus when $X + Y = a$, $\text{cov}(X, Y) = -\text{var}(Y)$. This establishes (i) the variance of a constant (*a*) is zero, (ii) the covariance of a random variable *Y* with a constant is zero. Note also that if *X* and *Y* were *positively* dependent, in the sense that $X - Y = a$, for some constant *a*, then in precisely the same way we can show that

$$\text{var}(X - Y) = 2\text{var}(Y) - 2\text{cov}(X,Y)$$

so that $\text{cov}(X,Y) = \text{cov}(Y) = \text{cov}(X)$.

Suppose finally that $X = aY$. In this case clearly

$$\text{cov}(X,Y) = \text{cov}(aY, Y) = E(aY^2) - aE(Y)^2$$
$$= a\,\text{var}(Y)$$

Even though *X* and *Y* are completely dependent, the covariance between them is a multiple of the variance of *Y*.

For this reason it is convenient to *normalise* the covariance and define what is known as the *correlation*, r(*x*, *y*), between *X* and *Y* as

$$r(X,Y) = \frac{\text{cov}(X,Y)}{\sqrt{\text{var}(X)\,\text{var}(Y)}}$$

For example in the case $X = aY$ then $\text{var}(X) = a^2\,\text{var}(Y)$ and $\text{cov}(X,Y) = a\,\text{var}(Y)$, so that $r(X,Y) = \dfrac{a\,\text{var}(Y)}{\sqrt{a^2\,\text{var}(Y)\,\text{var}(Y)}} = +1$. In similar fashion, suppose $X - Y = a$. As we have shown $\text{cov}(X,Y) = \text{cov}(Y) = \text{cov}(X)$ and so again $r(X,Y) = +1$. However, consider the case of negative dependence where $X + Y = a$. As we have shown $\text{var}(X) = \text{var}(Y)$ and $\text{cov}(X,Y) = -\text{var}(Y)$. Thus $r(X,Y) = \dfrac{-\text{var}(Y)}{\sqrt{\text{var}(X)^2}} = -1$. It should be clear that the correlation $r(X,Y)$ must lie in the range $[-1,1]$. In the case $r(X,Y) = -1$ the two random variables are perfectly, but *negatively* dependent, while in the case $r(X,X) = 1$ the two variables are perfectly, but positively dependent.

Note also that the two situations $X = aY$ and $X - Y = a$ both give a correlation $r(X,Y) = 1$, and so the correlation itself does not indicate the nature of the dependence between the two random variables.

Finally, a convenient notation for $\text{var}(X)$ is σ_x^2 where σ_x is called the *standard deviation* in the random variable *X*.

The expected value, $E(X)$, of *X* is often written μ_x.

With this notation

$$r(X,Y) = \frac{\text{cov}(X,Y)}{\sigma_x\sigma_y} = \frac{E(XY) - \mu_x\mu_y}{\sigma_x\sigma_y}$$
$$= \frac{\mu_{xy} - \mu_x\mu_y}{\sigma_x\sigma_y}$$

Example 1.5

In the coin-tossing experiment, we have already shown that

$$\text{var}(X) = \text{var}(Y) = \tfrac{3}{4}, \mu_x = \mu_y = \tfrac{3}{2}$$

while

$$\text{cov}(X,Y) = \mu_{xy} - \mu_x\mu_y = \tfrac{3}{2} - (\tfrac{3}{2})^2 = -\tfrac{3}{4}$$

Thus

$$r(X,Y) = \frac{-\tfrac{3}{4}}{\sqrt{\tfrac{3}{4}\cdot\tfrac{3}{4}}} = -1$$

More generally, suppose that X and Y are two random variables defined on a sample space in such a way that $Y = aX + b$, for some constants a, b. Then X, Y are dependent and the joint probability function, h, satisfies

$$h(X, Y) \neq 0 \text{ if and only if } y = ax + b$$

in which case $h(x, ax + b) = f(x)$, where f is the probability function for X.

Clearly

$$E(XY) = \sum_x x(ax + b)f(x)$$
$$= a\sum_x x^2 f(x) + b\sum_x xf(x)$$
$$= aE(X^2) + bE(X)$$

Also

$$E(Y) = aE(X) + b, \text{ since E is linear}$$

Thus

$$\text{cov}(X, Y) = E(XY) - E(X)E(Y)$$
$$= aE(X^2) + bE(X) - (aE(X) + b)E(X)$$
$$= a[E(X^2) - E(X)^2]$$
$$= a\,\text{var}(X)$$

Similarly

$$\text{var}(Y) = \text{var}(aX + b) = a^2\,\text{var}(X)$$

Thus

$$r(X, Y) = \frac{a\,\text{var}(X)}{\sqrt{a^2\,\text{var}(X)\,\text{var}(X)}} = \pm 1$$

depending on whether a is positive or negative.

1.3 THE BINOMIAL DISTRIBUTION

Consider once again the Bernoulli experiment of replicating n times an experiment which on each trial has probability p of success. For any elementary event $\{O_1, \ldots, O_n\}$

in this compound experiment define the random variable X_i on the sample space $\mathscr{S}^n$ by

$$X_i(\{O_1,\ldots,O_n\}) = X(O_i)$$

where X is the random variable which gives a reading 1 if O_i is a success and 0 otherwise.

Clearly

$$P(X = 1) = p \text{ and } P(X = 0) = (1 - p) \text{ and so}$$
$$E(X) = 1 \cdot p + 0(1 - p) = p$$

Since the trials are assumed to be independent the random variable X_i also has expected value p. An outcome of this experiment is a vector of the form $(0,\ldots,1,.0)$ with 0 or 1 in the ith place depending on whether a success or failure occurred on the ith trial. The probability distribution f_i for X_i then takes the following form.

Let $x = (x_1,\ldots,x_n)$ be defined by $x_i = 1$ if the ith trial is a success, and $x_i = 0$ if the ith trial is a failure.

For any $x = (x_1,\ldots,x_n)$ let $f_i(x) = p \qquad$ if and only if $x_i = 1$
$$(1 - p) \text{ if and only if } x_i = 0$$

The expected value of X_i is clearly the same as X, i.e.

$$E(X_i) = \sum x_i f_i(x)$$
$$= 1 f_i(\ldots 1 \ldots) + 0 f_i(\ldots 0 \ldots)$$
$$= 1p + 0(1 - p) = p.$$

Here $(\ldots 1 \ldots)$ means that a success occurred in the ith trial etc. Thus the variance of X_i is

$$\mathrm{var}(X_i) = E((X_i - E(X_i)^2)$$
$$= (1 - p)^2 f_i(..1..) + (0 - p)^2 f_i(..0..)$$
$$= p(1 - p)^2 + p^2(1 - p)$$
$$= p(1 - p)(1 - p + p) = p(1 - p)$$

Since the trials are independent

$$\mathrm{cov}(X_i, X_j) = 0 \text{ for all } i \neq j$$

Now define a new random variable $Y = X_1 + \cdots + X_n$ on $\mathscr{S}$. For any event $\{O_1,\ldots,O_n\}$ let $Y(\{O_1,\ldots,O_n\}) = \sum_{i=1}^{n} X_i(O_i)$. Thus if $x = (x_1,\ldots,x_n)$ is an outcome, Y takes on the value $\sum_{i=1}^{n} x_i$.

Clearly

$$E(Y) = E\left(\sum_{i=1}^{n} X_i\right) = \sum_{i=1}^{n} E(X_i) = np.$$

Moreover

$$\text{var}(Y) = \text{var}\left(\sum_{i=1}^{n} X_i \right)$$

$$= \text{var}(X_1) + \cdots + \text{var}(X_n)$$

$$+ \sum\sum_{i \neq j} \text{cov}(X_i, X_j)$$

$$= np(1 - p)$$

Finally, define a new random variable $\bar{Y}$ called the *sample mean* by $\bar{Y} = \dfrac{Y}{n}$.

Clearly

$$\text{E}(\bar{Y}) = \frac{1}{n}\text{E}(Y) = p$$

and

$$\text{var}(\bar{Y}) = \frac{1}{n^2}\text{var}(Y) = \frac{p(1 - p)}{n}$$

More generally, consider an experiment with sample space $\mathscr{S}$. The sample space when the experiment is replicated n times is $\mathscr{S}^n$. Suppose that each trial is independent, and let X be a random variable which is defined on the sample space $\mathscr{S}$, and let X_i be the random variable whose values correspond to the possible observations in the ith experiment. For each i, we may therefore assume that the expected value $\text{E}(X_i) = \mu_x$ and the variance $\text{var}(X_i) = \sigma_x^2$, where μ_x and σ_x are the expected value and standard deviation respectively of the random variable X. Now define

$$Y = \sum_{i=1}^{n} X_i \text{ and } \bar{Y} = \frac{Y}{n}$$

Then the sample mean has expected value

$$\text{E}(\bar{Y}) = \frac{1}{n}\text{E}\left(\sum_{i=1}^{n} X_i \right) = \frac{1}{n} \sum_{i=1}^{n} \text{E}(X_i)$$

$$= \frac{1}{n}(n\mu_x) = \mu_x$$

The variance of $\bar{Y}$ is

$$\text{var}(\bar{Y}) = \frac{1}{n^2}\text{var}(Y)$$

$$= \frac{1}{n^2}\left[\sum_{i=1}^{n} \text{var}(X_i) + 2\sum\sum_{i \neq j} \text{cov}(X_i, X_j) \right]$$

$$= \frac{\sigma_x^2}{n}$$

Example 1.6

In the coin-tossing experiment, let X_i, $i = 1, 2, 3$, be 0 or 1 depending on whether the coin shows a head or tail in the ith toss. From the discussion above $E(X_i) = \frac{1}{2}$, since the coin is fair. Since Y is the number of heads in three tosses, $Y = X_1 + X_2 + X_3$, and so $E(Y) = np = \frac{3}{2}$ as before. Moreover $\text{var}(Y) = np(1 - p) = \frac{3}{4}$, also as before. Suppose that we now compute $\bar{Y}$, the mean number of heads obtained in the three tosses. Clearly $E(\bar{Y}) = \frac{1}{3} \cdot \frac{3}{2} = \frac{1}{2}$ which is an estimate of the probability of obtaining a head in one toss. Note also that the variance in the variable X_i is $\frac{1}{2} \cdot \frac{1}{2} = \frac{1}{4}$. On the other hand the variance in $\bar{Y}$ is $\frac{1}{3} \text{var}(X_i) = \frac{1}{12}$. Since the variance is a measure of the 'degree of uncertainty' of an observation, repeating an experiment a number of times reduces the uncertainty by a corresponding degree.

We now turn to a more formal proof of the expected value and variance of the random variable Y, defined to be the number of successes in the experiment of replicating a Bernoulli trial n times. First of all we prove the simple equality

$$C(n,r) + C(n, r - 1) = C(n + 1, r)$$

To see this note that

$$C(n,r) + C(n, r - 1) = \frac{n!}{(n - r)! r!} + \frac{n!}{(n - (r - 1))! (r - 1)!}$$

$$= \frac{n!}{r! (n - r + 1)!} [(n - r + 1) + r]$$

$$= \frac{(n + 1)!}{r! (n + 1 - r)!} = C(n + 1, r)$$

To give an intuitive interpretation of this equality, select any one object, A, from a set of $(n + 1)$ objects. Now consider the set of all subsets of size r, none of which include A. Clearly there are $C(n,r)$ subsets. Now from the set of n objects, other than A, pick any $(r - 1)$ objects. Clearly there are $C(n, r - 1)$ such subsets. If A is added to such a subset, then we obtain a set with r objects. In this manner we obtain all subsets with r objects out of $(n + 1)$.

We seek now to show that if x and y are real numbers, and n is a non-negative integer then

$$(x + y)^n = \sum_{r=0}^{n} \binom{n}{r} y^r x^{n-r}$$

Here, for convenience, we use the notation $C(n,r) = \binom{n}{r}$. First of all in the case $n = 0$, we observe that $\binom{0}{0} = 1$. On the left-hand side we obtain $(x + y)^0 = 1$, and on the right $1 \cdot y^0 x^0 = 1$. Thus the identity is valid when $n = 0$. For any n, we note that $\binom{n}{0} = \binom{n}{n} = 1$. In the case $n = 1$, we obtain $(x + y)$ on the left. On the right we obtain

$$\binom{1}{0} y^0 x^1 + \binom{1}{1} y^1 x^0 = y + x$$

Thus we can assert the proposition H_1: that the equation is valid for $n = 1$. Suppose now that the equation is valid for n equal to a particular value, k, say. Call this proposition H_k. We seek to show that H_k implies H_{k+1}. For any integer, k, define $\binom{k}{-1} = 0$. Assume now that H_k is true. Then

$$(x + y)^{k+1} = (x + y) \sum_{r=0}^{k} \binom{k}{r} x^r y^{k-r}$$

$$= \sum_{r=0}^{k} \binom{k}{r} x^{r+1} y^{k-r} + \sum_{r=0}^{k} \binom{k}{r} x^r y^{k-r+1}$$

$$= \sum_{r=0}^{k+1} \left(\binom{k}{r-1} + \binom{k}{r} \right) x^r y^{k+1-r}$$

$$\left(\text{where} \binom{k}{-1} = 0 \text{ and } \binom{k}{0} = \binom{k+1}{0} = 1 \right)$$

$$= \sum_{r=0}^{k+1} \binom{k+1}{r} x^r y^{k+1-r}$$

Thus if H_k is true then H_{k+1} is true. Since H_1 is true, the hypothesis H_k is true for all positive integer k.

Consider again the Bernoulli experiment with n trials, and let $Y = \sum_{i=1}^{n} X_i$ as before, where the random variable defined on the ith trial has probability distribution f_i given by

$$f_i(X_i = 1) = p, \quad f_i(X_i = 0) = (1 - p).$$

We seek to determine the probability distribution, f, for Y. It is evident that the probability of obtaining a *specific* sequence of results $(O_1, \ldots, O_n)$ with r successes and $(n - r)$ failures is $p^r(1 - p)^{n-r}$. Since there are $C(n,r)$ different ways of specifying r successes we find that

$$f(r) = P(Y = r) = \binom{n}{r} p^r (1 - p)^{n-r}$$

for $r = 0, \ldots, n$. Moreover since $Y = 0, \ldots, n$ gives a disjoint partition for the sample space we require the sum of these probabilities to be 1. By the binomial theorem

$$\sum_{r=0}^{n} f(r) = \sum_{r=0}^{n} \binom{n}{r} p^r (1 - p)^{n-r} = (p + (1 - p))^n = 1^n = 1.$$

as required.

Any random variable Y which has probability distribution f given by $f(r) = \binom{n}{r} p^r (1 - p)^{n-r}$ is said to be *binomially distributed*. We can now directly compute the expected value and variance of the binomial distribution, using the properties of the distribution.

The expected value of the binomial distribution, Y, is

$$E(Y) = \sum_{Y=0}^{n} Y f(Y)$$

$$= \sum_{r=0}^{n} r \binom{n}{r} p^r (1-p)^{n-r}$$

$$= \sum_{r=1}^{n} \frac{n!}{(n-r)!\,(r-1)!} p^{r-1} p (1-p)^{(n-1)-(r-1)}$$

$$= np \sum_{r=1}^{n} \frac{(n-1)!}{((n-1)-(r-1))!\,(r-1)!} p^{r-1} (1-p)^{(n-1)-(r-1)}$$

$$= np \sum_{r=0}^{n-1} \binom{n-1}{r} p^r (1-p)^{n-1-r}$$

$$= np(p + (1-p))^{n-1} = np$$

Hence

$$E(Y) = np$$

The variance of the binomial distribution, Y, is

$$\text{var}(Y) = \sum_{Y=0}^{n} (Y - E(Y))^2 f(X)$$

$$= \sum_{r=0}^{n} (r - np)^2 \binom{n}{r} p^r (1-p)^{n-r}$$

$$= \sum_{r=0}^{n} (r^2 + n^2 p^2 - 2rnp) \binom{n}{r} p^r (1-p)^{n-r}$$

$$= \sum_{r=0}^{n} (r(r-1) + r - 2rnp + n^2 p^2) \binom{n}{r} p^r (1-p)^{n-r}$$

$$= \left[\sum r(r-1)n(n-1) \frac{(n-2)!}{r(r-1)(r-2)!\,(n-r)!} p^2 p^{r-2} (1-p)^{n-r} \right]$$

$$+ np - 2(np)^2 + n^2 p^2$$

$$= \left[n(n-1)p^2 \sum \binom{n-2}{r-2} p^{r-2} (1-p)^{n-r} \right] + np - n^2 p^2$$

$$= n^2 p^2 - np^2 + np - n^2 p^2$$

$$= np(1-p)$$

These formal proofs merely corroborate our earlier demonstration that $E(Y) = np$ and $\text{var}(Y) = np(1-p)$, when Y is a random variable which has the binomial distribution with parameters (n, p).

In some cases we consider a random variable which has a binomial distribution with parameters (n, p) but where the number of cases, n, approaches infinity, and the probability of success on a single trial, p, becomes vanishingly small. In this case the important parameter is the limit np, or λ, if it exists. The resulting distribution is known as the *Poisson distribution*. Let

$$\xi = \binom{n}{r} p^r (1 - p)^{n-r}$$

$$= \frac{(1-p)^n}{(1-p)^r} p^r \frac{n}{r} \frac{(n-1)}{(r-1)} \cdots \frac{(n-r+1)}{1}$$

Put

$$\lambda = np$$

Then

$$\xi = \left(1 - \frac{\lambda}{n}\right)^n \frac{\frac{\lambda r}{n}}{\left(1 - \frac{\lambda}{n}\right)^r} \frac{n(n-1)\cdots(n-r+1)}{r!}$$

$$= \left(1 - \frac{\lambda}{n}\right)^n \frac{\lambda^r}{(n-\lambda)^r} \frac{n(n-1)\cdots(n-r+1)}{r!}$$

$$= \left(1 - \frac{\lambda}{n}\right)^n \frac{\lambda^r}{r!} \frac{n}{n-\lambda} \frac{n-1}{n-\lambda} \frac{n-2}{n-\lambda} \cdots \frac{n-r+1}{n-\lambda}$$

Consider

$$\frac{n-k}{n-\lambda} = \frac{1 - k/n}{1 - \lambda/n}$$

If $n \to \infty$, and $p \to 0$, with $\lambda \to$ some integer, then

$$\lim_{n \to \infty} \frac{1 - k/n}{1 - \lambda/n} = 1$$

Hence

$$\xi = \lim_{n \to \infty} \frac{\lambda^r}{r!} \left(1 - \frac{\lambda}{n}\right)^n$$

Now

$$\lim_{n \to \infty} \left(1 - \frac{\lambda}{n}\right)^n = \exp(-\lambda) = e^{-\lambda}$$

Hence

$$\xi = \frac{\lambda^r}{r!} \exp(-\lambda)$$

If a random variable Y has probability function

$$f(r) = \frac{\lambda^r}{r!} \exp(-\lambda)$$

it is Poisson distributed with parameter λ. Furthermore

$$\sum_{r=0}^{\infty} \frac{\lambda^r}{r!} \exp(-\lambda) = 1$$

Also

$$E(Y) = \sum_{r=0}^{\infty} r \frac{\lambda^r}{r!} \exp(-\lambda)$$

$$= \lambda \sum_{r=1}^{\infty} \frac{\lambda^{r-1}}{(r-1)!} \exp(-\lambda) = \lambda = np$$

As an exercise the reader should also show that $\text{var}(Y) = \lambda = np$.
Hence as $n \to \infty$, the Poisson distribution can be used to approximate the binomial.

1.4 CONDITIONAL EXPECTED VALUES

Suppose that we know that an event B has occurred and we wish to compute the probability (in the light of this knowledge) that another event A occurs. This conditional probability we write as $P(A/B)$. Clearly we need to redefine our 'universe' so that $P(B/B) = 1$. In other words we may define

$$P(B/B) = \frac{P(B)}{P(B)}$$

Now if A occurs, and we know B has occurred then we are concerned with the probability of event $A \cap B$, both A and B occurring. We may therefore define the conditional probability as

$$P(A/B) = \frac{P(A \cap B)}{P(B)}$$

Suppose now that $\{B_1, \ldots, B_n\}$ is a disjoint partition of $\mathscr{S}$. Then clearly $\{A \cap B_1, \ldots, A \cap B_n\}$ is a partition of A, and thus

$$P(A) = \sum_{i=1}^{n} P(A \cap B_i)$$

Moreover,

$$P(A/B_i) = \frac{P(A \cap B_i)}{P(B_i)}$$

and so

$$P(A) = \sum_{i=1}^{n} P(B_i)P(A/B_i)$$

This expression for $P(A)$ is generally dubbed 'Bayes' theorem'. One useful application of the theorem is in the case that A is a datum (of information) and $\{B, \rightarrow B\}$ are two conflicting hypotheses. Suppose further we may assign an initial, or *a priori*, probability $P(B)$ that B is a true hypothesis, and we know the probability that the datum A can occur in the cases when the hypotheses B or $\rightarrow B$ are true. Then we can compute the *a posteriori* probability $P(B/A)$ that B is true given that A occurred, as follows: Now

$$P(B/A) = \frac{P(B \cap A)}{P(A)}$$

But

$$P(A/B) = \frac{P(B \cap A)}{P(B)} \text{ so } P(B \cap A) = P(A/B)P(B)$$

Moreover,

$$P(A) = P(B)P(A/B) + P(\rightarrow B)P(A/\rightarrow B)$$

Thus

$$P(B/A) = \frac{P(A/B)P(B)}{P(B)P(A/B) + P(\rightarrow B)P(A/\rightarrow B)}$$

With a collection of hypotheses $B_1, \ldots, B_n$ an experiment to compare hypotheses is essentially the collection of a datum, A, where the *a priori* probabilities $P(B_1), \ldots, P(B_n)$ are given and $P(A/B_1), \ldots, P(A/B_n)$ are computable. Bayes' theorem then gives the *a posteriori* probabilities $P(B_1/A), \ldots, P(B_n/A)$.

As an application of Bayes' theorem, suppose that two random variables X, Y can take on values $\{x_1, \ldots, x_j, \ldots, x_M\}$ and $\{y_1, \ldots, y_k, \ldots, y_N\}$. Very often we are interested in the conditional probability distribution and expected value for Y, say, *given* that we know a particular value for X has occurred.

Suppose we let A be the set of outcomes in which Y takes the value y_k, and B be the set of outcomes in which X takes the value x_j. Then, as we have seen,

$$P(A/B) = P(Y = y_k/X = x_j)$$

$$= \frac{P(A \cap B)}{P(B)}$$

$$= \frac{P(Y = y_k \text{ and } X = x_j)}{P(X = x_j)}$$

If the probability functions for Y, X are $g(Y), f(X)$ respectively, and $h(X,Y)$ is the joint probability function then

$$P(Y = y_k/X = x_j) = g(y_k/x_j)$$

$$= \frac{P(Y = y_k \text{ and } X = x_j)}{P(X = x_j)}$$

$$= \frac{h(x_j, y_k)}{f(x_j)}$$

$g(y_k/x_j)$ is the conditional probability of y_k given x_j, and $g(Y/X_j)$ is the *conditional probability function* of Y given X_j. Now

$$\sum_{k=1}^{N} g(y_k/x_j) = \sum_{k=1}^{N} \frac{h(x_j, y_k)}{f(x_j)}$$

$$= \frac{f(x_j)}{f(x_j)} = 1$$

i.e., $g(C/x_j)$ is a probability function. We can define

$$E(Y/X = x_j) = \sum_{k=1}^{N} y_k g(y_k/x_j)$$

to be the expected value of Y given x_j. Let us assume that

$$E(Y/X = x_j) = mx_j + b$$

so that if $X = x_j$, then Y is expected to be $mx_j + b$. Thus

$$\sum_{j=1}^{M} f(x_j) E(Y/X = x_j) = \sum_{j=1}^{M} \sum_{k=1}^{N} y_k g(y_k/x_j) f(x_j)$$

$$= \sum_{j=1}^{M} (mx_j + b) f(x_j)$$

But

$$g(y_k/x_j) f(x_j) = \frac{h(x_j, y_k)}{f(x_j)} f(x_j) = h(x_j, y_k)$$

and so the left-hand side of this equation gives

$$\sum_{j=1}^{M} \sum_{k=1}^{N} y_k h(x_j, y_k) = \sum_{k=1}^{N} y_k g(y_k) = \mu_Y$$

where

$$\mu_Y = E(Y)$$

Also the right-hand side of this equation gives

$$\sum_{j=1}^{M} (mx_j + b) f(x_j) = mE(X) + b\sum f(x_j)$$

$$= m\mu_X + b \text{ where } \mu_X = E(X)$$

Thus

$$\mu_Y = m\mu_X + b, \text{ or } E(Y) = \sum f(x_j) E(Y/x_j) = E_X(E(Y/X))$$

Here E_X means simply the expectation operator E over the random variable X. In the equation $E(Y/x_j) = mx_j + b$, multiply by $f(x_j)x_j$ for all j and add. The two sides of the equation are as follows.

LHS: $$\sum_{j=1}^{M} \sum_{k=1}^{N} x_j y_k h(x_j y_k) = E(XY)$$

RHS: $$\sum_{j=1}^{M} x_j f(x_j)(mx_j + b) = mE(X^2) + bE(X)$$

Hence

$$\mu_Y = m\mu_X + b$$

$$E(XY) = mE(X^2) + b\mu_X$$

Solving:

$$\mu_Y E(X^2) = m\mu_X E(X^2) + bE(X^2)$$

$$\mu_X E(XY) = m\mu_X E(X^2) + b\mu_X^2$$

Therefore

$$\mu_Y E(X^2) - \mu_X E(XY) = b(E(X^2) - \mu_X^2)$$

Thus

$$b = \frac{\mu_Y E(X^2) - \mu_X E(XY)}{E(X^2) - \mu_X^2}$$

$$m = \frac{\mu_Y - \left[\dfrac{\mu_Y E(X^2) - \mu_X E(XY)}{E(X^2) - \mu_X^2}\right]}{\mu_X}$$

$$= \frac{\mu_Y E(X^2) - \mu_Y \mu_X^2 - \mu_Y E(X^2) + \mu_X E(XY)}{\mu_X [E(X^2) - \mu_X^2]}$$

$$= \frac{E(XY) - \mu_Y \mu_X}{E(X^2) - \mu_X^2}$$

Now

$$\text{cov}(X,Y) = E(XY) - \mu_Y \mu_X$$

$$\text{var}(X) = E(X^2) - \mu_X^2$$

Hence

$$m = \frac{\text{cov}(X,Y)}{\text{var}(X)}$$

Therefore

$$E(Y/X = x_j) = \frac{\text{cov}(X,Y)}{\text{var}(X)}x_j + \frac{\mu_Y E(X^2) - \mu_X E(XY)}{E(X^2) - \mu_X^2}$$

Now

$$b = \frac{\mu_Y E(X^2) - \mu_X E(XY)}{E(X^2) - \mu_X^2}$$

$$= \frac{\mu_Y (E(X^2) - \mu_X^2) + \mu_Y \mu_X^2 - \mu_X E(XY)}{E(X^2) - \mu_X^2}$$

$$= \mu_Y - \mu_X \left[\frac{E(XY) - \mu_X \mu_Y}{E(X^2) - \mu_X^2} \right]$$

$$= \mu_Y - \mu_X \frac{\text{cov}(X,Y)}{\text{var}(X)}$$

Hence

$$E(Y/X = x_j) = \mu_Y + \frac{\text{cov}(X,Y)}{\text{var}(X)}[x_j - \mu_X]$$

We shall use this result in introducing the linear regression model in the next chapter.

1.5 CONTINUOUS RANDOM VARIABLES

Until now we have assumed that we can write

$$P(X = x_j) = f(x_j)$$

However, if X is a continuous random variable the occurrence of any exact value of X may be regarded as having zero probability. Instead of determining the probability that $X = a$, we are now interested in the probability that X lies in a range (a,b) say. Let us write

$$P(X \le a) = F(a) = P(X < a)$$

F is called the *cumulative probability function* of X. Now

$$P(a \le X \le b) = P((X \le b) \text{ and not } (X < a))$$

$$= P(X \le b) - P(X < a)$$

$$= F(b) - F(a)$$

Suppose $b - a$ is small and equal to ΔX. Then

$$P(a \le X \le a + \Delta X) = F(a + \Delta X) - F(a)$$

The probability of the interval relative to ΔX is

$$\frac{P(a \leq X \leq a + \Delta X)}{\Delta X} = \frac{F(a + \Delta X) - F(a)}{\Delta X}$$

Suppose we now let $\Delta X \to 0$. Then

$$\lim_{\Delta X \to 0} \frac{P(a \leq X \leq a + \Delta X)}{\Delta X} = \lim_{\Delta X \to 0} \frac{F(a + \Delta X) - F(a)}{\Delta X}$$

For those familiar with calculus, this is $\left.\dfrac{dF}{dX}\right|_{X = a}$. This expression we write as $f(a)$, the value of the *probability density function* of X at a. Thus

$$\left.\frac{dF}{dX}\right|_{X = a} = f(a)$$

Hence

$$F(a) = \int_{-\infty}^{a} f(X)dX$$

Therefore

$$P(a \leq X \leq b) = F(b) - F(a)$$

$$= \int_{-\infty}^{a} f(X)dX - \int_{-\infty}^{a} f(X)dX$$

$$= \int_{a}^{b} f(X)dX$$

In other words $f: \mathbf{R} \to \mathbf{R}$ is a function which has the property that the probability that the random variable X takes values between a and b is given by the area under the graph of f between a and b as shown in Figure 1.1.

Note that

$$P(-\infty \leq X \leq +\infty) = \int_{-\infty}^{+\infty} f(X)dX = 1$$

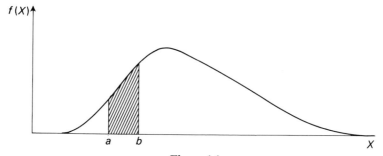

Figure 1.1

Following the previous definitions of E and var, define

$$E(X) = \int_{-\infty}^{+\infty} Xf(X)dX = \mu_X$$

$$\text{var}(X) = \int_{-\infty}^{+\infty} (X - \mu_X)^2 f(X)dX$$

$$= \sigma_X^2$$

$\sqrt{\text{var}(X)}$ is called the *standard deviation* of X and written σ_X. Write $\int_X dX$ for the *integral* over all X. As before E is linear: i.e.

$$E(aX) = \int aXf(X)dX = aE(X)$$

$$E(X + Y) = \int_X \int_Y (X + Y)h(XY)dXdY$$

Now

$$\int_Y Xh(XY)dY = Xf(X), \quad \int_X Yh(XY)dX = Yg(Y)$$

So

$$E(X + Y) = \int_X Xf(X)dX + \int_Y Yf(Y)dY$$

$$= E(X) + E(Y)$$

Moreover

$$\text{var}(aX) = \int_X (aX - a\mu_X)^2 f(X)$$

$$= \int a^2(X - \mu_X)^2 f(X) = a^2 \text{var}(X)$$

Similarly

$$\text{var}(X + Y) = E((X + Y - \mu_X - \mu_Y)^2)$$
$$= E((X - \mu_X)^2) + E((Y - \mu_Y)^2) + 2E((X - \mu_X)(Y - \mu_Y))$$
$$= \text{var}(X) + \text{var}(Y) + 2\text{cov}(X,Y)$$

Here

$$\text{cov}(X,Y) = \int_{XY} XYh(X,Y)dXdY - E(X)E(Y)$$

The normal distribution

Consider a probability density function (pdf) given by

$$f(X) = \frac{1}{\sqrt{2\pi}} \exp(-\tfrac{1}{2}X^2)$$

We can show that $\int_{-\infty}^{+\infty} \exp(-\tfrac{1}{2}X^2)dX = \sqrt{2\pi}$. Hence

$$\int_X f(X)dX = 1$$

If X has a pdf of this form it is called a *normal variate*. Now

$$E(X) = \frac{1}{\sqrt{2\pi}} \int_{-\infty}^{+\infty} X \exp(-\tfrac{1}{2}X^2)dX$$

$$= \frac{1}{\sqrt{2\pi}} \left\{ \int_{-\infty}^{0} X \exp(-\tfrac{1}{2}X^2)dX + \int_{0}^{+\infty} X \exp(-\tfrac{1}{2}X^2)dX \right\}$$

In the first part of the expression we change X to $-X$ and obtain

$$E(X) = \frac{1}{\sqrt{2\pi}} \left\{ \int_{0}^{\infty} (-X)\exp(-\tfrac{1}{2}X^2)dX + \int_{0}^{\infty} X \exp(-\tfrac{1}{2}X^2)dX \right\}$$

$$= 0$$

Also

$$\text{var}(X) = E(X^2) = \frac{1}{\sqrt{2\pi}} \int_{-\infty}^{\infty} X^2 \exp(-\tfrac{1}{2}X^2)dX$$

$$= \left[\frac{1}{\sqrt{2\pi}} X \exp(-\tfrac{1}{2}X^2) \right]_{-\infty}^{+\infty}$$

$$+ \frac{1}{\sqrt{2\pi}} \int_{\infty}^{+\infty} \exp(-\tfrac{1}{2}X^2)dX$$

$$= 0 + 1 = 1$$

Thus X is distributed *normally* with mean 0 and variance 1. In this case we say X is distributed as $N(0,1)$. Suppose Z is distributed as $N(0,1)$, and

$$Z = \frac{X - \mu}{\sigma} \text{ for some constants } \mu, \sigma$$

Then

$$E\left[\left[\frac{X - \mu}{\sigma} \right]^2 \right] = 1 \text{ and } E((X - \mu)^2) = \sigma^2$$

Also

$$E\left[\frac{X - \mu}{\sigma}\right] = 0 \text{ so } E(X - \mu) = 0 \text{ or } E(X) = \mu$$

In which case X has mean μ, variance σ^2, and is distributed as $N(\mu, \sigma^2)$. Also

$$1 = \int_Z f(Z)dZ = \int_X \frac{1}{\sqrt{2\pi}} \exp\left[-\tfrac{1}{2}\left[\frac{X - \mu}{\sigma}\right]^2\right]\frac{dX}{\sigma}$$

$$= \int_X \frac{1}{\sigma\sqrt{2\pi}} \exp\left[-\tfrac{1}{2}\left[\frac{X - \mu}{\sigma}\right]^2\right]dX$$

Hence the pdf for X is

$$f(X) = \frac{1}{\sigma\sqrt{2\pi}} \exp\left[-\tfrac{1}{2}\left[\frac{X - \mu}{\sigma}\right]^2\right]$$

In general if f takes this form $f(Z)$ it is written as $\phi(Z)$. The cumulative probability function is written as

$$\Phi(a) = \int_{-\infty}^{a} \phi(Z)dZ$$

Let X be distributed as $N(\mu, \sigma^2)$, and $Z = \dfrac{X - \mu}{\sigma}$ be distributed as $N(0,1)$. Then

$$P(a \leq X \leq b) = P\left[\frac{a - \mu}{\sigma} \leq Z \leq \frac{b - \mu}{\sigma}\right]$$

$$= \Phi\left[\frac{b - \mu}{\sigma}\right] - \Phi\left[\frac{a - \mu}{\sigma}\right]$$

Now the normal distribution is symmetric about 0

i.e.,

$$\Phi(-Z) = 1 - \Phi(Z)$$

Thus the normal distribution may be represented by Figure 1.2.

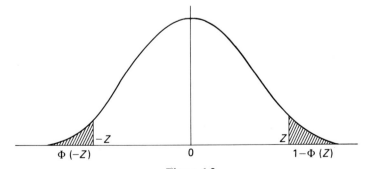

Figure 1.2

So

$$P(-a \leq Z \leq a) = \Phi(a) - \Phi(-a)$$
$$= \Phi(a) - (1 - \Phi(a))$$
$$= 2\Phi(a) - 1$$

Let $\Phi(Z_p) = p$, i.e., $P(Z \leq Z_p) = p$. Then

$$P(-Z_p \leq Z \leq Z_p) = 2\Phi(Z_p) - 1$$
$$= 2p - 1$$

For example, if $p = 0.975$, then $Z_p = 1.96$. Thus

$$P(-1.96 \leq Z \leq 1.96) = 2(0.975) - 1$$
$$= 1.950 - 1$$
$$= 0.950$$

The interval $(-1.96, +1.96)$ is called the two-sided 95 per cent confidence interval for Z. Now

$$P(-1.96 \leq Z \leq 1.96)$$

$$= P\left(-1.96 \leq \frac{X - \mu}{\sigma} \leq 1.96\right)$$

$$= P(\mu - 1.96\sigma \leq X \leq \mu + 1.96\sigma)$$

In general then $(\mu - 1.96\sigma, \mu + 1.96\sigma)$ is the two-sided 95 per cent confidence interval for X distributed as $N(\mu, \sigma^2)$. More generally $(\mu - \sigma Z_p, \mu + \sigma Z_p)$ is the two-sided $(2p - 1)$ confidence interval for X distributed as $N(\mu, \sigma^2)$.

As an application of the use of the normal distribution, consider the problem of computing the probability of obtaining r successes out of n trials in the Bernoulli experiment when the probability of a single success in a trial is p. Let X be the random variable defined to be the number of successes. As we showed previously, $E(X) = np$ and $\mathrm{var}(X) = np(1 - p)$. We may suppose that X is approximately normally distributed as $N(np, np(1 - p))$ and take as an approximation to $P(X = x)$ the value

$$\int_{x-}^{x+} \phi\left(\frac{x - np}{\sqrt{np(1 - p)}}\right) dx = \Phi\left(\frac{x + \frac{1}{2} - np}{\sqrt{np(1 - p)}}\right) - \Phi\left(\frac{x - \frac{1}{2} - np}{\sqrt{np(1 - p)}}\right)$$

For example suppose $n = 5$, $p = \frac{1}{2}$. Then $E(X) = \frac{5}{2}$ and $\sigma_x = \sqrt{5 \cdot \frac{1}{2} \cdot \frac{1}{2}} = 1.12$. Now $P(X = 5) = p^n = (\frac{1}{2})^5 = 0.0312$. Let $Z_1 = \dfrac{x + \frac{1}{2} - np}{\sqrt{np(1 - p)}}$ and $Z_0 = \dfrac{x - \frac{1}{2}np}{\sqrt{np(1 - p)}}$. Then for $x = 5$,

$$Z_1 = \frac{5.5 - 2.5}{1.12} = 2.68$$

and

$$Z_0 = \frac{4.5 - 2.5}{1.12} = 1.79$$

Thus $P(X = 5) \simeq \Phi(2.68) - \Phi(1.79) = 0.4963 - 0.4625 = 0.0338$. Putting in the other

values for x and $Z = \dfrac{x - np}{\sqrt{np(1 - p)}}$ gives Table 1.5.

Table 1.5

X	$P(X)$ from binomial	Z	(Z_0, Z_1)	$\Phi(Z_1) - \Phi(Z_0)$
5	0.0312	2.23	(1.79, 2.68)	0.0338
4	0.1563	1.34	(0.89, 1.79)	0.1500
3	0.3125	0.45	(0.00, 0.89)	0.3133
2	0.3125	−0.45	(−0.89, 0.00)	0.3133
1	0.1563	−1.34	(−1.79, −0.89)	0.1500
0	0.0312	−2.23	(−2.68, −1.79)	0.0330

1.6 SAMPLING FROM A POPULATION

Suppose now that we are interested in the variation of a variable X across a population, but that we do not know the manner in which the variable is distributed. As a first guide to the nature of the distribution we should like to know the true values for the parameters called the expected value, μ_x, and variance, σ_x^2, of X. However, since we typically face a population that is effectively infinite in size, the best we can hope for is to obtain estimations $\hat{\mu}_x$ and $\text{vâr}(X)$ for these two parameters. Obviously we are interested in the relationship between these *estimators* $\hat{\mu}_x$, $\text{vâr}(X)$ and the true values μ_x, $\text{var}(X)$ of the parameters.

One method of estimating the expected value is to take a sample of n independent observations of the variable. As before we can regard this as obtaining a sequence of observations $(x_1, \ldots, x_n)$ of the variable $(X_1, \ldots, X_n)$, where each X_i is simply a copy of X. Define the new random variable $\bar{X}$ by $\bar{X} = \dfrac{1}{n} \sum_{i=1}^{n} X_i$. A value for $\bar{X}$ is simply a

reading $\dfrac{1}{n} \sum_{i=1}^{n} x_i$ obtained from the n different observations. Then

$$\text{E}(\bar{X}) = \text{E}\left(\frac{1}{n} \sum_{i=1}^{n} X_i\right) = \frac{1}{n}\text{E}\left(\sum_{i=1}^{n} X_i\right) = \frac{1}{n} \sum_{i=1}^{n} \text{E}(X_i)$$

(since each observation is assumed to be independent of the others)

$$= \frac{1}{n}(\mu_x + \cdots + \mu_x) = \mu_x$$

Thus the expected value of $\bar{X}$ is simply the expected value of the randon variable. If we define as our estimator $\hat{\mu}_x$ for the expected value of X that experimental procedure where we compute the mean of n observations of X, then clearly $\hat{\mu}_x = \dfrac{1}{n} \sum_{i=1}^{n} X_i$. Moreover, as we have shown $\text{E}(\hat{\mu}_x) = \mu_x$. Now consider how the variance of $\bar{X}$ is related to the true variance of the random variable X. For convenience write μ_x as μ. By definition

$$\mathrm{var}(\bar{X}) = \mathrm{E}((\bar{X} - \mathrm{E}(\bar{X}))^2)$$

$$= \mathrm{E}((\bar{X} - \mu)^2)$$

$$= \mathrm{E}\left(\left(\frac{1}{n}\sum_i X_i - \mu\right)^2\right)$$

$$= \mathrm{E}\left(\frac{1}{n^2}\left(\sum_i (X_i - \mu)\right)^2\right)$$

As we have shown previously

$$\mathrm{var}(X_1 + X_2) = \mathrm{var}(X_1) + \mathrm{var}(X_2) + 2\mathrm{cov}(X_1, X_2)$$

where

$$\mathrm{cov}(X_1, X_2) = \mathrm{E}((X_1 - \mu_{x_1})(X_2 - \mu_{x_2}))$$

The expression $\mathrm{E}\left(\left(\sum_i (X_i - \mu)\right)^2\right)$ is clearly $\mathrm{var}\left(\sum_{i=1}^{n} X_i\right)$ since each X_i has expected value μ. Moreover, all observations are independent, and so $\mathrm{cov}(X_i, X_j) = 0$ for all $i \neq j$. Thus

$$\mathrm{var}(\bar{X}) = \frac{1}{n^2}\left(\sum_{i=1}^{n} \mathrm{var}(X_i)\right)$$

But each replicate X_i has variance $\mathrm{var}(X) = \sigma_x^2$. Thus

$$\mathrm{var}(\bar{X}) = \frac{1}{n^2}(n\sigma_x^2) = \frac{\sigma_x^2}{n}$$

In other words the true standard deviation of the *sample mean* $\bar{X}$ is

$$\frac{\sigma_x}{\sqrt{n}}$$

Now we seek an estimator for the population variance. Clearly a plausible candidate for $\mathrm{v\hat{a}r}(X)$ is $V = \frac{1}{n}\sum_{i=1}^{n}(X_i - \bar{X})^2$, where we essentially use $\frac{1}{n}$ as a proxy for the probability of obtaining the reading. Consider however the expected value of V. To compute $\mathrm{E}(V)$ proceed as follows. First of all, consider the following:

$$\sum_i ((X_i - \bar{X})^2 + (\bar{X} - \mu)^2)$$

$$= \sum_i (X_i^2 + \bar{X}^2 - 2\bar{X}X_i + \bar{X}^2 + \mu^2 - 2\mu\bar{X})$$

But

$$\sum_i (2\bar{X}^2 - 2\bar{X}X_i) = 2n\bar{X}^2 - 2\bar{X}\sum_i X_i = 0$$

since
$$\sum_i X_i = n\bar{X}$$

Thus the expression becomes

$$\sum_i (X_i^2 - 2\mu\bar{X} + \mu^2)$$

$$= \sum_i (X_i - \mu)^2$$

Hence

$$\mathrm{E}\left(\sum_i (X_i - \bar{X})^2\right) = \mathrm{E}\left(\sum_i (X_i - \mu)^2 - \sum_i (\bar{X} - \mu)^2\right).$$

As we have seen

$$n \operatorname{var}(\bar{X}) = \mathrm{E}\left(\sum_i (\bar{X} - \mu)^2\right)$$

$$= n\mathrm{E}((\bar{X} - \mu)^2)$$

$$= \frac{n \cdot \sigma_x^2}{n} = \sigma_x^2$$

Moreover,

$$\mathrm{E}\left(\sum_i (X_i - \mu)^2\right) = \sum_i \mathrm{E}((X_i - \mu)^2) = n\sigma_x^2$$

since each replicate X_i has variance σ_x^2. Thus

$$\mathrm{E}\left(\sum_i (X_i - \bar{X})^2\right) = \sigma_x^2(n - 1)$$

Hence

$$\mathrm{E}(V) = \mathrm{E}\left(\frac{1}{n}\sum_i (X_i - \bar{X})^2\right) = \left(\frac{n - 1}{n}\right)\sigma_x^2$$

Since it is preferable to use an indicator vâr(X) for the variance of X one which has expected value the true value var(X) we use

$$S^2 = \frac{1}{n - 1}\sum_{i=1}^n (X_i - \bar{X})^2$$

as our estimator for the variance. Clearly $\mathrm{E}(S^2) = \sigma_x^2$.

An estimator $\hat{\theta}$ for a population parameter θ is called *unbiased* if the expected value $\mathrm{E}(\hat{\theta})$ is equal to θ. The *bias* in the estimator $\hat{\theta}$ is defined to be $B_{\hat{\theta}} = \theta - \mathrm{E}(\hat{\theta})$. Thus we have shown that the estimator $\bar{X}$ and S^2 are unbiased estimators for μ_x and σ_x^2. More generally define the *risk* associated with an estimator $\hat{\theta}$ for θ by

$$R(\hat{\theta}, \theta) = \mathrm{E}((\hat{\theta} - \theta)^2)$$

Now

$$R(\hat{\theta}, \theta) = E((\hat{\theta} - E(\hat{\theta})) - (\theta - E(\hat{\theta})))^2)$$
$$= E((\hat{\theta} - E(\hat{\theta}))^2) + E((\theta - E(\hat{\theta}))^2)$$
$$- 2E((\hat{\theta} - E(\hat{\theta}))(\theta - E(\hat{\theta})))$$

Now $\theta - E(\hat{\theta})$ is a constant, so

$$E((\hat{\theta} - E(\hat{\theta}))(\theta - E(\hat{\theta})))$$
$$= (E(\hat{\theta}) - E(\hat{\theta}))(\theta - E(\hat{\theta})) = 0$$

Moreover

$$E((\hat{\theta} - E(\hat{\theta}))^2) = \mathrm{var}(\hat{\theta})$$

and

$$E((\theta - E(\hat{\theta}))^2) = (\theta - E(\hat{\theta}))^2 = B_{\hat{\theta}}^2$$

Thus

$$R(\hat{\theta}, \theta) = \mathrm{var}(\hat{\theta}) + B_{\hat{\theta}}^2$$

Clearly, if $\hat{\theta}_1$ and $\hat{\theta}_2$ are both unbiased estimators of the parameter θ, and $\mathrm{var}(\hat{\theta}_1) < \mathrm{var}(\hat{\theta}_2)$ then $R(\hat{\theta}_1, \theta) < R(\hat{\theta}_2, \theta)$. Since the risk is a measure of the spread of an estimator about the expected value of the parameter, the lower the risk the better. An unbiased estimator $\hat{\theta}$ for a parameter θ which has lower risk than any other unbiased estimator is called a *best unbiased estimator* (BUE). If the estimator is formed by taking a linear combination of replicates of an experiment then the estimator is called linear. A linear unbiased estimator which has lower risk than any other linear unbiased estimator is, naturally enough, called a *best linear unbiased estimator* (BLUE).

Note for example that the sample mean $\bar{X}$ is linear, since it is a linear combination $\bar{X} = \frac{1}{n} \sum X_i$. Moreover, we can show that $\bar{X}$ is BLUE.

A second important property of an estimator concerns the behaviour of the estimator as the scale of the experiment increases. For example, suppose that we perform n replicates of a measuring experiment on a population and use the n individual observations to generate an estimator $\hat{\theta}(n)$ for θ. For example, in the previous discussion we defined $\hat{X}(n) = \frac{1}{n} \sum_i X_i = \bar{X}$. Then the estimation procedure is said to be *consistent* if $R(\hat{\theta}(n), \theta)$ approached 0 as n approaches infinity. For example the sample mean $\hat{X}(n)$ is unbiased. Thus

$$R(\hat{X}(n), \mu_x) = \mathrm{var}(\hat{X}(n)) = \frac{1}{n}\sigma_x^2$$

Clearly as $n \to \infty$, $R(\hat{X}(n), \mu_x) \to 0$ so $\hat{X}(n)$ is consistent. In choosing between two consistent estimators, it is often convenient to choose that estimator which has lowest variance. In particular if $\hat{\theta}_1$ is a consistent estimator, and $\mathrm{var}(\hat{\theta}_1) < \mathrm{var}(\hat{\theta}_2)$ for any other consistent estimator, then $\hat{\theta}_1$ is said to be *efficient*. Finally, it is not always possible to choose an unbiased estimator. However, if $\hat{\theta}(n)$ is an estimation procedure and the bias $B_{\hat{\theta}(n)}$ approaches zero as n approaches infinity, then the procedure is said to be *asymptotically unbiased*.

Example 1.7

Suppose θ is a random variable with expected value μ and variance σ^2. We seek the most appropriate estimator $\hat{\theta}^2$ for θ^2.

Two candidates suggest themselves in the n-replicated experiment. We may either define

$$A_1(n) = \hat{\theta}_1^2 = \left(\frac{1}{n}\sum_i \theta_i\right)^2$$

or

$$A_2(n) = \hat{\theta}_2^2 = \frac{1}{n}\left(\sum_i \theta_i\right)^2$$

By definition

$$\sigma^2 = E((\theta - \mu)^2)$$
$$= E(\theta^2 + \mu^2 - 2\mu\theta)$$
$$= E(\theta^2) - \mu^2$$

Thus $E(\theta^2) = \mu^2 + \sigma^2$. Note that this is true for any parameter with mean μ and variance σ^2. Now consider the case $n = 2$ and the two estimators $A_1(2) = A_1$ and $A_2(2) = A_2$.

Clearly

$$E(A_1) = E((\tfrac{1}{2}(\theta_1 + \theta_2))^2)$$
$$= \tfrac{1}{4}E(\theta_1^2 + \theta_2^2 + 2\theta_1\theta_2)$$
$$= \tfrac{1}{4}(2\sigma^2 + 2\mu^2 + 2E(\theta_1)E(\theta_2))$$
$$= \tfrac{1}{2}(\sigma^2 + \mu^2 + \mu^2)$$
$$= \mu^2 + \frac{\sigma^2}{2}$$

On the other hand

$$E(A_2) = E(\tfrac{1}{2}(\theta_1^2 + \theta_2^2))$$
$$= \tfrac{1}{2}(\mu^2 + \sigma^2 + \mu^2 + \sigma^2)$$
$$= \mu^2 + \sigma^2$$

Thus the bias in $A_1 = \tfrac{1}{2}\sigma^2$ and the bias in $A_2 = \sigma^2$. Clearly if we now replicate the experiment n times then the bias in $A_1(n)$ is $\dfrac{1}{n}\sigma^2$ while the bias in $A_2(n)$ is σ^2. Thus $A_1(n)$ is a consistent estimator, while $A_2(n)$ is not.

1.7 CONFIDENCE INTERVALS FOR THE PARAMETERS OF A DISTRIBUTION

Suppose that we know that a random variable X is normally distributed with true variance σ, but do not know the expected value μ of the variable. As we have shown the sample mean $\bar{X}$ for sample size n will have variance $\dfrac{\sigma^2}{n}$. Moreover $\bar{X}$ will be normally distributed, with expected value μ. Thus

$$P\left(\mu - 1.96\frac{\sigma}{\sqrt{n}} \le \bar{X} \le \mu + 1.96\frac{\sigma}{\sqrt{n}}\right) = 0.95$$

If a particular value $\bar{x}$ is obtained for the sample mean then clearly

$$P\left(\bar{x} - 1.96\frac{\sigma}{\sqrt{n}} \le \mu \le \bar{x} + 1.96\frac{\sigma}{\sqrt{n}}\right) = 0.95$$

Thus we obtain a 95 per cent confidence interval for the unknown expected value of the random variable. In general, of course, the variance of the random variable is unknown and we need to use an estimator S^2 for σ^2. Define

$$S^2 = \frac{1}{n-1}\sum_i (X_i - \bar{X})^2$$

That is to say for any sequence of observations $(x_1, \dots, x_n)$ define the value s^2 of S^2 to be $\dfrac{1}{n-1}\sum_i (x_i - \bar{x})^2$ where $\bar{x} = \sum_i x_i$. As we have shown S^2 is an unbiased estimator, since $E(S^2) = \sigma^2$, and we may conveniently use S^2 as an estimator for σ^2. However, since S^2 is based on a random variable, it will itself be distributed in some fashion. In obtaining confidence intervals for the expected value of X we need to take account of the variance of S^2 itself, and we are required also to know the nature of the distribution of S^2. To deal with the distribution of S^2, we must first mention the *gamma distribution*.

For a positive real number α define the gamma function by

$$\Gamma(\alpha) = \int_0^\infty y^{\alpha-1} e^{-y} dy$$

Integrating by parts, for $\alpha > 1$, gives

$$\Gamma(\alpha) = [-y^{\alpha-1} e^{-y}]_0^\infty + \int_0^\infty (\alpha - 1)y^{\alpha-2} e^{-y} dy$$

However, the first term on the right is zero, and so

$$\Gamma(\alpha) = (\alpha - 1)\Gamma(\alpha - 1)$$

On the other hand

$$\Gamma(1) = \int_0^\infty e^{-y} dy = [-e^y]_0^\infty = 1$$

Thus if α is a positive integer, greater than 1,

$$\Gamma(\alpha) = (\alpha - 1)\Gamma(\alpha - 1) = (\alpha - 1)(\alpha - 2)\cdots\Gamma(1) = (\alpha - 1)!$$

For the case $\alpha = 1$ define $(0)! = \Gamma(1) = 1$. Let α, β be positive real numbers and define the probability density function for the gamma distribution by

$$\gamma(x:\alpha, \beta) = \frac{1}{\Gamma(\alpha)\beta^{\alpha}} \cdot x^{\alpha - 1} e^{-x/\beta} \text{ if } x > 0$$

$$= 0 \text{ if } x \le 0$$

To show that γ is a probability density function we need to show that

$$\int_0^{\infty} \gamma(x:\alpha, \beta) = 1$$

Now

$$\int_0^{\infty} \frac{x^{\alpha - 1} e^{-x/\beta}}{\beta^{\alpha}} dx$$

$$= \int_0^{\infty} y^{\alpha - 1} e^{-y} dy \text{ where } y = \frac{x}{\beta}$$

$$= \Gamma(\alpha)$$

Thus $\int_0^{\infty} \gamma(x:\alpha, \beta) = 1$. A random variable which has a gamma distribution with parameters α, β we shall say is distributed as $\gamma(\alpha, \beta)$. It can be shown that any random variable which is $\gamma(\alpha, \beta)$ distributed has expected value $\alpha\beta$ and variance $\alpha\beta^2$. In the case that the parameters α, β take the values $\alpha = \frac{k}{2}$ and $\beta = 2$ then the expected value and variance are $\frac{k}{2} \cdot 2 = k$ and $\frac{k}{2} \cdot 4 = 2k$ respectively. The distribution $\gamma\left(\frac{k}{2}, 2\right)$ is called the χ^2 (chi-squared) distribution. Since χ^2 only has one parameter, k, we may write it as $\chi^2(k)$. An important characteristic of the gamma distribution is that if $\{X_1, \ldots, X_n\}$ are independent random variables such that each X_i is distributed as $\gamma(\alpha_i, \beta)$ then the variable $Y = C\left(\sum_i X_i\right)$ is distributed as $\gamma\left(\sum_i \alpha_i, C\beta\right)$. In particular $E(Y) = C\beta\sum_i \alpha_i$ and var$(Y) = C^2\beta^2\sum_i \alpha_i$. Consider now a variable X distributed as $N(0,1)$ (that is to say normally with expected value 0 and variance 1). Then we can show that X^2 is distributed as $\gamma(\frac{1}{2}, 2)$ or $\chi^2(1)$. To see this, note that the cumulative probability is given by

$$P(X^2 \le a) = P(-\sqrt{a} \le X \le \sqrt{a})$$

$$= 2\int_0^{\sqrt{a}} \frac{1}{\sqrt{2\pi}} \exp\left(-\frac{x^2}{2}\right) dx \text{ if } a > 0$$

$$P(X^2 \le a) = 0 \text{ if } a \le 0$$

Write $x = \sqrt{y}$.

Then $P(X^2 \leq a) = \displaystyle\int_0^a \frac{1}{\sqrt{2\pi}} \frac{1}{y^{1/2}} e^{-y/2} \, dy$

with probability density function

$$g(y) = \frac{1}{\sqrt{2\pi}} y^{-1/2} e^{-y/2}$$

Now

$$\gamma(y : \tfrac{1}{2}, 2) = \frac{y^{-1/2} e^{-y/2}}{\Gamma(\tfrac{1}{2})\sqrt{2}}$$

Hence

$$g(y) = \frac{y^{-1/2} e^{-y/2}}{\Gamma(\tfrac{1}{2})\sqrt{2}} \cdot \frac{\Gamma(\tfrac{1}{2})}{\sqrt{\pi}} = \gamma(y : \tfrac{1}{2}, 2)$$

But both $g(y)$ and $\gamma(y : \tfrac{1}{2}, 2)$ are probability density functions in the range $[0, \infty]$, and so it must be the case that $\Gamma(\tfrac{1}{2}) = \sqrt{\pi}$. Thus $X^2 = Y$ has pdf $\gamma(\tfrac{1}{2}, 2)$, and so X^2 is distributed as $\chi^2(1)$. More generally, suppose that $X_1, \ldots, X_n$ are distributed as $N(\mu_i, \sigma_i)$. Then for each $i = 1, \ldots, n$ $\left(\dfrac{X_i - \mu_i}{\sigma_i} \right)$ is distributed as $N(0, 1)$ and so $\left(\dfrac{X_i - \mu_i}{\sigma_i} \right)^2$ is distributed as $\gamma(\tfrac{1}{2}, 2)$ or $\chi^2(1)$. But then $\sum_i \left(\dfrac{X_i - \mu_i}{\gamma_i} \right)^2$ is distributed as $\gamma(n/2, 2)$ or $\chi^2(n)$. The integer n we call the *number of degrees of freedom of the distribution* $\chi^2(n)$.

This property we shall call the additivity of the chi-squared distribution. In other words if $X_1^2, \ldots, X_n^2$ are independently distributed as χ^2 with $k_1, \ldots, k_n$ degrees of freedom respectively, then $\sum_i X_i^2$ is distributed as χ^2 with $k_1 + \cdots + k_n$ degrees of freedom.

Consider now the problem of estimating the population variance by $S^2 = \dfrac{1}{n-1} \sum_i (X_i - \bar{X})^2$, where each X_i is normally distributed. In this case each sample is drawn from a population with expected value μ and variance σ^2. As we have seen $\sum_i \left(\dfrac{X_i - \mu}{\sigma} \right)^2$ is distributed as $\chi^2(n)$. But we have also shown that

$$\frac{1}{\sigma^2} \sum_i (X_i - \mu)^2 = \frac{1}{\sigma^2} \sum_i (X_i - \bar{X})^2 + \frac{n}{\sigma^2} (\bar{X} - \mu)^2$$

Moreover, $\bar{X}$ has variance $\dfrac{\sigma^2}{n}$ and so $\left(\dfrac{\bar{X} - \mu}{\sigma/\sqrt{n}} \right)$ is distributed as $N(0, 1)$. Thus $\dfrac{n}{\sigma^2} (\bar{X} - \mu)^2$ is distributed as $\chi(1)$. It follows that $\dfrac{1}{\sigma^2} \sum_i (X_i - \bar{X})^2$ is distributed as $\chi^2(n-1)$. But then $(n-1) \dfrac{S^2}{\sigma^2}$ is distributed as $\chi^2(n-1)$. Now define, for a particular number of degrees of freedom, the value χ_p^2 by

$$P(X^2 < \chi_p^2) = p$$

where X^2 is distributed as $\chi^2(n-1)$.

Then

$$P\left(\chi_{0.025}^2 < (n-1)\frac{S^2}{\sigma^2} < \chi_{0.975}^2\right) = 0.95$$

For example with $n = 15$,

$$\chi_{0.975}^2 = 26.1$$

$$\chi_{0.025}^2 = 5.63$$

If we let $C^2 = \dfrac{\chi^2}{n-1}$ then we obtain

$$P\left(C_{0.025}^2 < \frac{S^2}{\sigma^2} < C_{0.975}^2\right) = 0.95$$

$$\text{or } P\left(0.402 < \frac{S^2}{\sigma^2} < 1.86\right) = 0.95, \text{ in the case } n = 15$$

Thus if a particular reading s^2 is obtained for S^2 in an experiment with fifteen observations, a 95 per cent confidence interval for the true variance σ^2 is $\left(\dfrac{s^2}{1.86}, \dfrac{s^2}{0.402}\right)$. Note than in general a $\chi^2(k)$ variable has expected value k and variance $2k$. Thus the expected value of $\dfrac{\chi^2}{k}$ is 1 and as k approaches infinity, the variance approaches zero. Since $\dfrac{S^2}{\sigma^2}$ is distributed as C^2, $E\left(\dfrac{S^2}{\sigma^2}\right) = 1$ and, as the size of the sample increases, var(S^2) approaches zero. Thus S^2 is both an unbiased and a consistent estimator for σ^2.

Having obtained the nature of the distribution of the estimator S^2 for the population variance, we are now in a position to compute confidence intervals for the population expected value. As we have shown previously the 95 per cent confidence interval for μ, when the population variance σ^2 is known, is $\left[\bar{x} - 1.96\dfrac{\sigma}{\sqrt{n}}, \bar{x} + 1.96\dfrac{\sigma}{\sqrt{n}}\right]$. We should expect that when we use the estimator S^2 for σ^2 then we should obtain a confidence interval

$$\left[\bar{x} - a(n)\frac{S}{\sqrt{n}}, \bar{x} + a(n)\frac{S}{\sqrt{n}}\right]$$

which is dependent on the sample size, n, and which is wider than the previous confidence interval (i.e., $a(n) > 1.96$) because of the variance in S^2. Because S^2 is a consistent estimator we should expect $a(n)$ to approach 1.96, as n approaches infinity.

To see that this is indeed the case, we introduce the F-distribution and (students) t-distribution.

Suppose that U is a χ^2 variable with k degrees of freedom and V is a χ^2-variable with r degrees of freedom. When U and V are independent, then the joint probability density function of U and V is

$$g(u,v) = \gamma(u:(k/2),2)\gamma(v:(r/2),2)$$

$$= \frac{\mu^{(k/2)-1}v^{(r/2)-1}e^{-(u+v)/2}}{\Gamma(k/2)\Gamma(r/2)2^{(k+r)/2}}$$

Now define a new random variable by $F = \dfrac{U}{k}\Big/\dfrac{V}{r}$. Then the probability density function for F, with parameters k,r is

$$g(f:k,r) = \frac{\Gamma\dfrac{(k+r)}{2}(k/r)^{k/2}}{\Gamma(k/2)\Gamma(r/2)} \frac{f^{(k/2)-1}}{(1+kf/r)^{k+r/2}}$$

A random variable with a probability density function of this form is said to be distributed as $F(k,r)$, where k and r are the two degrees of freedom associated with the distribution. In particular, if X is distributed as $N(0,1)$ and V is distributed as $\chi^2(r)$ then, since X^2 is distributed as $\chi^2(1)$, the new variable $Y^2 = \dfrac{rX^2}{V}$ is distributed as $F(1,r)$. The variable $Y = X\sqrt{r}/\sqrt{v}$ then has the t-distribution with r degrees of freedom, with probability density function

$$g(t:r) = \frac{\Gamma(1+r/2)}{\sqrt{\pi r}\,\Gamma(r/2)} \frac{1}{\left(1+\dfrac{t^2}{r}\right)^{(1+r)/2}}$$

Note that $g(-t:r) = g(t:r)$ and so $P(Y \geq t) = P(Y \leq -t)$. Thus $P(Y \leq -t) = 1 - P(Y \leq t)$. Clearly the t-distribution is symmetric about zero. With r degrees of freedom, define the value $t_p(r)$ by $P(Y \leq t_p(r)) = p$. Then, by symmetry $P(-t_p(r) \leq Y \leq t_p(r)) = P(Y \leq t_p(r)) - P(Y < -t_p(r)) = p - (1-p) = 2p - 1$. For example, if we let $p = 0.975$ and $r = 14$, then $t_{0.975}(14) = 2.145$, and so

$$P(-2.145 \leq Y \leq 2.145) = 0.95$$

The interval $(-2.145, 2.145)$ is called the *two sided 95 per cent confidence interval* for the variable Y distributed as $t(14)$. The values of $t_p(r)$ for $p = 0.975$ and degree of freedom of r from 1 to infinity are:

r	1	2	3	4	5	6	7	8	9	10	∞
$t_p(r)$	12.71	4.30	3.18	2.78	2.57	2.45	2.36	2.30	2.26	2.23	1.96

As we noted earlier if Z is distributed as $N(0,1)$ and

$$P(Z \leq Z_p) = p$$

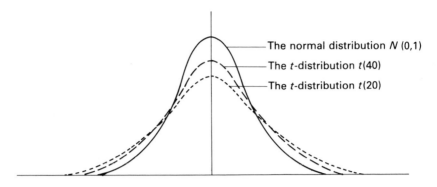

The normal distribution $N(0,1)$

The t-distribution $t(40)$

The t-distribution $t(20)$

Figure 1.3

then in the case $p = 0.975$, $Z_p = 1.96$. Here we see that $t_{0.975}(r) \to 1.96$ as $r \to \infty$, and indeed more generally $t_p(r) \to Z_p$ as $r \to \infty$. In general then the t-distribution is 'flatter' than the normal distribution, and as the parameter r increases, then the distribution $t(r)$ approaches $N(0,1)$.

As we have seen, the variable $(n-1)\dfrac{S^2}{\sigma^2}$ is distributed as $\chi^2(n-1)$, where S^2 is the estimator of the population variance, drawn from a sample of size n. Moreover, the sample mean $\bar{X}$ has expected value μ, and variance $\dfrac{\sigma^2}{n}$. Thus $\left(\dfrac{\bar{X}-\mu}{\sigma}\right)\sqrt{n}$ is distributed as $N(0,1)$. Moreover

$$\left(\frac{\bar{X}-\mu}{\sigma}\right)\sqrt{n}\cdot\sqrt{\frac{(n-1)\sigma^2}{(n-1)S^2}}=\left(\frac{\bar{X}-\mu}{S\sqrt{n}}\right)$$

is t-distributed with $(n-1)$ degrees of freedom. (To obtain this, we have to assume that S^2 and $(\bar{X}-\mu)/\sigma$ are *independent* random variables. We shall show this in a later section.) If we let $t = t_{0.975}(n-1)$ be the t-value defined by

$$P(Y \le t_{0.975}(n-1)) = 0.975$$

then just as before:

$$P(\mu - tS/\sqrt{n}) \le \bar{X} \le \mu + tS/\sqrt{n}) = 0.95$$

Thus the interval $(\mu - tS/\sqrt{n}, \mu + tS/\sqrt{n})$ is the 95 per cent confidence interval for the sample mean. In other words if we believe that the population has mean μ, then the sample mean $\bar{X}$ should lie in this interval, with probability 0.95. Alternatively, if values $\bar{x}$ and S^2 are obtained for the sample mean and sample variance, then

$$\bar{x} - tS/\sqrt{n} \le \mu \le \bar{x} + tS/\sqrt{n}$$

is a 95 per cent confidence interval for the population mean, μ. As we expected, the value t, dependent on the sample size n, approaches 1.96 as the sample size approaches infinity.

Example 1.8

Suppose that we take ten observations of a random variable X which is normally distributed. The mean is $\bar{x} = 0.6$ and we obtain $\sum_i (x_i - \bar{x})^2 = 3.6$. We wish to determine whether the population mean μ is zero. Now $P(\bar{x} - tS/\sqrt{n} \le \mu) = 0.95$ if we choose $t = t_{0.95}(9) = 1.833$. In other words we may assert with 95 per cent confidence that μ lies in the interval $(\bar{x} - tS/\sqrt{n}, \infty)$. Clearly if $\bar{x} > t(S/\sqrt{n})$ then this interval does not contain zero, and so we may, with 95 per cent confidence, reject the hypothesis that $\mu = 0$. Now $S^2 = \frac{1}{9}(3.6) = 0.4$ and $(S^2/\sqrt{n}) = 0.126$ and so $\bar{x} - t(S/\sqrt{n}) = 0.6 - (1.833)(0.4/\sqrt{10}) \simeq 0.369$. Thus $P(\bar{x} > tS/\sqrt{N}) > 0.95$ and so with probability 95 per cent we may reject the hypothesis that $\mu = 0$. In general if the probability associated with an interval is $1 - p$, then the *significance level* is p. In the above test the hypothesis that $\mu = 0$ is rejected at the 5 per cent significance level.

The above method of constructing confidence intervals for the mean of a population can be extended to the case when two samples are taken from the population.

Suppose that two samples of size n, m are obtained from two populations normally distributed as $N(\mu_1, \sigma^2)$ and $N(\mu_2, \sigma^2)$. Let S_1^2 and S_2^2 be the estimates for the population variance, and $\bar{X}_1, \bar{X}_2$ the sample means. As we know $\dfrac{(n-1)S_1^2}{\sigma^2}$ and

$\dfrac{(m-1)S_2^2}{\sigma^2}$ are independently distributed as χ^2 with $(n-1)$ and $(m-1)$ degrees of

freedom. Thus $\dfrac{1}{\sigma^2}[(n-1)S_1^2 + (m-1)S_2^2]$ is distributed as $\chi^2(n+m-2)$. Moreover,

$\bar{X}_1, \bar{X}_2$ are independently distributed as $N(\mu_1, \sigma^2), N(\mu_2, \sigma^2)$ and so $\bar{X}_1 - \bar{X}_2$ is distri-

buted as $N\left(\mu_1 - \mu_2, \dfrac{\sigma^2}{n} + \dfrac{\sigma^2}{m}\right)$. Since a t variable with r degrees of freedom is of the

form $X\sqrt{r/v}$ where X is $N(0,1)$ and V is $\chi^2(r)$ we see that

$$Y = \frac{\bar{X}_1 - \bar{X}_2 - (\mu_1 - \mu_2)}{\sigma\sqrt{1/n + 1/m}} \sqrt{\frac{(n+m-2)\sigma^2}{(n-1)S_1^2 + (m-1)S_2^2}}$$

$$= \frac{(\bar{X}_1 - \bar{X}_2) - (\mu_1 - \mu_2)}{\sqrt{\dfrac{(n-1)S_1^2 + (m-1)S_2^2}{(n+m-2)}}(1/n + 1/m)}$$

is t-distributed with $(n+m-2)$ degrees of freedom. Suppose we let $S_{12}^2 = \dfrac{(n-1)S_1^2 + (m-1)S_2^2}{(n+m-2)}$ and $r = \dfrac{1}{1/n + 1/m} = \dfrac{nm}{m+n}$. Then S_{12}^2 is an estimate of the population variance weighted by the relative sizes of the two samples, while the variance of $\bar{X}_1 - \bar{X}_2$ is $\dfrac{\sigma^2}{r}$. Thus

$$Y = \frac{[(\bar{X}_1 - \bar{X}_2) - (\mu_1 - \mu_2)]}{S_{12}} \sqrt{r}$$

is t distributed with $(n + m - 2)$ degrees of freedom. A two-sided test on the difference of population means is then given by

$$2p - 1 = P\left((\bar{x}_1 - \bar{x}_2) - t\frac{S_{12}}{\sqrt{r}} \le \mu_1 - \mu_2 \le (\bar{x}_1 - \bar{x}_2) + t\frac{S_{12}}{\sqrt{r}}\right)$$

where $t = t_p(n + m - 2)$ is the t value such that

$$P(Y \le t_p(n + m - 2)) = p$$

Example 1.9

Frequently one is interested in the hypothesis that $\mu_1 = \mu_2$. For example suppose $n = 10$, $m = 7$, $\bar{x} = 4.2$, $\bar{y} = 3.4$, $S_1^2 = 49$ and $S_2^2 = 32$. Then the t value for the two-sided confidence interval is 2.131. Now $S_{12}^2 = \dfrac{9(49) + 7(32)}{15} = 42.2$ so $S_{12} = 6.5$, and

$\sqrt{r} = \sqrt{\dfrac{70}{17}} = \sqrt{4.11} = 2.03$. Thus the 95 per cent confidence interval for $\mu_1 - \mu_2$ is

$$\left(0.8 \pm 2.131\left(\frac{6.5}{2.03}\right)\right) = (-6.02 + 7.62)$$

Since this interval clearly includes zero, we may accept the hypothesis that $\mu_1 = \mu_2$ at the 5 per cent significance level.

We earlier showed that if a sample of size n is obtained and the estimate S^2 of variance calculated, then

$$P\left(C_{0.025}^2 \le \frac{S^2}{\sigma^2} \le C_{0.975}^2\right) = 0.95$$

where C_p^2 is that value of the $\dfrac{\chi^2}{n-1}$ variable such that $P(C^2 \le C_p^2) = p$. This of course gives a 95 per cent confidence interval

$$\left[\frac{S^2}{C_{0.975}^2}, \frac{S^2}{C_{0.025}^2}\right]$$

for the population variance.

It is often the case that two samples of size n, m are obtained from two populations, and estimates S_1^2, S_2^2 of the population variances σ_1^2, σ_2^2 obtained. A typical question is whether the samples are drawn from the same population (i.e., $\sigma_1^2 = \sigma_2^2$).

As we have seen $(n-1)\dfrac{S_1^2}{\sigma_1^2}$, $(m-1)\dfrac{S_2^2}{\sigma_2^2}$ are distributed as $\chi^2(n-1)$, $\chi^2(m-1)$ respectively. Then $F = \dfrac{S_1^2}{\sigma_1^2} \bigg/ \dfrac{S_2^2}{\sigma_2^2}$ has an F-distribution with $(n-1)$, $(m-1)$ degrees of freedom

and so
$$P\left(F_{0.025} \le \frac{S_1^2\,\sigma_2^2}{\sigma_1^2\,S_2^2} \le F_{0.975}\right) = 0.95$$

where $F_{0.025}$, $F_{0.975}$ are the appropriate F values.

Note that if
$$P\left(\frac{S_1^2\,\sigma_2^2}{\sigma_1^2\,S_2^2} \le F_{0.975}\right) = 0.975$$

then
$$P\left(\frac{S_2^2\,\sigma_1^2}{\sigma_2^2\,S_1^2} \ge \frac{1}{F_{0.975}}\right) = 0.975 = 1 - 0.025$$

and so
$$P\left(\frac{S_2^2\,\sigma_1^2}{\sigma_2^2\,S_1^2} \le \frac{1}{F_{0.975}}\right) = 0.025$$

Thus for any particular number of degrees of freedom $F_{0.025} = \dfrac{1}{F_{0.975}}$. More generally if we defined $F_p(k, r)$ by

$$P(F \le F_p(k, r)) = p$$

then $F_p(k, r) = \dfrac{1}{F_{1-p}(k, r)}$.

Example 1.10

In example 1.9, we assumed $S_1^2 = 49$ and $S_2^2 = 32$. Suppose we wish to examine whether or not $\sigma_1^2 > \sigma_2^2$. We set

$$P\left(\frac{S_1^2}{S_2^2}\cdot\frac{\sigma_2^2}{\sigma_1^2} \le F_{0.95}\right) = 0.95$$

and $F_{0.95} = 4.10$ since there are $(9,6)$ degrees of freedom. Then

$$P\left(\frac{\sigma_2^2}{\sigma_1^2} \le (4.10)\tfrac{32}{49} = 2.67\right) = 0.95$$

Since the right-hand side of the inequality is greater than one, we can reject the hypothesis that $\sigma_1^2 > \sigma_2^2$, at the 5 per cent significance level.

On the other hand if the hypothesis under consideration is that $\sigma_1^2 = \sigma_2^2$, then we use the two-sided test

$$P\left(\frac{1}{F_{0.975}}\frac{S_2^2}{S_1^2} \le \frac{\sigma_2^2}{\sigma_1^2} \le F_{0.975}\cdot\frac{S_2^2}{S_1^2}\right) = 0.95$$

to obtain the 95 per cent confidence interval $(0.16, 2.67)$ for $\dfrac{\sigma_2^2}{\sigma_1^2}$.

1.8 THE CENTRAL LIMIT THEOREM

In section 1.6 we gave a justification for the use of the sample mean $\bar{X}$ and sample variance S^2 in terms of the lack of *bias* of these two estimators. The second useful property of an estimator $\hat{\theta}_n$ for θ was that the variance $\text{var}(\hat{\theta}_n)$ approached zero as the scale of the experiment, n, increased. Another way of expressing this is that the random variable θ_n defined by the estimator lies close to some constant c, say, as the scale n increases.

More formally, say that a random variable θ_n *converges* to a constant c if and only if, for any $\varepsilon > 0$ the limit

$$\lim_{n \to \infty} P(|\theta_n - c| < \varepsilon) = 1$$

As we have seen the same mean $\bar{X}_n$ (for a sample of size n) has expected value μ and variance $\dfrac{\sigma^2}{n}$. Thus we would expect $\bar{X}_n$ to *converge*, in the above sense, to μ. To show this formally we use *Chebyshev's inequality*. Suppose that $u(X)$ is a non-negative function of a random variable X, and c is a constant. Let

$$A = \{x : u(x) \geq c\} \text{ and } B = \{x : u(x) < c\}$$

Then

$$E(u(X)) = \int_A u(x) f(x) dx + \int_B u(x) f(x) dx$$

$$\geq \int_A u(x) f(x) dx$$

$$\geq c \int_A f(x) dx = cP(u(x) \geq c)$$

Here f is the pdf for X.
Thus

$$P(u(x) \geq c) \leq \frac{1}{c} E(u(x)).$$

Now take $u(X) = (X - \mu)^2$, and $c = k^2 \sigma^2$ for any constant k, where μ, σ are the expected value and variance of X.
Then

$$P((X - \mu)^2 \geq k^2 \sigma^2) \leq \frac{1}{k^2 \sigma^2} E((X - \mu)^2)$$

But $(X - \mu)^2 \geq k^2 \sigma^2$ if and only if X lies outside the range $(\mu - k\sigma, \mu + k\mu)$, or $|X - \mu| \geq k\sigma$. Moreover $E((X - \mu)^2) = \sigma^2$ and so

$$P(|X - \mu| \geq k\sigma) \leq \frac{1}{k^2}, \text{ which is Chebyshev's inequality.}$$

For a normal variate, X, a 95 per cent confidence interval is $(\mu - 1.96\sigma, \mu + 1.96)$. Thus

$$P(|X - \mu| \geq 1.96\sigma) \simeq 0.05$$

Chebyshev's inequality implies that the probability on the left is less than $\frac{1}{(1.96)^2} \simeq 0.26$, which is true enough in this case.

In general the inequality implies that the probability that an observation occurs in the range $(\mu - k\sigma, \mu + k\sigma)$ is at least $1 - \frac{1}{k^2}$. So for example more than 75 per cent of all observations lie within two standard deviations of the expected value.

Consider now the sample mean $\bar{X}_n$ drawn from a population with mean μ, variance σ^2. The variance of $\bar{X}_n$ is $\frac{\sigma^2}{n}$, and so by Chebyshev's inequality

$$P\left(|\bar{X}_n - \mu| \geq k\frac{\sigma}{\sqrt{n}}\right) \leq \frac{1}{k^2}$$

For any $\varepsilon > 0$, put $k = \frac{\varepsilon\sqrt{n}}{\sigma}$. Then $P(|\bar{X}_n - \mu| \geq \varepsilon) \leq \frac{\sigma^2}{n\varepsilon^2}$. In the limit, $\lim_{n \to \infty} P(|\bar{X}_n - \mu| \geq \varepsilon) = 0$ and so $\lim_{n \to \infty} P(|\bar{X}_n - \mu| < \varepsilon) = 1$. Thus the random variable $\bar{X}_n$ *converges* to the parameter μ.

In section 1.6 we defined an estimation procedure $\{\hat{\theta}_n\}$ for a parameter θ to be *consistent* if the risk

$$R(\hat{\theta}_n, \theta) = \text{var}(\hat{\theta}_n) + (\theta - E(\hat{\theta}_n))^2$$

approaches zero as n approaches infinity. We shall show in a later chapter that if an estimation procedure is *consistent* then the estimator $\hat{\theta}_n$ converges to the parameter θ. Thus convergence of an estimator to the parameter may be regarded as the consistency of the estimator.

As an explicit example, consider the case where Y_n is the number of successes in n trials of a Bernoulli experiment, drawn from a population with parameter p. As we have seen, the expected value of Y_n is np and the variance is $np(1 - p)$.

Consider $\hat{p}_n = \frac{1}{n}Y_n$ as an estimator for p. Clearly the variance is $\frac{p(1 - p)}{n}$ and expected value is p.

Thus $P\left(|\hat{p}_n - p| \geq k\sqrt{\frac{p(1 - p)}{n}}\right) \leq \frac{1}{k^2}$. For any $\varepsilon > 0$ put $k = \varepsilon\sqrt{\frac{n}{p(1 - p)}}$. Thus $P(|\hat{p}_n - p| \geq \varepsilon) \leq \frac{p(1 - p)}{n\varepsilon}$. Clearly as $n \to \infty$, $P(|\hat{p}_n - p| \geq \varepsilon) \to 0$ and so $\lim_{n \to \infty} P(|\hat{p}_n - p| < \varepsilon) = 1$. Thus the estimator $\hat{p}_n = \frac{1}{n}Y_n$ converges to the true population parameter p. The convergence of the estimator $\hat{p}$ to the true parameter, in this case a probability p, can be used to give an *experimental* definition of probability. That is to say, an event has probability p, if a consistent procedure, of sampling n replicates of the event and computing the estimator $\hat{p}$, converges to the value p. In a situation where the event is obtaining a head, say, in the coin-tossing experiment, it is possible to conceive of experiments consisting of an infinite number of replicates of the coin toss.

Aside from the usefulness of the convergence property in defining probability, it is helpful to know that in principle replication of the experiment leads to a value for a population parameter that more closely approximates the true value. Note that in showing that the sample mean $\bar{X}_n$ converges to the population parameter μ, we were not required to assume that $\bar{X}_n$ had a particular distribution. To show that estimator S_n^2, for the second order parameter σ^2, converges to σ^2, we need to make some assumptions about the underlying distribution. For example if we assume that each observation is drawn from a population which is normally distributed as $N(\mu, \sigma)$ then as we have shown

$$P\left(C_{1-p}^2 \le \frac{S_n^2}{\sigma^2} \le C_p^2\right) = 2p - 1$$

where $C^2 = \dfrac{\chi^2}{n-1}$. Without proving the assertion, it should be plausible that C^2 converges to 1 as $n \to \infty$, and so S_n^2 should converge to σ^2.

When the underlying distribution of a random variable X is unknown, we can nonetheless use an approximation to the distribution of X if our estimator X_n, drawn from a sample of size n, has a particular distribution, called the *limiting distribution*, as the sample size is increased arbitrarily.

To indicate the idea of limiting distribution, the binomial, Poisson and chi-square distributions all behave like the normal distribution in the limit.

For example, consider the binomial distribution $B(n, p)$ with parameters n (number of trials) and p (probability of a single success). As we saw in section 1.3 if $\lim_{n \to \infty} np = \lambda$ (a constant) then

$$\lim_{n \to \infty} \binom{n}{r} p^r (1 - p)^{n-r} = \frac{\lambda^r}{r!} \exp(-\lambda)$$

That is to say, the limiting distribution of the binomial distribution is the Poisson distribution with probability function $f(r) = \dfrac{\lambda^r}{r!} \exp(-\lambda)$, expected value $\mu = \lambda$ and variance $\sigma^2 = \lambda$. Let Y_λ be a random variable which has a Poisson distribution with $\mu = \lambda$ and $\sigma^2 = \lambda$, and consider the new random variable $\dfrac{Y_\lambda - \lambda}{\sqrt{\lambda}} = Z_\lambda$. It can be shown in the limit as λ approaches infinity, that Z_λ is normally distributed with mean zero and variance one. Therefore we can infer that the limiting distribution of the binomial distribution is the normal distribution. In other words if X_n is distributed as $B(n, p)$ then X_n is 'approximately' distributed as $N(np, \sqrt{np(1-p)})$ where we mean by this that the limiting distribution of $\dfrac{X_n - np}{\sqrt{np(1-p)}}$ is $N(0, 1)$.

In the same way if Y_n is distributed as $\chi^2(n)$ with expected value n and variance $2n$ then the random variable $\dfrac{Y_n - n}{\sqrt{2n}}$ has a limiting normal distribution $N(0, 1)$.

Suppose that X is a random variable with unknown distribution, but with known expected value μ and variance σ^2. If $\{X_1, \ldots, X_n\}$ are replicates of X, obtained from independent observations in a sample of size n then the sample mean $\bar{X}_n$ has expected value μ and variance $\dfrac{\sigma^2}{\sqrt{n}}$.

The *central limit theorem* asserts that if μ is finite and σ^2 is positive, then the random variable $Y_n = \dfrac{(\bar{X}_n - \mu)\sqrt{n}}{\sigma}$ has limiting normal distribution $N(0,1)$. For a fixed positive integer n, we may regard the variable Y_n as being *approximately* distributed as $N(0, 1)$.

In the case that the true population variance is unknown then we may use the estimator $S_n^2 = \dfrac{1}{n-1}\sum_i (X_i - \bar{X})^2$ for the variance. As in section 1.7 the random variable $\dfrac{(\bar{X}_n - \mu)\sqrt{n}}{S_n}$ is then *approximately* distributed as the *t*-distribution with $(n-1)$ degrees of freedom. This permits us to construct confidence intervals for the population mean and variance as before.

1.9 EXERCISES

1. A pack of cards has 52 cards (four suits each with thirteen face values). In a given five-card poker hand the various possibilities are:
   (a) a pair (with the same face value);
   (b) two pairs;
   (c) trio (three cards with the same face value);
   (d) straight (five cards in sequence, not necessarily of the same suit);
   (e) flush (five cards of the same suit);
   (f) full house (one pair and one trio);
   (g) quartet (four cards with the same face value);
   (h) straight flush (straight, with all cards the same suit).
   Show that the probability diminishes from pair to straight flush. In three-card 'brag' show the sequence is pair, flush, straight, trio, straight flush.

2. Consider a jury consisting of twelve people. Suppose that the probability that any juror finds the plaintiff guilty is p. The plaintiff is found guilty by the jury if k jurors find the plaintiff guilty. For each decision rule $k = 1, \ldots, 12$, compute the probability that the first juror and the jury as a whole disagree in their judgement.

Chapter 2

Regression Analysis

In the previous chapter we considered sampling of a single random variable both in the case when the underlying distribution was known and when it was unknown. In the case of a normally distributed random variable X, we made use of the sample mean $\bar{X}$ as an estimator for the population mean μ_x, and showed that $\bar{X}$ was distributed normally as $N\left(\mu_x, \frac{\sigma_x^2}{T}\right)$, where we now use T to refer to the sample size. Alternatively, given a set of observations $\{X_1, \ldots, X_T\}$ then the errors $e_i = X_i - \mu_x$ are drawn from a population with zero mean and variance σ_x^2. In this chapter we develop the discussion of section 1.4 and consider the case where the 'errors' are generated by a linear relationship between a number of variables $\{X, Y, Z, \ldots\}$ etc.

2.1 BIVARIATE REGRESSION

Suppose that we wish to analyse the relationship between two random variables X, Y and obtain a series of observations $\{(Y_1, X_1), \ldots, (Y_T, X_T)\}$. Here $i = 1, \ldots, T$ may often be identified with the time the observation occurred. Note that T is the number of observations, rather than n as in the earlier chapter. Let us make the hypothesis that the random variables are linearly related. That is to say for any observation X_i, the true value of Y_i is $\alpha + \beta X_i$. Another way of expressing this is that the expected value of Y_i given X_i is $E(Y_i/X_i) = \alpha + \beta X_i$. Alternatively we may write

$$Y_i = \alpha + \beta X_i + e_i$$

where e_i is an error term with zero expected value. We assume for the moment that the errors are independent, so $\text{cov}(e_i, e_j) = 0$ for $i \neq j$. X is called the *independent* variable and Y the *dependent* variable.

Given the sample the problem is to obtain *estimates* $\hat{\alpha}$, $\hat{\beta}$ for the parameters α, β. This in turn allows us to write $\hat{Y}_i = \hat{\alpha} + \hat{\beta}X_i$ for the estimated true value of Y_i given X_i and $Y_i = \hat{Y}_i + \hat{e}_i$ where $\hat{e}_i$ is an estimate for the true error. In section 1.4 it was shown that when the expected value of Y_i given X_i is $\alpha + \beta X_i$ then the true values of α, β are given by the equation

$$E(Y_i/X_i) = \mu_y + \frac{\text{cov}(X,Y)}{\text{var}(X)}(X_i - \mu_x)$$

Here μ_y, μ_x are the true expected values of the random variables Y, X and $\text{cov}(X,Y)$, $\text{var}(X)$ are the true covariance between X, Y and variance of X. In the case that we do not know these (true) population parameters we may nonetheless estimate $\text{cov}(X,Y)$ and $\text{var}(X)$. Thus for a sample $\{Y_1, X_1), \ldots, (Y_T, X_T)\}$ consisting of T different observations of the pairs of random variables, define

$$S_{xx} = \sum_{i=1}^{T} (X_i - \bar{X})^2 = \sum_{i=1}^{T} x_i^2$$

$$S_{yy} = \sum_{i=1}^{T} (Y_i - \bar{Y})^2 = \sum_{i=1}^{T} y_i^2$$

$$S_{xy} = \sum_{i=1}^{T} (X_i - \bar{X})(Y_i - \bar{Y})$$

$$= \sum_{i=1}^{T} x_i y_i$$

Here $x_i = X_i - \bar{X}$ and $y_i = Y_i - \bar{Y}$ are observations about the sample means of X, Y respectively. The obvious candidates for the estimators for the (population) co-variance, $\text{cov}(X,Y)$, and variance, $\text{var}(X)$, are

$$\hat{\text{cov}}(X, Y) = \frac{1}{T-1} S_{xy}, \quad \hat{\text{var}}(X) = \frac{1}{T-1} S_{xx}$$

Moreover the estimated values of μ_y and μ_x can be taken to be $\bar{Y}$, $\bar{X}$ respectively. Thus the estimator for the expected value of Y given X_i is

$$\hat{E}(Y_i/X_i) = \bar{Y} + \frac{S_{xy}}{S_{xx}}(X_i - \bar{X})$$

In other words if we write $\hat{E}(Y_i/X_i) = \hat{Y}_i$ then $\hat{Y}_i = \hat{\alpha} + \hat{\beta}X_i$ where the estimator $\hat{\beta} = \dfrac{S_{xy}}{S_{xx}}$

while

$$\hat{\alpha} = \bar{Y} - \bar{X}\frac{S_{xy}}{S_{xx}}$$

By making the coordinate change from X_i to $x_i = X_i - \bar{X}$ we may write

$$\hat{Y}_i = \hat{\alpha} + \hat{\beta}x_i$$

where $\hat{\beta} = \dfrac{S_{xy}}{S_{xx}}$ as before, but $\hat{\alpha} = \bar{Y}$. Although this definition of the estimators $\hat{\alpha}, \hat{\beta}$ is consistent with the earlier analysis of a linear expected value of Y given X, we need to provide further justification for these estimators. It is to this we now turn. Our first justification for the use of the estimators $\hat{\alpha}, \hat{\beta}$ is that these estimators minimise the sum of squared errors. To see this suppose that a and b are constants used to estimate the expected value

$$\hat{Y}_i = a + bx_i$$

But then the actual value of Y_i, given X_i, is

$$Y_i = \hat{Y}_i + \hat{e}_i$$

where $\hat{e}_i$ is the estimate of the error.

Thus
$$R = \sum_{i=1}^{T} \hat{e}_i^2 = \sum_{i=1}^{T} (Y_i - a - bx_i)^2$$

is the sum of squared errors (dependent of course on a, b). We can show that R is minimised when $a = \hat{\alpha}, b = \hat{\beta}$. To see this,

$$R = \sum_i Y_i^2 + Ta^2 + b^2 \sum_i x_i^2$$

$$- 2a \sum_i Y_i - 2b \sum_i x_i Y_i + 2ab \sum_i x_i$$

But $\sum_i x_i = \sum_i (X_i - \bar{X}) = \sum_i X_i - T\bar{X} = 0$ and $\sum_i x_i^2 = S_{xx}, \sum_i x_i Y_i = S_{xy}$. For convenience, we suppress indices on summations.

Completing the squares in this expression gives

$$R = T(\bar{Y} - a)^2 + S_{xx}\left(\frac{S_{xy}}{S_{xx}} - b\right)^2 + \sum\left(Y_i - \bar{Y} - \frac{S_{xy}}{S_{xx}}x_i\right)^2$$

Since all three expressions on the right are square terms and non-negative, the expression is minimised when $a = \bar{Y} = \hat{\alpha}$ and $b = \dfrac{S_{xy}}{S_{xx}} = \hat{\beta}$, in which case of course, $R = \sum (Y_i - \hat{\alpha} - \hat{\beta}x_i)^2$. An alternative proof, involving calculus, is as follows.

$$\frac{\partial R}{\partial a} = -2\sum_i (Y_i - a - bx_i)$$

$$\frac{\partial R}{\partial b} = -2b\sum_i x_i(Y_i - a - bx_i)$$

Setting $\dfrac{\partial R}{\partial a} = \dfrac{\partial R}{\partial b} = 0$ we obtain

1. $\sum Y_i - b\sum x_i - Ta = 0.$

But $\qquad\qquad\qquad \sum x_i = 0$, thus $a = 1/T\sum Y_i = \bar{Y}$

2. $S_{xy} - bS_{xx} - a\sum x_i = 0.$

Thus $$b = \frac{S_{xy}}{S_{xx}}$$

Of course to verify that setting $a = \hat{\alpha}$ and $b = \hat{\beta}$ minimises R we need to check the second order conditions. However, this is not necessary in this case since we have verified this already by completing squares. The estimators $\hat{\alpha}, \hat{\beta}$ are known as the *least square estimators* in the bivariate regression model.

The estimates $\hat{e}_i = Y_i - (\hat{\alpha} + \hat{\beta}x_i)$ of the errors we may assume are drawn from a population with mean zero and variance σ^2. This gives us a regression equation

$$\hat{Y}_i = \bar{Y} + \frac{S_{xy}}{S_{xx}}(X_i - \bar{X})$$

essentially an estimate of the relationship between Y and X, with the errors being the vertical distance between an observation (Y_i, X_i) and the point $(\hat{Y}_i, X_i)$ on the regression line. Note that the regression line contains the point $(\hat{Y}_i, X_i) = (\bar{Y}, \bar{X})$.

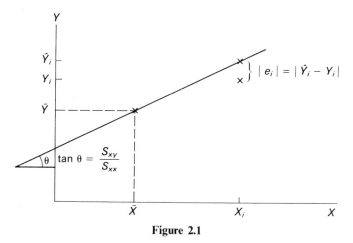

Figure 2.1

The assumption that the errors are distributed with mean zero and variance σ^2 allows us to compute the expected values and variances of the estimators $\hat{\alpha}, \hat{\beta}$ as follows.

Consider the estimator $\hat{\alpha}$

$$E(\hat{\alpha}) = E(\bar{Y}) = E\left(\frac{1}{T}\sum Y_i\right)$$

$$= \frac{1}{T}\sum E[Y_i]$$

$$= \frac{1}{T}\sum (\alpha + \beta x_i) = \alpha$$

Thus $\hat{\alpha}$ has expected value the true value α. As we have mentioned $\hat{\alpha}$ is said to be *unbiased*.

Moreover

$$\text{var}(\hat{\alpha}) = E[(\hat{\alpha} - \alpha)^2] = E[(\bar{Y} - \alpha)^2]$$

$$= E\left[\left(\frac{1}{T}\sum Y_i - \alpha\right)^2\right]$$

$$= E\left[\left(\frac{1}{T}\sum(Y_i - \beta x_i) - \alpha\right)^2\right]$$

$$= E\left[\left(\frac{1}{T}\sum(Y_i - \alpha - \beta x_i)\right)^2\right]$$

$$= \frac{1}{T^2}E\left[\sum e_i^2\right] \text{ since the errors are independent.}$$

But e_i is distributed with mean 0, variance σ^2, so $E[e_i^2] = \text{var}(e_i) = \sigma^2$ and

$$\text{var}(\hat{\alpha}) = \frac{1}{T^2}E\left[\sum e_i^2\right] = \frac{T\sigma^2}{T^2} = \frac{\sigma^2}{T}$$

Consider the estimator $\hat{\beta}$

$$\hat{\beta}: E[\hat{\beta}] = E\left[\frac{S_{xy}}{S_{xx}}\right]$$

$$E\left[\frac{\sum x_i Y_i}{\sum x_i^2}\right]$$

We may regard the x_i's as constants, since they are given as data:

Thus

$$E(\hat{\beta}) = \frac{\sum x_i E(Y_i)}{\sum x_i^2}$$

$$= \frac{\sum x_i(\alpha + \beta x_i)}{S_{xx}} = \beta\frac{S_{xx}}{S_{xx}} = \beta$$

and

$$\text{var}(\hat{\beta}) = \text{var}\left[\frac{\sum x_i Y_i}{\sum x_i^2}\right] = \frac{1}{S_{xx}^2}E\left(\left(\sum e_i x_i\right)^2\right)$$

$$= \frac{1}{S_{xx}^2}\sum x_i^2 \text{ var}(e_i), \text{ since } \{e_i\} \text{ are independent}$$

$$= \frac{1}{S_{xx}^2}S_{xx}\sigma^2 = \frac{\sigma^2}{S_{xx}}$$

Hence $\hat{\alpha}, \hat{\beta}$ are distributed with means α, β are variances $\dfrac{\sigma^2}{T}, \dfrac{\sigma^2}{S_{xx}}$. Furthermore $\hat{\alpha}, \hat{\beta}$ are both linear in Y_i, i.e.

$$\hat{\alpha} = \sum_i \frac{Y_i}{T} = \sum c_i Y_i \text{ where } c_i = \frac{1}{T}$$

and

$$\hat{\beta} = \sum_i \frac{x_i Y_i}{S_{xx}} = \sum d_i Y_i \text{ where } d_i = \frac{x_i}{S_{xx}}$$

We previously said that an estimator $\hat{\theta}$ for a population parameter was a best linear unbiased estimator (BLUE) if (i) it was linear in the observations of the sample, (ii) it was an unbiased estimator of θ, and (iii) it had lower variance than any other linear, unbiased estimator for θ. The previous analysis shows that the estimators $\hat{\alpha}, \hat{\beta}$ are linear in the dependent variables $Y_1, \ldots, Y_T$. In the case that the errors, e_i, are uncorrelated (in the sense that the covariance $\text{cov}(e_i, e_j) = 0$ for each $i \neq j$) then the *Gauss–Markov theorem* asserts that the estimators $\hat{\alpha}, \hat{\beta}$ are best linear unbiased estimators. This is proved more formally below. To indicate the proof, we proceed as follows.

1. $\hat{\alpha}$: Let $a = \sum c_i Y_i$ where a is a linear unbiased estimator for α.

Thus

$$\alpha = E(a) = \sum c_i E(Y_i) = \sum c_i(\alpha + \beta x_i)$$

and so

$$\sum c_i = 1, \sum c_i x_i = 0$$

Moreover

$$\text{var}(a) = E[(a - \alpha)^2] = E\left[\left(\sum c_i Y_i - \alpha\right)^2\right]$$

$$= E\left[\left(\sum c_i(\alpha + \beta x_i + e_i) - \alpha\right)^2\right]$$

$$= E\left[\left(\sum c_i e_i\right)^2\right]$$

$$= \sum c_i^2 E(e_i^2) + \sum_{i \neq j} c_i c_j E(e_i e_j)$$

Now e_i, e_j are assumed to be independent for $i \neq j$, so

$$E(e_i)E(e_j) = E(e_i e_j) = 0 \text{ for } i \neq j$$

Hence

$$\text{var}(a) = \sum c_i^2 E(e_i^2) = \sum c_i^2 \sigma^2$$

Now $\text{var}(a)$ is a minimum when $\sigma^2 \sum c_i^2$ is a minimum subject to the constraints that $\sum c_i = 1, \sum c_i x_i = 0$. This is true when $c_i = \dfrac{1}{T}$. Hence var (a) is minimum when

$a = \dfrac{1}{T}\sum Y_i = \bar{Y} = \hat{\alpha}$. But this is the least squares estimator, so $\hat{\alpha}$ has minimum variance among the linear unbiased estimators.

2. $\hat{\beta}$: Let $b = \sum d_i Y_i$, $E(b) = \beta$.

Then

$$\beta = E(b) = \sum d_i E(Y_i) = \sum d_i(\alpha + \beta x_i).$$

Hence

$$\sum d_i x_i = 1, \quad \sum d_i = 0.$$

Now

$$\mathrm{var}(b) = E[(b - \beta)^2]$$

$$= E\left[\left(\sum d_i Y_i - \beta\right)^2\right]$$

$$= E\left[\left(\sum d_i(\alpha + \beta x_i + e_i) - \beta\right)^2\right]$$

$$= E\left[\left(\sum d_i e_i\right)^2\right]$$

$$= \sigma^2 \sum d_i^2 \text{ as before.}$$

Subject to the restrictions $\sum d_i = 0$, $\sum d_i x_i = 1, \sum d_i^2$ is minimised if $d_i = \dfrac{x_i}{\sum x_i^2} = \dfrac{x_i}{S_{xx}}$. Hence var$(b)$ is minimum if $b = \sum \dfrac{x_i Y_i}{\sum x_i^2} = \dfrac{S_{xy}}{S_{xx}}$. But $\hat{\beta} = \dfrac{S_{xy}}{S_{xx}}$. Hence $\hat{\beta}$ has a minimum variance among the linear unbiased estimators.

A second justification for use of the least square estimators is the method of maximum likelihood. As an illustration consider again estimation of a population mean from the sample mean. In the case that the random variable is distributed as $N(\mu,\sigma^2)$ then the probability density function for each X_i is $f(X_i) = \dfrac{1}{\sigma\sqrt{2\pi}}\exp\left(-\tfrac{1}{2}\left(\dfrac{X_i - \mu}{\sigma}\right)^2\right)$. If the T observations are independent then the joint probability density function for $X_1,\ldots,X_T$ is

$$L(X_1,\ldots,X_T) = \prod_{i=1}^{T} f(X_i)$$

In the case that we use *estimators* $\hat{\mu}, \hat{\sigma}^2$ for the population mean and variance then the estimated probability density function for X_i is

$$f(X_i : \hat{\mu}, \hat{\sigma}) = \dfrac{1}{\hat{\sigma}\sqrt{2\pi}}\exp\left(-\tfrac{1}{2}\left(\dfrac{X_i - \hat{\mu}}{\hat{\sigma}}\right)^2\right)$$

and the likelihood function for $X_1, \ldots, X_T$ is

$$L(X_1, \ldots, X_T : \hat{\mu}, \hat{\sigma}) = \prod_{i=1}^{T} f(X_i : \hat{\mu}, \hat{\sigma}).$$

If we choose those estimators μ^*, σ^* for $\hat{\mu}, \hat{\sigma}$ such that $L(X_1, \ldots, X_T : \hat{\mu}, \hat{\sigma})$ is maximised then these estimators are called *maximum likelihood estimators* (MLE). For example, the likelihood function for the population mean is

$$L(X_1, \ldots, X_T : \hat{\mu}, \hat{\sigma}) = \prod_{i=1}^{T} f(X_i : \hat{\mu}, \hat{\sigma})$$

$$= \left(\frac{1}{\hat{\sigma}\sqrt{2\pi}} \right)^T \exp\left[-\tfrac{1}{2} \sum_i \left(\frac{X_i - \hat{\mu}}{\hat{\sigma}} \right)^2 \right]$$

Then

$$\frac{\partial}{\partial \hat{\mu}} [\log L] = 0 \quad \text{when} \quad \sum_i \frac{X_i - \hat{\mu}}{\hat{\sigma}} = 0$$

Thus $\mu^* = \dfrac{1}{T} \sum_{i=1}^{T} X_i$ is the maximum likelihood estimator.

In the case of bivariate regression the likelihood of obtaining $\{Y_1, \ldots, Y_T\}$ given the values of the independent variables $\{X_1, \ldots, X_T\}$ is simply the likelihood of obtaining the errors $\{e_1, \ldots, e_T\}$. If we assume that these errors are uncorrelated (i.e., independent), and normally distributed with mean 0 and variance σ^2 then the likelihood function becomes

$$L(e_i, \ldots, e_T : a, b) = \left(\frac{1}{\sigma\sqrt{2\pi}} \right)^T \exp\left[-\frac{1}{2\sigma^2} \sum_i^n e_i^2 \right]$$

However, $e_i = Y_i - a - bx_i$ where a, b are the estimators we seek. Now let

$$R = \sum_i e_i^2 = \sum_i (Y_i - a - bx_i)^2$$

and let $\underline{e} = (e_1, \ldots, e_T)$ be the *vector* of errors. Then

$$L(\underline{e} : a, b) = \left(\frac{1}{\sigma\sqrt{2\pi}} \right)^T \exp\left[-\frac{1}{2\sigma^2} R \right]$$

Clearly $L(\underline{e} : a, b)$ is maximised when R is minimised. But as we have seen previously, R is minimised when $a = \bar{Y} = \hat{\alpha}$ and $b = \dfrac{S_{xy}}{S_{xx}} = \hat{b}$. Thus $\hat{\alpha}$ and $\hat{\beta}$ are the *maximum likelihood estimators*. This method also gives a maximum likelihood estimator for the variance σ^2 of errors. Taking log (to base e) in the above expression we obtain

$$\log L = -\frac{T}{2} \log 2\pi - \frac{T}{2} \log \sigma^2 - \frac{1}{2\sigma^2} R$$

Then $\dfrac{\partial}{\partial \sigma} \log L = -\dfrac{T}{2\sigma^2} \cdot 2\sigma + \dfrac{R}{\sigma^3} = 0$ if $\sigma^2 = \dfrac{R}{T}$. Thus the maximum likelihood estimator $\hat{\sigma}^2$ for σ^2 is $\hat{\sigma}^2 = \dfrac{R}{T} = \dfrac{1}{T}\sum\limits_{i=1}^{T}(Y_i - \hat{\alpha} - \hat{\beta}x_i)^2$. In the case discussed in section 1.6 of estimation of a sample variance from observations $\{Y_1, \ldots, Y_T\}$ it was shown that the expected value

$$\text{E}\left(\frac{1}{T}\sum_{i=1}^{T}(Y_i - \bar{Y})^2\right) = \frac{T-1}{T}\cdot\sigma^2$$

In the next section, in just the same way, it is shown that the expected value of the maximum likelihood estimator is

$$\text{E}(\hat{\sigma}^2) = \frac{T-2}{T}\sigma^2$$

That is to say the maximum likelihood estimator for $\hat{\sigma}^2$ is *biased*. Instead an unbiased estimator for σ^2 is

$$\hat{\sigma}^2 = \frac{R}{T-2} = \frac{1}{T-2}\sum_{i=1}^{T}(Y_i - \hat{\alpha} - \hat{\beta}x_i)^2$$

2.2   CONFIDENCE INTERVALS ON THE ESTIMATORS

To obtain confidence intervals on the estimators $\hat{\alpha}, \hat{\beta}$ we can proceed as in the discussion in Chapter 1 of a sample of a single variable. First of all, suppose that the true parameters are α, β. Then the sum of squared errors is

$$R(\alpha, \beta) = \sum_{i=1}^{T}(Y_i - \alpha - \beta x_i)^2 = \sum_{i=1}^{T} e_i^2$$

But we have shown that

$$R(\alpha, \beta) = T(\bar{Y} - \alpha)^2 + S_{xx}\left(\frac{S_{xy}}{S_{xx}} - \beta\right)^2$$

$$+ \sum_i\left(Y_i - \bar{Y} - \frac{S_{xy}}{S_{xx}}x_i\right)^2$$

$$= T(\hat{\alpha} - \alpha)^2 + S_{xx}(\hat{\beta} - \beta)^2 + \sum_i \hat{e}_i^2$$

where $\hat{e}_i = Y_i - \hat{\alpha} - \hat{\beta}x_i$ is our estimate of the error in the ith observation. Write $R(\hat{\alpha}, \hat{\beta}) = \sum\limits_i \hat{e}_i^2$. Now we know that

$$\text{E}(\hat{\alpha}) = \alpha, \ \text{var}(\hat{\alpha}) = \frac{\sigma^2}{T}$$

$$\text{E}(\hat{\beta}) = \beta, \ \text{var}(\hat{\beta}) = \frac{\sigma^2}{S_{xx}}$$

Suppose that the true errors e_i are normally distributed as $N(0, \sigma)$. Then for each $i = 1, \ldots, T$, $\dfrac{e_i}{\sigma} = \dfrac{Y - \alpha - \beta x_i}{\sigma}$ is distributed as $N(0, 1)$ and so $\dfrac{1}{\sigma^2} R(\alpha, \beta) = \dfrac{1}{\sigma^2} \sum_{i=1}^{T} e_i^2$ is distributed as $\chi^2(T)$. But also $(\hat{\alpha} - \alpha)$ will be normally distributed as $N\left(0, \dfrac{\sigma^2}{T}\right)$ and $(\hat{\beta} - \beta)$ will be normally distributed as $N\left(0, \dfrac{\sigma^2}{S_{xx}}\right)$. Thus $T\left(\dfrac{\hat{\alpha} - \alpha}{\sigma}\right)^2$ and $S_{xx}\left(\dfrac{\hat{\beta} - \beta}{\sigma}\right)^2$ will both be distributed as $\chi^2(1)$. Moreover

$$\frac{R(\alpha, \beta)}{\sigma^2} = T\frac{(\hat{\alpha} - \alpha)^2}{\sigma^2} + S_{xx}\frac{(\hat{\beta} - \beta)^2}{\sigma^2} + \frac{1}{\sigma^2}\sum_i \hat{e}_i^2$$

and so

$$\frac{1}{\sigma^2}\sum_i \hat{e}_i^2 = \frac{1}{\sigma^2} R(\hat{\alpha}, \hat{\beta})$$

will be distributed as $\chi^2(T - 2)$. Note here that we use the fact that the three random variables $\dfrac{(\hat{\alpha} - \alpha)}{\sigma}\sqrt{T}$, $\dfrac{(\hat{\beta} - \beta)}{\sigma}\sqrt{S_{xx}}$ and $\dfrac{\sqrt{R(\hat{\alpha}, \hat{\beta})}}{\sigma}$ are independent.

If we take expected values then

$$E\left(\frac{R(\alpha, \beta)}{\sigma^2}\right) = E\left(\frac{T(\hat{\alpha} - \alpha)^2}{\sigma^2}\right) + E\left(\frac{S_{xx}}{\sigma^2}(\hat{\beta} - \beta)^2\right)$$

$$+ E\left(\frac{R(\hat{\alpha}, \hat{\beta})}{\sigma^2}\right)$$

However

$$E\left(\frac{R(\alpha, \beta)}{\sigma^2}\right) = E\left(\sum_i^T \frac{e_i^2}{\sigma^2}\right) = T$$

since the errors are independent with mean 0 and variance σ^2. Moreover

$$E\left(\frac{T(\hat{\alpha} - \alpha)^2}{\sigma^2}\right) = E\left(\frac{S_{xx}}{\sigma^2}(\hat{\beta} - \beta)^2\right) = 1$$

Thus

$$E\left(\frac{R(\hat{\alpha}, \hat{\beta})}{\sigma^2}\right) = T - 2$$

Hence if we define $S^2 = \dfrac{1}{T - 2} R(\hat{\alpha}, \hat{\beta}) = \dfrac{1}{T - 2}\sum_i \hat{e}_i^2$ we see that $E(S^2) = \sigma^2$ and so S^2 is an *unbiased* estimator for σ^2.

We have therefore shown

1. In the case where the errors $\{e_i : i = 1, \ldots, T\}$ are independent, the estimator

$S^2 = \dfrac{1}{T-2} R(\hat{\alpha}, \hat{\beta})$ is an unbiased estimator for the variance of errors.

2. In the case where the error terms are independent *and* distributed as $N(0, \sigma^2)$, the random variable $\dfrac{1}{\sigma^2} R(\hat{\alpha}, \hat{\beta})$ is distributed as $\chi^2(T-2)$.

As in Chapter 1, if we define $C^2 = \dfrac{1}{T-2} \chi^2(T-2)$, with $T-2$ degrees of freedom, and

$C_p^2 = \dfrac{1}{T-2} \chi_p^2$ where χ_p^2 is the chi-square value such that $P(X^2 < \chi_p^2) = p$, for X^2 a chi-square variable, then

$$P\left(C_{0.025}^2 < \frac{S^2}{\sigma^2} < C_{0.975}^2 \right) = 0.95$$

The only difference between this case and the single variable sample is that the number of degree of freedom is $T-2$, where T is the number of observations.

Precisely as in the previous chapter, the assumption that the errors are normally distributed allows us to conclude that both $\dfrac{\hat{\alpha} - \alpha}{S/\sqrt{T}}$ and $\dfrac{\hat{\beta} - \beta}{S/\sqrt{S_{xx}}}$ are t-distributed with $(T-2)$ degree of freedom. As before if we let t be the t value at the 97.5 per cent level with $T-2$ degree of freedom, then

$$P\left(-t \le \frac{\alpha - \hat{\alpha}}{S/\sqrt{T}} \le t \right) = 0.95$$

or

$$P\left(\hat{\alpha} - t \cdot \frac{S}{\sqrt{T}} \le \alpha \le \hat{\alpha} + t \cdot \frac{S}{\sqrt{T}} \right) = 0.95$$

Thus if $\left| \dfrac{\hat{\alpha}\sqrt{T}}{S} \right| < t$ the 95 per cent confidence interval for α includes zero. In this case the hypothesis that $\alpha = 0$ cannot be rejected as the 5 per cent significance level. Since S^2 is our *estimate* for the variance of the errors, $\dfrac{S}{\sqrt{T}} = S_\alpha$ is the estimate of the standard deviation, known as the standard error in $\hat{\alpha}$. The value $\left| \dfrac{\hat{\alpha}}{S_\alpha} \right| = t_\alpha$ is called the t-value for the estimator $\hat{\alpha}$. In the same way the random variable $\dfrac{\hat{\beta} - \beta}{\sigma/\sqrt{S_{xx}}}$ is distributed as $N(0, 1)$ and so $\dfrac{\hat{\beta} - \beta}{S/\sqrt{S_{xx}}}$ has a t-distribution with $T-2$ degree of freedom. Again if we let t be the appropriate value at the 97.5 per cent with $T-2$ degree of freedom, then

$$P\left(\hat{\beta} - t \cdot \frac{S}{\sqrt{S_{xx}}} \leq \beta \leq \hat{\beta} + t \cdot \frac{S}{\sqrt{S_{xx}}}\right) = 0.95$$

Similarly $\frac{S}{\sqrt{S_{xx}}} = S_\beta$ is the standard error in β. Thus if $\left|\frac{\hat{\beta}}{S_\beta}\right| = t_\beta < t$ then the 95 per cent confidence interval for β includes 0, and so the hypothesis that $\beta = 0$ cannot be rejected as the 5 per cent significance level.

As we have seen $T\frac{(\hat{\alpha} - \alpha)^2}{\sigma^2}$ and $S_{xx}\frac{(\hat{\beta} - \beta)^2}{\sigma^2}$ are independent, and both are distributed as $\chi^2(1)$, and so

$$\frac{1}{\sigma^2}[T(\hat{\alpha} - \alpha)^2 + S_{xx}(\hat{\beta} - \beta)^2]$$

is distributed as $\chi^2(2)$. Moreover $\frac{1}{\sigma^2}R(\hat{\alpha}, \hat{\beta}) = \frac{T-2}{\sigma^2} \cdot S^2$ is distributed as $\chi^2(T-2)$.

Thus
$$F = \frac{1}{\sigma^2}\frac{[T(\hat{\alpha} - \alpha)^2 + S_{xx}(\hat{\beta} - \beta)^2]}{\frac{1}{\sigma^2}(T-2)S^2} \cdot \frac{T-2}{2}$$

$$= \frac{1}{2S^2}[T(\hat{\alpha} - \alpha)^2 + S_{xx}(\hat{\beta} - \beta)^2]$$

is F-distributed with $(2, T-2)$ degrees of freedom. Then $P(F \leq F_{0.95}) = 0.95$ is a simultaneous test on $\hat{\alpha}, \hat{\beta}$. For a particular value of $Y_i = \hat{\alpha} + \hat{\beta}x_i + e_i$ the variance in Y_i is the sum of variance in $\hat{\alpha}, \hat{\beta}$ as well as e_i.
Thus

$$\mathrm{var}(Y_i) = \mathrm{var}(\hat{\alpha} + \hat{\beta}x_i + \hat{e}_i)$$

$$= \frac{\sigma^2}{T} + x_i^2\frac{\sigma^2}{S_{xx}} + \sigma^2$$

$$= \sigma^2\left[1 + \frac{1}{T} + \frac{x_i^2}{S_{xx}}\right]$$

An estimator var(Y_i), for the variance in Y_i is then

$$\mathrm{var}(Y_i) = S^2\left(1 + \frac{1}{T} + \frac{x_i^2}{S_{xx}}\right)$$

Since the estimator for Y_i is $\hat{\alpha} + \hat{\beta}x_i$, clearly $\frac{Y_i - \hat{\alpha} - \hat{\beta}x_i}{\sqrt{\mathrm{var}(Y_i)}}$ is t-distributed with $T-2$

degree of freedom. Consequently, if we let t be the t-value at the 97.5 per cent level, then

$$0.95 = P(\hat{\alpha} + \hat{\beta}x_i - t \cdot \sqrt{\text{var}(Y_i)} \leq Y_i \leq \hat{\alpha} + \hat{\beta}x_i + t\sqrt{\text{var}(Y_i)})$$

Thus a 95 per cent confidence interval for Y_i, given x_i is $[\hat{\alpha} + \hat{\beta}x_i - t\sqrt{\text{var}(Y_i)}$, $\hat{\alpha} + \hat{\beta}x_i + t\sqrt{\text{var}(Y_i)}]$. Note that $\hat{Y}_i = \hat{\alpha} + \hat{\beta}x_i$ is the equation for the regression line and so for each value of x_i the confidence interval is an interval $t\sqrt{\text{var}(Y_i)}$ above and below the regression line. Moreover, this interval is dependent on the value x_i, and is smallest where $x_i = 0$, i.e., at the mean point $X_i = \bar{X}$.

To illustrate, suppose the following seven pairs of observations $(Y_1, X_1), \ldots$ are made. Clearly $\bar{X} = 0$ and so $x_i = X_i$. The estimated values $\hat{Y}_i$ are as given, and the confidence interval is a minimum of ± 9.57 at $x_i = 0$ and a maximum of ± 10.84 at $x_i = 300$. See Table 2.1.

Table 2.1

x_i	Y_i	$\hat{Y}_i = \hat{\alpha} + \hat{\beta}x_i$	Interval $(\pm)$
−300	40	39.6	10.84
−200	45	46.4	10.15
−100	50	53.2	9.72
0	65	60.0	9.57
100	70	66.8	9.72
200	70	73.6	10.15
300	80	80.4	10.84

2.3   THE PRODUCT MOMENT CORRELATION COEFFICIENT

If X, Y are two random variables with expected values μ_x, μ_y and variances σ_x^2, σ_y^2 then the covariance between X and Y is defined to be

$$\text{cov}(X, Y) = E((X - \mu_x)(Y - \mu_y))$$

and the correlation between X and Y by

$$r(X, Y) = \text{cov}\left(\frac{X - \mu_x}{\sigma_x}, \frac{Y - \mu_y}{\sigma_y}\right) = \frac{\text{cov}(X, Y)}{\sigma_x \sigma_y}$$

In general we do not know the true covariance and variances, but as before may use as estimators the sum of products viz

$$\hat{\text{cov}}(X, Y) = \frac{1}{T - 1} \sum_{i=1}^{T} (X_i - \bar{X})(Y_i - \bar{Y}) = \frac{1}{T - 1} S_{xy}$$

$$\hat{\sigma}_x^2 = \frac{1}{T - 1} \sum_{i}^{T} (X_i - \bar{X})^2 \qquad = \frac{1}{T - 1} S_{xx}$$

$$\hat{\sigma}_y^2 = \frac{1}{T - 1} \sum_{i}^{T} (Y_i - \bar{Y})^2 \qquad = \frac{1}{T - 1} S_{yy}$$

Thus $r = \hat{r}(X, Y) = \dfrac{S_{xy}}{\sqrt{S_{xx}S_{yy}}}$ is the estimated (product moment) correlation coefficient

obtained from the sequences of observations $\{Y_1, \ldots, Y_T\}$, $\{X_1, \ldots, X_T\}$. Since $\hat{\beta} = \dfrac{S_{xy}}{S_{xx}}$

we can also write $r = \hat{\beta}\sqrt{S_{xx}/S_{yy}}$.

Another way of expressing this is as follows. Suppose we *normalise* the original variables Y, X by dividing by our estimate of their respective standard deviations $\hat{\sigma}_y, \hat{\sigma}_x$. Then the regression equation would become

$$\frac{Y}{\hat{\sigma}_y} = \frac{\bar{Y}}{\hat{\sigma}_y} + \beta^* \frac{(X - \bar{X})}{\hat{\sigma}_x}$$

where

$$\beta^* = \frac{S_{xy}}{\hat{\sigma}_x \hat{\sigma}_y} \cdot \frac{\hat{\sigma}_x^2}{S_{xx}}$$

$$= \frac{S_{xy}}{\sqrt{S_{xx}S_{yy}}} = r$$

Thus the correlation coefficient r is identical to the least square beta coefficient, β^*, obtained in a regression equation involving normalised variables. We have defined $R = R(\hat{\alpha}, \hat{\beta}) = \sum_i (Y_i - \hat{\alpha} - \hat{\beta}x_i)^2$ to be the estimate of the sum of squared errors or *residuals*. We can relate R to the correlation coefficient r, as follows.

First of all we relate R to the total variation in the sample.

The total *variation* in the variable Y about its mean is $S_{yy} = \sum_i (Y_i - \bar{Y})^2$. On the other hand, for each value x_i the estimated value for the dependent variable Y is $\hat{Y}_i = \bar{Y} + \hat{\beta}x_i$. Therefore $\sum (\hat{Y}_i - \bar{Y})^2 = \hat{\beta}^2 S_{xx} = \hat{\beta}S_{xy}$ is the variation in Y *explained* by the regression. We seek to show that

$$R(\hat{\alpha}, \hat{\beta}) = S_{yy} - \hat{\beta}^2 S_{xx}$$

But as we showed in section 2.1, for any coefficients a, b, if we define $R(a, b) = \sum (Y_i - a - bx_i)^2$ then $R(a, b) = T(\hat{\alpha} - a)^2 + S_{xx}(\hat{\beta} - b)^2 + R(\hat{\alpha}, \hat{\beta})$. In particular if we set $a = \bar{Y}$ and $b = 0$ then we obtain

$$S_{yy} = \hat{\beta}^2 S_{xx} + R(\hat{\alpha}, \hat{\beta}) = \hat{\beta}S_{xy} + R(\hat{\alpha}, \hat{\beta})$$

Clearly $R(\hat{\alpha}, \hat{\beta})$ is the *variation unexplained* by the regression. On the other hand, as we have seen $r^2 = \hat{\beta}^2 \dfrac{S_{xx}}{S_{yy}}$.

Thus

$$r^2 = \frac{S_{yy} - R(\hat{\alpha}, \hat{\beta})}{S_{yy}}$$

so that r^2 may be interpreted as the ratio of explained variation to total variation. Clearly if $R(\hat{\alpha}, \hat{\beta}) = 0$, so that all observations lie on the regression line, then $r^2 = 1$ so $r = \pm 1$. In this case the only two possibilities are $\hat{\beta} = \pm 1$ and clearly if $\hat{\beta} = +1$ then $r = 1$, and if $\hat{\beta} = -1$ then $r = -1$.

Previously we showed, on the assumption that the errors were normally distributed that $\dfrac{R(\hat{\alpha}, \hat{\beta})}{\sigma^2}$ was a chi-square variate with $T - 2$ degree of freedom. This allowed us to construct an F-test for the two parameters $\hat{\alpha}, \hat{\beta}$. In precisely the same way, the variable

$$\frac{1}{S^2} S_{xx}(\hat{\beta} - \beta)^2$$

is F-distributed with $(1, T - 2)$ degree of freedom. Here $S^2 = \dfrac{1}{T - 2} R(\hat{\alpha}, \hat{\beta})$ is the estimate for variance. Thus $F = \dfrac{(\hat{\beta} - \beta)^2 S_{xx}}{R/T - 2}$, where $R = R(\hat{\alpha}, \hat{\beta})$, is the sum of square errors. Suppose we put $\beta = 0$. Then $F_0 = \dfrac{\hat{\beta}^2 S_{xx}}{R/T - 2}$ and $\sqrt{F_0}$ is the t-value $\left|\dfrac{\hat{\beta}}{S_\beta}\right|$ for the β coefficient.

Moreover

$$r^2 = \hat{\beta}^2 \frac{S_{xx}}{S_{yy}}$$

and

$$1 - r^2 = \frac{R(\hat{\alpha}, \hat{\beta})}{S_{yy}}$$

Thus

$$\frac{r^2}{1 - r^2} = \frac{\hat{\beta}^2 S_{xx}}{R(\hat{\alpha}, \hat{\beta})}$$

and so

$$F_0 = (T - 2) \frac{r^2}{1 - r^2}$$

Thus the t-test on the β-coefficient can be regarded as a test on the correlation coefficient r.

Before proceeding to regression analysis with many variables, we note another interpretation of the correlation coefficient. Consider the correlation coefficient between the observed values Y_i for Y and the estimated, or fitted, values $\hat{Y}_i = \hat{\alpha} + \hat{\beta} x_i$ from the regression equation.

Then

$$r(Y, \hat{Y}) = \frac{S_{y\hat{y}}}{\sqrt{S_{\hat{y}\hat{y}} S_{yy}}}$$

But

$$S_{y\hat{y}} = \sum_i (Y_i - \bar{Y})(\hat{Y}_i - \bar{Y}) = \hat{\beta} S_{xy}$$

and

$$S_{\hat{y}\hat{y}} = \sum_i \hat{\beta}^2 x_i^2 = \hat{\beta}^2 S_{xx}$$

Thus

$$r(Y, \hat{Y}) = \frac{S_{xy}}{\sqrt{S_{xx} S_{yy}}} \quad \text{when } \hat{\beta} > 0$$

$$= r(X, Y)$$

The correlation coefficient between X and Y may be identified therefore with the correlation coefficient between the variable Y and the fitted, or estimated, variable $\hat{Y}$. As we have seen, if all observations lie on the regression line, the fit is perfect and $r(X, Y) = \pm 1$. If $\hat{\beta} > 0$ then $r(Y, \hat{Y}) = r(X, Y)$. On the other hand if $\hat{\beta} < 0$, then $r(x, y) = -1$, while $r(Y, \hat{Y}) = +1$. More generally we may identify $r(Y, \hat{Y})$ with $r(X, Y)$, and regard $r(Y, \hat{Y})$ as a measure of the *goodness of fit* of the regression line.

2.4 REGRESSION WITH TWO INDEPENDENT VARIABLES

In the previous sections we showed how to construct a regression given a sample $\{(Y_1, X_1), \ldots, (Y_T, X_T)\}$ of observations for the two variables Y, X. In this section we extend the analysis to regression between a dependent variable Y, and two independent variables X, Z. Just as before define $\bar{X} = \frac{1}{T} \sum X_i$, $\bar{Z} = \frac{1}{T} \sum Z_i$, and let $x_i = X_i - \bar{X}$, $z_i = Z_i - \bar{Z}$ for $i = 1, \ldots, T$. Again we make the hypothesis that

$$Y_i = \alpha + \beta_1 x_i + \beta_2 z_i + e_i$$

where e_i is an error variable with variance σ^2. We seek estimates $\hat{\alpha}, \hat{\beta}_1, \hat{\beta}_2$ for α, β_1, β_2 so as to minimise the sum of square errors.
Let

$$E = \sum (Y_i - a - bx_i - cz_i)^2$$

1.

$$\frac{\partial E}{\partial a} = -2 \sum (Y_i - a - bx_i - cz_i) = 0$$

so

$$\sum Y_i - na = 0 \quad \text{or} \quad a = \hat{\alpha} = \frac{\sum Y_i}{T}$$

2.
$$\frac{\partial E}{\partial b} = -2\sum x_i(Y_i - a - bx_i - cz_i) = 0$$

$$S_{xy} - bS_{xx} - cS_{xz} = 0$$

where $S_{xz} = \sum x_i z_i = \sum (X_i - \bar{X})(Z_i - \bar{Z})$. This is zero when $b = \hat{\beta}_1$, $c = \hat{\beta}_2$.

i.e.

$$S_{xy} - \hat{\beta}_1 S_{xx} - \hat{\beta}_2 S_{xz} = 0$$

Similarly,

$$\frac{\partial E}{\partial c} = -2\sum z_i(Y_i - a - bx_i - cz_i) = 0$$

i.e.

$$S_{zy} - \hat{\beta}_1 S_{xz} - \hat{\beta}_2 S_{zz} = 0$$

Solving these equations we obtain

$$\hat{\beta}_1 = \frac{S_{zz}S_{xy} - S_{xz}S_{zy}}{[S_{xx}S_{zz} - S_{xz}^2]}$$

and

$$\hat{\beta}_2 = \frac{S_{xx}S_{zy} - S_{xz}S_{xy}}{[S_{xx}S_{zz} - S_{xz}^2]}$$

In the bivariate case we saw that $\hat{\beta} = \dfrac{S_{xy}}{S_{xx}}$ and var $(\hat{\beta}) = \dfrac{\sigma^2}{S_{xx}}$. Now $\hat{\beta}_1 = \dfrac{S_{xy} - \dfrac{S_{xz}S_{zy}}{S_{zz}}}{S_{xx} - \dfrac{S_{xz}^2}{S_{zz}}}$

which is the same as in the bivariate case if $z_i = 0$ for all i, so we guess that

$$\text{var}(\hat{\beta}_1) = \frac{\sigma^2}{S_{xx} - \dfrac{S_{xz}^2}{S_{zz}}} = \sigma^2 \frac{S_{zz}}{(S_{xx}S_{zz} - S_{xz}^2)}$$

and similarly

$$\text{var}(\hat{\beta}_2) = \sigma^2 \frac{S_{xx}}{(S_{xx}S_{zz} - S_{xz}^2)}$$

We can also show that $E(\hat{\beta}_1) = \beta_1$, $E(\hat{\beta}_2) = \beta_2$:

$$E[\hat{\beta}_1] = E\left[\frac{S_{zz}S_{xy} - S_{xz}S_{zy}}{(S_{xx}S_{zz} - S_{xz}^2)}\right]$$

$$= \frac{S_{zz}\sum x_i E(Y_i) - S_{xz}\sum z_i E(Y_i)}{(S_{xx}S_{zz} - S_{xz}^2)}$$

$$= \frac{S_{zz}\sum x_i(\alpha + \beta_1 x_i + \beta_1 z_i) - S_{xz}\sum z_i(\alpha + \beta_1 x_i + \beta_2 z_i)}{(S_{xx}S_{zz} - S_{xz}^2)}$$

$$= \frac{\beta_1 S_{zz}S_{xx} + \beta_2 S_{zz}S_{xz} - \beta_1 S_{xz}^2 - \beta_2 S_{xz}S_{zz}}{(S_{xx}S_{zz} - S_{xz}^2)}$$

$$= \beta_1$$

Just as before we defined

$$r^2 = \frac{\text{explained variation}}{\text{total variation}}$$

$$= \frac{S_{yy} - R}{S_{yy}}$$

$$= 1 - \frac{R}{S_{yy}}$$

In this case R is given by $R = S_{yy} - \beta_1 S_{xy} - \beta_2 S_{zy}$, in a similar fashion to the bivariate case.
Hence

$$r^2 = \frac{\hat{\beta}_1 S_{xy} + \hat{\beta}_2 S_{zy}}{S_{yy}}$$

If $\hat{\beta}_2 = 0$, or $z_i = 0$ for all i, then $r^2 = \dfrac{S_{xy}^2}{S_{xx}S_{yy}}$ as before. For the bivariate regressions between x, y and z let us write

$$r_{xy} = \frac{S_{xy}}{\sqrt{S_{xx}S_{yy}}}, \quad r_{zy} = \frac{S_{zy}}{\sqrt{S_{zz}S_{yy}}} \quad \text{and} \quad r_{xz} = \frac{S_{xz}}{\sqrt{S_{xx}S_{zz}}}$$

Now

$$\hat{\beta}_1 = \frac{S_{zz}S_{xy} - S_{xz}S_{zy}}{[S_{xx}S_{zz} - S_{xz}^2]} = \left(\frac{r_{xy} - r_{yz}r_{zx}}{1 - r_{xz}^2}\right)\sqrt{\frac{S_{yy}}{S_{xx}}}$$

and

$$\hat{\beta}_2 = \left(\frac{r_{zy} - r_{yz}r_{zx}}{1 - r_{xz}^2}\right)\sqrt{\frac{S_{yy}}{S_{zz}}}$$

Hence

$$r^2 = \frac{r_{xy}^2 + r_{zy}^2 - 2r_{xz}r_{yz}r_{xy}}{1 - r_{xz}^2}$$

If $\hat{y}_i = \hat{\alpha} + \hat{\beta}_1 x_i + \hat{\beta}_2 z_i$

then $r_{y\hat{y}}$ = correlation between observed and fitted dependent variables

$\quad\quad = r$

Partial correlation

If we regress Y_i against z_i to obtain $\hat{Y}_i = \bar{Y} + a z_i$ then the unexplained residuals are $u_i = Y_i - \hat{Y}_i = (Y_i - \bar{Y}) - a z_i = Y_i - a z_i$. Then $\sum u_i^2 = S_{uu}$ = unexplained variation, so

$$1 - r_{yz}^2 = \frac{\text{unexplained variation}}{\text{total variation}} = \frac{\sum u_i^2}{\sum (Y_i - \bar{Y})^2} = \frac{S_{uu}}{S_{yy}}$$

Similarly, if we regress x_i against z_i to obtain

$$\hat{X}_i = \bar{X} + b z_i, \text{ then } v_i = X_i - \hat{X}_i = (X_i - \bar{X}) - b z_i$$

then $\sum v_i^2 = S_{vv}$ = unexplained variation, and

$$1 - r_{xz}^2 = \frac{\sum v_i^2}{\sum (X_i - \bar{X})^2} = \frac{\sum v_i^2}{S_{xx}} = \frac{S_{vv}}{S_{xx}}$$

Now the correlation coefficient of u on v is given by

$$r_{uv} = \frac{S_{uv}}{\sqrt{S_{uu} S_{vv}}} = \frac{S_{uv}}{\sqrt{S_{yy}(1 - r_{yz}^2) S_{xx}(1 - r_{xz}^2)}}$$

where

$$S_{uv} = \sum (y_i - a z_i)(x_i - b z_i)$$

and

$$a = r_{yz}\sqrt{\frac{S_{yy}}{S_{zz}}} \quad b = r_{xz}\sqrt{\frac{S_{xx}}{S_{zz}}}$$

Therefore

$$r_{uv} = \frac{\dfrac{S_{yz}}{\sqrt{S_{yy} S_{xx}}} - r_{xz} r_{yz} - r_{xz} r_{yz} + r_{xz} r_{yz}}{\sqrt{(1 - r_{yz}^2)(1 - r_{xz}^2)}}$$

$$= \frac{r_{yx} - r_{xz} r_{yz}}{\sqrt{(1 - r_{yz}^2)(1 - r_{xz}^2)}}$$

The correlation coefficient r_{uv} is the estimate of the covariance between the errors in the regression equation of Y with Z and X with Z, and may be regarded therefore as the correlation between Y and X when the 'influence' of Z is removed. For this reason,

r_{uv} is called the *partial correlation* between Y and X, and is written $r_{xy,z}$. Note that the expression r_{uv} is symmetric in x and y, so that $r_{yx,z} = r_{xy,z}$.

In the same way of course, the effect of X on the correlation between Y and Z can be factored out to give the partial correlation $r_{yz,x}$. More generally, if $X_1, \ldots, X_K$ is a set of random variables, then we may compute the correlation coefficient r_{12} between X_1 and X_2, say, but also factor out the influence of $X_2, \ldots, X_K$ to obtain a partial correlation coefficient

$$r_{12,3\ldots K}$$

We shall discuss this procedure below.

2.5 ELEMENTS OF LINEAR ALGEBRA

In section 2.7 of this chapter we shall introduce the matrix approach to regression analysis. Before we can do this however we shall mention some aspects of matrix or linear algebra that will prove useful. In the general linear regression model we obtain a series of observations $\{Y_1, \ldots, Y_i, \ldots, Y_T\}$, say, for the *dependent* variable, Y, and for each *independent* variable, X_j, for $j = 1, \ldots, K$, a parallel series $\{X_{1j}, \ldots, X_{ij}, \ldots, X_{Tj}\}$. For simplicity suppose the jth variable has mean $\bar{X}_j$, so that we may write $x_{ij} = X_{ij} - \bar{X}_j$ for $j = 1, \ldots, K$. First of all, suppose that for each $i = 1, \ldots, T$, the observation Y_i is related to the observations of $X_1, \ldots, X_K$ by

$$Y_i = \beta_0 + \beta_1 x_{i1} + \beta_2 x_{i2} + \beta_3 x_{i3} + \cdots + \beta_K x_{iK}$$

where $\beta_0, \ldots, \beta_K$ are constants.

This set of T equations can be more conveniently written

$$
\begin{bmatrix} Y_1 \\ \\ \\ \\ Y_i \\ \\ \\ \\ Y_T \end{bmatrix}
=
\begin{bmatrix} 1 & x_{11} & x_{12} & x_{1j} & x_{1K} \\ & \cdot & & \cdot & \cdot \\ & \cdot & & \cdot & \cdot \\ 1 & x_{i1} & \cdots & x_{ij} & x_{iK} \\ & \cdot & & \cdot & \cdot \\ & \cdot & & \cdot & \cdot \\ 1 & x_{T1} & x_{T2}\ldots x_{Tj} & x_{TK} \end{bmatrix}
\begin{bmatrix} \beta_0 \\ \beta_1 \\ \\ \cdot \\ \cdot \\ \cdot \\ \beta_K \end{bmatrix}
$$

The matrix on the right containing the observations $\{x_{ij}\}$ can either be written as (x_{ij}) or as X. Note that there are T rows and $(K + 1)$ columns in the matrix, the ith row corresponds to the set of K observations for the independent variables corresponding to Y_i, while the $(j + 1)$th column corresponds to the T different observations associated with the jth independent variable. The column formed by $(Y_1, \ldots, Y_T)$ may be written Y and the column formed by $(\beta_0, \ldots, \beta_K)$ may be written β. Then the set of T equations may be more conveniently written in matrix notation as

$$Y = X\beta$$

Note that $X\beta$ is a column of T different entries whose ith entry is the summation $\beta_0 + \sum_{j=1}^{K} \beta_j x_{ij}$. Since each entry in the column Y is a real number (belongs to $\mathbf{R}$), the set of columns with T entries can be identified with $\mathbf{R} \times, \ldots, \times \mathbf{R}$ (T times) or $\mathbf{R}^T$. Such a column is also called a *vector* in $\mathbf{R}^T$. Two column vectors

$$Y = \begin{bmatrix} Y_1 \\ \cdot \\ \cdot \\ \cdot \\ Y_T \end{bmatrix} \quad Z = \begin{bmatrix} Z_1 \\ \cdot \\ \cdot \\ \cdot \\ Z_T \end{bmatrix}$$

say, may be added to give a third

$$\begin{bmatrix} Y_1 + Z_1 \\ \cdot \\ \cdot \\ \cdot \\ Y_T + Z_T \end{bmatrix} = Y + Z$$

A column vector, Y, may be multiplied by a real number α to give a new column vector

$$\alpha \begin{bmatrix} Y_1 \\ \cdot \\ \cdot \\ \cdot \\ Y_T \end{bmatrix} = \begin{bmatrix} \alpha Y_1 \\ \cdot \\ \cdot \\ \cdot \\ \alpha Y_T \end{bmatrix}$$

In the earlier set of equations we neglected to add in error terms, so if we let

$$U = \begin{bmatrix} e_1 \\ \cdot \\ \cdot \\ \cdot \\ e_T \end{bmatrix}$$

be the column vector of errors, the matrix equation we shall be examining is

$$Y = X\beta + U$$

Another way of representing the vector equation is to let

$$x_j = \begin{bmatrix} x_{1j} \\ \cdot \\ \cdot \\ \cdot \\ x_{ij} \\ x_{Tj} \end{bmatrix}$$

be the vector of T observations associated with the jth independent variable. Neglecting the error terms, we may write the set of equations as

$$Y = \beta_0[1] + \beta_1 x_1 + \ldots \beta_j x_j + \ldots \beta_K x_K$$

where [1] stands for the column vector all of whose entries are 1. It is convenient to let x_0 stand for the column for 1's, so we may write

$$Y = \sum_{j=0}^{K} \beta_j x_j$$

When a vector Y in $\mathbf{R}^T$ can be expressed in terms of a set of vectors $\{x_j\}$ then Y is said to be a linear combination of $\{x_j\}$.

More abstractly, suppose that $V = \{v_1, \ldots, v_K\}$ is a set of vectors, each one of which belongs to $\mathbf{R}^T$. A vector v is a *linear combination* of the set V if $v = \sum_{j=1}^{K} \beta_j v_j$. If every vector in $\mathbf{R}^T$ can be expressed as a linear combination of the set V, then V is called a *span* for $\mathbf{R}^T$. In general if V is a span for $\mathbf{R}^T$ then V must include at least T different vectors. Even when V is a span for $\mathbf{R}^T$, the expression $v = \sum_{j=1}^{K} \beta_j v_j$ need not be unique.

However, the set V is said to be *linearly independent* if it is the case that $\sum_{j=1}^{K} \alpha_j v_j = 0$ implies that $\alpha_1 = \ldots = \alpha_K = 0$. A necessary condition for the set V to be linearly independent is that $K \leq T$. If V is both linearly independent and a span for $\mathbf{R}^T$, then V is called a *basis* for $\mathbf{R}^T$. In this case each vector $v \in \mathbf{R}^T$ may be written as a unique combination $v = \sum_{j=1}^{K} \beta_j v_j$, where $\{\beta_1, \ldots, \beta_K\}$ are called the *coefficients* of v with respect to $\{v_1, \ldots, v_K\}$. To see that the coefficients are unique, suppose that $\{\beta_1, \ldots, \beta_K\}$ and $\{\alpha_1, \ldots, \alpha_K\}$ are both coefficients for v.

Then
$$0 = v - v = \sum_{j}^{K} \beta_j v_j - \sum_{j}^{K} \alpha_j v_j = \sum_{j=1}^{K} (\beta_j - \alpha_j) v_j$$

By linear independence $\beta_j - \alpha_j = 0$ for $j = 1, \ldots, K$, and so the coefficients $\beta_j = \alpha_j$ for $j = 1, \ldots, K$. Note also that if $\{v_1, \ldots, v_K\}$ is a basis for $\mathbf{R}^T$ then it is necessary that $K = T$. Every basis for $\mathbf{R}^T$ must contain the same number of elements, T, and this number is called the *dimension* of the vector space. Now consider the vector equation

$$Y = \sum_{j=0}^{K} \beta_j x_j$$

For convenience write $y_i = Y_i - \beta_0$, and let y be the column vector whose ith entry is y_i. We then obtain the vector equation

$$y = \sum_{j=1}^{K} \beta_j x_j$$

Four possibilities present themselves.

1. $K > T$. It is impossible for the vectors $\{x_j : j = 1, \ldots, K\}$ to be linearly independent. In this case there is no unique *solution* $\{\beta_1, \ldots, \beta_K\}$ for the coefficients.
2. $K \leq T$ but $\{x_j : j = 1, \ldots, K\}$ are not linearly independent. Again there can be no unique and exact solution to the equation.
3. $K = T$ and $\{x_j : j = 1, \ldots, K\}$ are linearly independent. In this case, for every vector $y \in \mathbf{R}^T$ there is an *exact* and *unique* solution or set of coefficients $\{\beta_1, \ldots, \beta_K\}$. In this case the vector of errors $U = y - \sum_{j=1}^{K} \beta_j x_j$ is identically zero.
4. $K < T$ and $\{x_j : j = 1, \ldots, K\}$ are linearly independent. The span of $V = \{x_j : j = 1, \ldots, K\}$ is the set of all possible linear combinations $\sum_{j=1}^{K} \beta_j x_j$, and will be a K-dimensional plane (or subspace) in $\mathbf{R}^T$. Clearly, not all vectors in $\mathbf{R}^T$ will belong to this span.

If $K < T$ then a vector y in $\mathbf{R}^T$ cannot be written as a linear combination of V. However, any vector y in $\mathbf{R}^T$ can be written as

$$y = \sum_{j=1}^{K} \beta_j x_j + U(y)$$

where $U(y)$ is an error vector belonging to a $(T - K)$ dimensional subspace of $\mathbf{R}^T$. The regression model essentially is concerned with the selection of an appropriate procedure for selecting the error vector, and thus the coefficients $\{\beta_1, \ldots, \beta_K\}$, for a given set of data $\{y, x_1, \ldots, x_K\}$. Note that this can only be done when the variables $\{x_j : j = 1, \ldots, K\}$ are linearly independent, and $K < T$.

Consider the case now where $T = K$ and $\{x_1, \ldots, x_K\}$ are linearly independent, and $y = \sum_{j=1}^{K} \beta_j x_j$. As we have mentioned $\{\beta_1, \ldots, \beta_K\}$ are the coefficients of y with respect to the new basis $\{x_1, \ldots, x_K]$. Originally we expressed y as a vector $(y_1, \ldots, y_K)$.

Another way of writing this is

$$y = \sum_{j=1}^{K} y_j e_j$$

where e_j is the vector $(0, \ldots, 0, 1, 0, \ldots, 0)$ with a 1 in the jth position. However, we can also write the relationship between y and $\{x_1, \ldots, x_K\}$ as

$$y = X\beta$$

where X is the matrix whose jth column is the vector x_j. Note also that the column vector β is precisely the column of coefficients of y in terms of the new basis $\{x_1, \ldots, x_K\}$. For this reason we may call X a *basis change* matrix. Define the inverse X^{-1} to the matrix X to be the matrix X^{-1} such that

$$X^{-1}(y) = \beta.$$

Note that because of the linear independence of the column vectors of X, for each y there exists exactly óne β satisfying the equation $y = X\beta$. Thus X^{-1} can indeed be represented by a matrix. It is important here to note that we can only write X^{-1} for the matrix inverse to X, when $T = K$, so X is a square $K \times K$ matrix.

There is a well defined procedure for obtaining the inverse to a $K \times K$ matrix, in terms of the *determinant* and *cofactors* of the matrix.

For a real number, a, define the determinant, $\det(a)$ to be a. For a 2×2 matrix

$$A = \begin{bmatrix} a_{11} & a_{12} \\ a_{21} & a_{22} \end{bmatrix}$$

define $\det(A)$, or $|A|$ to be $a_{11}a_{22} - a_{21}a_{12}$. For a 3×3 matrix, A, define the (i, j) cofactor, A_{ij}, to be the *determinant* of the 2×2 matrix obtained from A by deleting the ith row and jth column, and multiplying by $(-1)^{i+j}$. Thus if

$$A = \begin{bmatrix} a_{11} & a_{12} & a_{13} \\ a_{21} & a_{22} & a_{23} \\ a_{31} & a_{32} & a_{33} \end{bmatrix}$$

the *cofactor*

$$A_{11} = \begin{vmatrix} a_{22} & a_{23} \\ a_{32} & a_{33} \end{vmatrix} = (-1)^2(a_{22}a_{33} - a_{23}a_{32})$$

The determinant of A, written $|A|$, is $a_{11}A_{11} + a_{12}A_{12} + a_{13}A_{13}$.

More generally if A is a $K \times K$ matrix, then we may define, by induction, the cofactor A_{ij} in the (i, j)th place to be the determinant of the $(K - 1) \times (K - 1)$ matrix obtained by deleting the ith row and jth column and then multiplying by $(-1)^{i+j}$.

The determinant of A is then

$$|A| = \sum_{j=1}^{K} a_{1j}A_{1j}$$

Moreover it can be shown that, for each $i = 1, \ldots, K$,

$$\sum_{j=1}^{K} a_{ji} A_{ri} = \sum_{j=1}^{K} a_{ij} A_{ir} = |A| \quad \text{if } j = r$$

$$= 0 \quad \text{if } j \neq r$$

Let us write

$$(A_{ij}) = \begin{bmatrix} A_{11} & A_{12} & \cdot & \\ A_{21} & \cdot & \cdot & \\ \cdot & \cdot & \cdot & \\ \cdot & & & \\ \cdot & \cdot & \cdot & \end{bmatrix}$$

for the $K \times K$ cofactor matrix. For a general $T \times K$ matrix, B, with T rows and K columns, the transpose B' of B is the $K \times T$ matrix (with K rows and T columns) obtained by writing columns as rows and vice versa. If C is a $K \times P$ matrix (with K rows and P columns) whose columns are $c_1, \ldots, c_p$, say, then the composition, BC, is the $T \times P$ matrix whose jth column is the vector $B(c_j)$. Thus

$$BC = \begin{bmatrix} b_{11} & \cdot & b_{1r} & \cdot & b_{1K} \\ \cdot & & & & \\ b_{21} & & b_{ir} & & b_{iK} \\ \cdot & & & & \\ b_{T1} & \cdot & \cdot & \cdot & b_{TK} \end{bmatrix} \begin{bmatrix} c_{11} & \cdot & c_{ij} & \cdot & c_{1P} \\ \cdot & & & & \cdot \\ \cdot & & c_{rj} & & \cdot \\ \cdot & & & & \cdot \\ c_{K1} & \cdot & c_{Kj} & \cdot & c_{KP} \end{bmatrix}$$

$$= \begin{bmatrix} \cdot & \sum b_{1r} c_{rj} & \cdot \\ & \cdot & \\ \cdot & \sum_{r=1}^{K} b_{ir} c_{rj} & \cdot \\ & \cdot & \\ \cdot & \cdot & \cdot \end{bmatrix}$$

whose entry in the ith row and jth column is $\sum_{r=1}^{K} b_{ir} c_{rj}$. Now consider the matrix composition $(a_{ij})(A_{ij})'$ where $(A_{ij})'$ is the transpose of the cofactor matrix. By definition the entry in the (i, j)th position is $\sum_{r=1}^{K} a_{ir} A_{jr}$ which is 0 if $i \neq r$ and is $|A|$ if $i = r$. (Note we have A_{jr} here rather than A_{rj} because we have the transpose of (A_{ij})). Thus $(a_{ij})(A_{ij})'$ is equal to the matrix whose (i, j)th entries are $|A|$ if $i = j$, and zero otherwise.

Let I, or I_K, be the identity $K \times K$ matrix, with 1 in each diagonal entry, and zero elsewhere. We may write $|A|I$ for the diagonal matrix with $|A|$ in each diagonal position. Then

$$(a_{ij})(A_{ij})' = |A|I$$

Now consider a matrix equation $y = A\beta$ and suppose there exists an inverse A^{-1} such that $A^{-1}(y) = \beta$. In this case $y = A(A^{-1}(y))$. Clearly this is the case if $AA^{-1} = I$, the identity matrix. But we have shown that

$$I = \frac{1}{|A|} (a_{ij})(A_{ij})'$$

Thus

$$A^{-1} = \frac{1}{|A|} (A_{ij})'$$

at least in the case $|A| \neq 0$. A $K \times K$ (square) matrix is called *non-singular* if $|A| \neq 0$. For such a matrix the inverse A^{-1} is defined. Note also that if the column vectors of A are linearly independent then the matrix is a basis change matrix and so should be non-singular.

Suppose however the column vectors are linearly dependent. In this case we should expect $|A|$ to be zero. To see that this is indeed the case, proceed as follows.

Given a matrix $A = (a_{ij})$ form a new matrix B by adding a multiple (α) of the rth column of A to the jth column of A. The jth column of B is then $(a_{ij} + \alpha a_{ir})_{i=1,\ldots,K}$. However, the cofactors $(B_{ij})_{i=1,\ldots,K}$ associated with the jth column of B are identical to the cofactors associated with the jth column of A.

Thus

$$|B| = \sum_{i=1}^{K} (a_{ij} + \alpha a_{ir}) A_{ij}$$

However, if $r \neq j$ then $\sum_{i=1}^{K} a_{ir} A_{ij} = 0$

Thus

$$|B| = \sum_{i=1}^{K} a_{ij} A_{ij} = |A|$$

Suppose now that the column vectors of a matrix A are not linearly independent. Write the K columns of A as $a_1, \ldots, a_K$. The vector a_1, say, is linearly dependent on the remainder, and so

$$a_1 = \sum_{j=2}^{K} \alpha_j a_j$$

Form the new matrix B from A by substituting, for the first column, the new column $b_1 = a_1 - \sum_{j=2}^{K} \alpha_j a_j$. But this column is a zero column, and so

$$|B| = |A| = \sum_{i=1}^{K} b_{i1} A_{i1} = 0$$

Consequently, if the column vectors of a square matrix are not linearly independent, then the matrix is singular, with zero determinant. For a square $K \times K$ matrix, A, the *rank* of A, written rank(A), is the maximal number of linearly independent column vectors. Thus if rank(A) $< K$ then $|A| = 0$ and if rank(A) $= K$ then $|A| \neq 0$. As an example consider a data matrix

$$X = \begin{bmatrix} 1 & x_1 & z_1 \\ \cdot & \cdot & \cdot \\ \cdot & \cdot & \cdot \\ \cdot & \cdot & \cdot \\ 1 & x_T & z_T \end{bmatrix}$$

generated by a stream of T-observations for two variables X, Z about their means $\bar{X}$ and $\bar{Z}$. Consider the square matrix

$$X'X = \begin{bmatrix} 1 & \cdots & 1 \\ x_1 & \cdots & x_T \\ z_1 & \cdots & z_T \end{bmatrix} \begin{bmatrix} 1 & x_1 & z_1 \\ \cdot & \cdot & \cdot \\ \cdot & \cdot & \cdot \\ \cdot & \cdot & \cdot \\ 1 & x_T & z_T \end{bmatrix}$$

$$= \begin{bmatrix} T & 0 & 0 \\ 0 & S_{xx} & S_{xz} \\ 0 & S_{xz} & S_{zz} \end{bmatrix}$$

Note here that the $(1,1)$ term is $\sum_T 1.1 = T$, while the terms $(1,j)$ or $(j,1)$ for $j \neq 1$ are

$\sum_{i=1}^{T} x_i = 0$ or $\sum_{i=1}^{T} z_i = 0$. The $(2,2)$ term is $\sum_{i=1}^{T} x_i^2 = \sum (X_i - \bar{X})^2 = S_{xx}$. The other terms in the matrix follow in a similar fashion. Suppose now we consider a data matrix

$$X = [1 \, x_1 \ldots x_j \ldots x_K]$$

associated with K variables $\{x_1, \ldots, x_K\}$. Then

$$X'X = \begin{bmatrix} T & 0 & \cdot & 0 \\ 0 & S_{11} & \cdot & S_{1K} \\ \cdot & \cdot & \cdot & \cdot \\ 0 & S_{K1} & \cdot & S_{KK} \end{bmatrix}$$

where

$$S_{ij} = \sum_{t=1}^{T} (X_{ti} - \bar{X}_i)(X_{tj} - \bar{X}_j) = \sum_{t=1}^{T} x_{ti} x_{tj}$$

is the *co-variation* between the ith and jth variables. An important point is that the matrix $X'X$ is a symmetric $(K + 1) \times (K + 1)$ matrix; that is to say its (i,j)th entry is identical to its (j, i)th entry.

To compute the inverse of $X'X$ in the two variable case, the determinant is easily seen to be

$$|X'X| = T[S_{xx}S_{zz} - S_{xz}^2]$$

The cofactor matrix is

$$\begin{bmatrix} (S_{xx}S_{zz} - S_{xz}^2) & 0 & 0 \\ 0 & TS_{zz} & -TS_{xz} \\ 0 & -TS_{xz} & TS_{xx} \end{bmatrix}$$

and so

$$(X'X)^{-1} = \frac{1}{S_{xx}S_{zz} - S_{xz}^2} \begin{bmatrix} \dfrac{1}{T}(S_{xx}S_{zz} - S_{xz}^2) & 0 & 0 \\ 0 & S_{zz} & -S_{xz} \\ 0 & -S_{xz} & S_{xx} \end{bmatrix}$$

Suppose now that z and x are almost dependent in the sense that $z_t = x_t + e_t$, where e_t is a small error term. Write $S_{xe} = \sum_t x_t e_t$ etc. Then

$$X'X = \begin{bmatrix} T & 0 & 0 \\ 0 & S_{xx} & S_{xx} + S_{xe} \\ 0 & S_{xx} + S_{xe} & S_{xx} + 2S_{xe} + S_{ee} \end{bmatrix}$$

Since we may subtract the second column from the third, leaving the determinant unchanged, we find that

$$|X'X| = \begin{vmatrix} T & 0 & 0 \\ 0 & S_{xx} & S_{xe} \\ 0 & S_{xx} + S_{xe} & S_{xe} + S_{ee} \end{vmatrix}$$

If the errors are small in comparison to the observations, the determinant $|X'X|$ will be close to zero, and so the matrix $X'X$ will be almost singular. More generally if the variables $\{x_1, \ldots, x_K\}$ are 'almost' linearly dependent then the co-variation matrix will be almost singular. As we shall see this presents problems in the general regression model.

The fact that the covariation matrix $X'X$ is square and symmetric allows us to *diagonalise* the matrix.

2.6   QUADRATIC FORMS

Suppose therefore that $A = (a_{ij})$ is a $K \times K$ matrix. Under some conditions it is possible to transform A into a diagonal matrix

$$\Lambda = \begin{bmatrix} \lambda_1 & \cdots & & & 0 \\ & & & & \cdot \\ \cdot & & \lambda_r & & \cdot \\ & & & & \\ \cdot & & & & \\ 0 & & \cdots & & 0 \end{bmatrix}$$

where r is the rank of A (and of course $r \leq K$). Suppose there exists a vector x in $\mathbf{R}^K$ such that

$$A(x) = \lambda x$$

where λ is a real number. Then x is called an *eigenvector* of A, and λ is the *eigenvalue* corresponding to x. This eigenequation may be written

$$(A - \lambda I)(x) = 0$$

where $A - \lambda I$ is the matrix

$$\begin{bmatrix} a_{11} - \lambda & a_{12} & \cdots \\ a_{21} & a_{22} - \lambda & \cdots \\ & \cdot & \\ & \cdot & \\ & \cdot & \end{bmatrix}$$

If rank $(A - \lambda I) = K$, so that the vectors of the matrix are linearly independent, then the only solution to the eigenequation is $x = 0$. For a non-zero solution to exist we require that $|A - \lambda I| = 0$. This is called the *characteristic equation* of A. Once the eigenvalues $\{\lambda_i\}$ are known, the eigenvectors $\{x_i\}$ may be found, and the matrix A written in diagonal form, as the following example illustrates.

Example 2.1

Suppose that

$$A = \begin{bmatrix} 2 & 1 & -1 \\ 0 & 1 & 1 \\ 2 & 0 & -2 \end{bmatrix}$$

Then the characteristic equation is $|A - \lambda I| = 0$ or

$$(2 - \lambda)[(1 - \lambda)(-2 - \lambda)] - 1(-2) - 1(-2(1 - \lambda))$$
$$= -\lambda(\lambda^2 - \lambda - 2) = -\lambda(\lambda - 2)(\lambda + 1) = 0$$

The characteristic equation therefore has three roots $\lambda = 0, +2, -1$. Having obtained the three eigenvalues we may then compute the eigenvectors. For example, consider $\lambda_1 = 0$. The appropriate eigenequation is $A(x_1) = 0$. It should be easy to see that if

$$x_1 = \begin{bmatrix} 1 \\ -1 \\ 1 \end{bmatrix} \text{ then } A(x_1) = 0$$

In similar fashion the eigenvectors

$$x_2 = \begin{bmatrix} 2 \\ 1 \\ 1 \end{bmatrix}, \quad x_3 = \begin{bmatrix} 1 \\ -1 \\ 2 \end{bmatrix}$$

correspond to $\lambda_2 = 2$, $\lambda_3 = -1$. Now write

$$P = \begin{bmatrix} 1 & 2 & 1 \\ -1 & 1 & -1 \\ 1 & 1 & 2 \end{bmatrix}$$

for the eigenvector matrix (whose columns are the eigenvectors).

It should be clear that the three column vectors x_1, x_2, x_3 are linearly independent, since $|P| \neq 0$. Thus P has an inverse P^{-1} which can easily be calculated to be

$$P^{-1} = \tfrac{1}{3} \begin{bmatrix} 3 & -3 & -3 \\ 1 & 1 & 0 \\ -2 & 1 & 3 \end{bmatrix}$$

Suppose now that we choose $\{x_1, x_2, x_3\}$ as a basis for $\mathbf{R}^3$. With respect to this new basis, the matrix A can be written as

$$\Lambda = P^{-1} A P$$

where Λ is the diagonal, eigenvalue 3×3 matrix

$$\Lambda = \begin{bmatrix} 0 & 0 & 0 \\ 0 & 2 & 0 \\ 0 & 0 & -1 \end{bmatrix}$$

This example illustrates a number of properties of the eigenvalues. First of all the characteristic equation for a $K \times K$ matrix will be a polynomial of degree K in λ i.e.

$$\lambda^K - b_1 \lambda^{K-1} - b_2 \lambda^{K-2} \pm b_{K-1} = 0.$$

Such a polynomial need not have all its roots real. However, if the matrix **A** is symmetric (i.e. $a_{ij} = a_{ji}$ for all i, j) then the roots $\lambda_1, \ldots, \lambda_K$ will be real. In this case we may write the polynomial equation as

$$(\lambda - \lambda_1) \ldots (\lambda - \lambda_K) = 0$$

The number of non-zero roots to this equation will be identical to the *rank* of the matrix. The coefficient b_1 of the polynomial equation can be seen to be $\lambda_1 + \cdots + \lambda_K$.

For a general $K \times K$ matrix, A, the trace of A is defined by

$$\text{trace (A)} = \sum_{i=1}^{K} a_{ii}$$

Thus the coefficient $b_1 = \text{trace}(\wedge)$. Moreover b_1 can also be shown to be equal to the trace of the original matrix A. Thus we have trace $(\wedge) = \text{trace}(A)$. Secondly, the final term in the polynomial equation $b_{K-1} = \lambda_1 \ldots \lambda_K$ which is the determinant, $|\wedge|$, of the eigenvalue matrix $\wedge$. It can also be shown that $|A| = |\wedge|$.

To illustrate in Example 2.1, trace $(\wedge) = 1 = \text{trace}(A)$ and $|\wedge| = 0 = |A|$.

The procedure for diagonalising a matrix is most useful when the original matrix, A, is symmetric. In this case there is a natural *quadratic* form associated with A. For two vectors $x, y \in \mathbf{R}^K$ define the *quadratic form* associated with A to be the real number

$$x'A(y) = (x_1 \ldots x_K) \begin{bmatrix} \sum_{j=1}^{K} a_{1j}y_j \\ \\ \sum_{j=1}^{K} a_{Kj}y_j \end{bmatrix}$$

$$= \sum_{i=1}^{K} x_i \sum_{j=1}^{K} a_{ij}y_j = \sum_{i=1}^{K} \sum_{j=1}^{K} x_i a_{ij} y_j$$

Now consider $A(x)'y$ where $A(x)'$, the transpose of the column vector, is a row vector. Then

$$A(x)'y = \left[\ldots \sum_{j=1}^{K} a_{ij}x_j \ldots \right] \begin{bmatrix} y_1 \\ y_K \end{bmatrix}$$

$$= \sum_{i=1}^{K} y_i \sum_{j=1}^{K} a_{ij}x_j$$

$$= \sum_{i=1}^{K} \sum_{i=1}^{K} x_i a_{ji} y_j$$

When A is *symmetric* then $a_{ij} = a_{ji}$ and so $x'A(y) = A(x)'y$. In the case that A is the $K \times K$ identity matrix, I, then $x'I\,y = \sum_{i=1}^{K} x_i y_i = x'y$ also known as the *scalar product* of x and y. It is also useful to note here that

$$xy' = \begin{bmatrix} x_1 \\ \cdot \\ \cdot \\ \cdot \\ x_K \end{bmatrix} [y_1 \ldots y_K]$$

$$= \begin{bmatrix} x_1 y_1 & x_1 y_2 & x_1 y_K \\ x_2 y_1 & & \\ \cdot & & \\ \cdot & & \\ \cdot & & \\ x_K y_1 & & x_K y_K \end{bmatrix}$$

is a $K \times K$ matrix, with trace equal to $x'y$.

Suppose now that A is a symmetric matrix and that λ_1, λ_2 are two distinct eigenvalues with corresponding eigenvectors x_1, x_2. Now

$$A(x_1)'x_2 = (\lambda_1 x_2)'x_2 = \lambda_1(x_2' x_2)$$
$$= x_1' A(x_2) = x_1'(\lambda_2 x_2) = \lambda_2(x_1' x_2)$$

Thus $\lambda_1(x_1' x_2) = \lambda_2(x_1' x_2)$. Since $\lambda_1 \neq \lambda_2$ this implies that $(x_1' x_2) = 0$, so the scalar product of x_1 and x_2 is zero.

Two such vectors are called *orthogonal*. It is possible to show that a symmetric $K \times K$ matrix A has K orthogonal eigenvectors $x_1, \ldots, x_K$. If the rank of the matrix is r, then $K - r$ of these eigenvectors will be associated with the zero eigenvalue. Suppose we let $P = (x_1 \ldots x_K)$ be the basis change matrix, whose columns correspond to these orthogonal eigenvectors. Then

$$P'P = \begin{bmatrix} x_1' \\ \\ x_K' \end{bmatrix} [x_1 \ldots x_K]$$

$$= \begin{bmatrix} x_1' x_1 & x_1' x_2 & x_1' x_K \\ x_2' x_1 & & \\ & & \\ & & x_K' x_K \end{bmatrix}$$

$$= \begin{bmatrix} x_1' x_1 & 0 & 0 \\ 0 & x_2' x_2 & \\ & & \\ 0 & & x_K' x_K \end{bmatrix}$$

where the (i, i)th diagonal element corresponds to the scalar product $x_i' x_i$.

The scalar product, $x_i' x_i$, of a vector with itself is also written $||x_i||^2$, where $||x_i||$ is the *norm* associated with the vector x_i. Suppose we *normalise* each vector x_i for $i = 1, \ldots, K$ by writing $q_i = \dfrac{1}{||x_i||} x_i$. Then $q_i' q_i = \dfrac{1}{||x_i||^2} x_i' x_i = 1$. The *orthonormal* vectors $q_1, \ldots, q_K$ will still be *eigenvectors* of A. To see this observe that

$$A(q_i) = A\left[\frac{1}{||x_i||} x_i\right] = \frac{1}{||x_i||} A[x_i] = \frac{\lambda_i x_i}{||x_i||}$$

$$= \lambda_i q_i$$

Let $Q = (q_1 \ldots q_K)$ be the basis change matrix corresponding to the orthonormal eigenvectors. The (i, i)th diagonal entry in $Q'Q$ will now be $q_i' q_i = \frac{1}{||x_i||^2} x_i' x_i = 1$ and so $Q'Q = I$, where I is the $K \times K$ identity matrix. Thus the *orthonormal* matrix Q has as inverse Q^{-1} the transpose matrix Q'. In this case we may write

$$\Lambda = Q'AQ$$

where Λ is the eigenvalue matrix whose non-zero diagonal entries are $\lambda_1, \ldots, \lambda_r$ and r is the rank of A.

Example 2.2

Consider the symmetric matrix

$$A = \begin{bmatrix} 0 & 0 & 1 \\ 0 & 1 & 0 \\ 1 & 0 & 0 \end{bmatrix}$$

Clearly

$$x'A(x) = (x_1 x_2 x_3) \begin{bmatrix} x_3 \\ x_2 \\ x_1 \end{bmatrix} = x_2^2 + 2x_1 x_3$$

The characteristic equation of A is

$$O = \begin{bmatrix} -\lambda & 0 & 1 \\ 0 & 1-\lambda & 0 \\ 1 & 0 & -\lambda \end{bmatrix} = -\lambda(1-\lambda)(-\lambda) - (1-\lambda)$$

$$= (1-\lambda)(\lambda^2 - 1)$$

Thus the eigenvalues are $\lambda_1 = 1$, $\lambda_2 = 1$, $\lambda_3 = -1$. For the case $\lambda = 1$, the eigenvectors satisfy $Ax = x$. Letting $x' = (x_1, x_2, x_3)$ we obtain the equations: $x_3 = x_1$, $x_2 = x_2$, $x_1 = x_3$. One solution to these equations is $x_1 = x_3 = 1$, $x_2 = 0$, giving an eigenvector $v_1' = (1, 0, 1)$. A second solution is $x_1 = x_3 = 0$, $x_2 = 1$, giving an eigenvector $v_2' = (0, 1, 0)$. Now $||v_1||^2 = 2$ and $||v_2||^2 = 1$. Thus the two normalised eigenvectors associated with the eigenvalue $\lambda = 1$ are

$$q_1' = \frac{1}{\sqrt{2}}(1, 0, 1)$$

and
$$q_2' = (0, 1, 0)$$

In similar fashion, for the case $\lambda = -1$ we obtain the equation: $x_3 = -x_1$, $x_2 = -x_2$, $x_1 = -x_3$. The only solution to these equations is $x_2 = 0$, $x_1 = -x_3$, giving an eigenvector $v_3' = (1, 0, -1)$ which when normalised is $q_3 = \dfrac{1}{\sqrt{2}}(1, 0, -1)$. Note that these three eigenvectors q_1, q_2, q_3 are orthonormal. Let

$$Q = \frac{1}{\sqrt{2}} \begin{bmatrix} 1 & 0 & 1 \\ 0 & \sqrt{2} & 0 \\ 1 & 0 & -1 \end{bmatrix}$$

It can readily be shown that the transpose

$$Q' = \frac{1}{\sqrt{2}} \begin{bmatrix} 1 & 0 & 1 \\ 0 & \sqrt{2} & 0 \\ 1 & 0 & -1 \end{bmatrix}$$

is inverse to Q. Moreover,

$$Q'AQ = \wedge = \begin{bmatrix} 1 & 0 & 0 \\ 0 & 1 & 0 \\ 0 & 0 & -1 \end{bmatrix}$$

Another way of writing this is as

$$A = Q \wedge Q'$$

Consider now the quadratic form $x'A(x)$. As we have shown $x'Ax = x'Q \wedge Q'x$. But $x'Q = (Q'x)'$ and so $x'Ax = (Q'x)' \wedge (Q'x) = z' \wedge z$ where $z = Q'x$. In the example

$$Q'x = \frac{1}{\sqrt{2}} \begin{bmatrix} 1 & 0 & 1 \\ 0 & \sqrt{2} & 0 \\ 1 & 0 & -1 \end{bmatrix} \begin{bmatrix} x_1 \\ x_2 \\ x_3 \end{bmatrix}$$

$$= \begin{bmatrix} x_1 + x_2 \\ \sqrt{2}x_2 \\ x_1 - x_3 \end{bmatrix}$$

Thus $x'Ax = 1(x_1 + x_2)^2 + 1(\sqrt{2}x_2)^2 - (x_1 - x_3)^2$.

As this example illustrates, this procedure allows us to express a quadratic form, A, in the following way. Let Q be the orthogonal eigenvector matrix. For any vector $x \in \mathbf{R}^K$ let $z = Q'x$. This gives the *normal form* of the expression. Then

$$x'Ax = (Q'x)' \wedge (Q'x) = z' \wedge z'$$

$$= \sum_{i=1}^{K} \lambda_i z_i^2$$

If the r is rank of A, then only r of the eigenvalues can be non-zero. Let s be the number of eigenvalues that are strictly negative. This is often called the *index* of the form. By definition exactly $r - s$, eigenvalues will be strictly positive. The *canonical quadratic form* for A is then

$$x'Ax = -\sum_{i=1}^{s} |\lambda_i| z_i^2 + \sum_{j=s+1}^{r} \lambda_i z_i^2$$

where we have simply collected together negative and positive eigenvalues.

There are five possible cases:

1. $s = K$: A is called *negative definite*
2. $r < K$ and $s = r$: A is *negative semi-definite*
3. $s = 0$ and $r = K$: A is *positive definite*
4. $r < K$ and $s = 0$: A is *positive semi-definite*
5. $s \neq 0, r - s \neq 0$: A is sometimes called a 'saddle of index s'.

Consider the case $s = 0$ and $r = K$. In this case, for any $x \in \mathbf{R}^K$ with $x \neq 0$,

$$x'Ax = \sum_{i=1}^{K} \lambda_i z_i^2 > 0$$

since $\lambda_1, \ldots, \lambda_K$ are all non-zero. This explains the terminology 'positive definite'. On the other hand suppose that A has less than maximal rank (i.e. $r < K$). Then there exists at least one eigenvector associated with zero eigenvalue. Let $\{z_{r+1}, \ldots, z_K\}$ be the set of such eigenvectors. These eigenvectors are also said to belong to the *kernel* of A. Since $Az = 0$ for any vector z in the kernel, it is clearly possible to find a vector $x \neq 0$ such that

$$x'Ax = \sum_{i=r+1}^{K} \lambda_i z_i^2 = 0$$

Here $\lambda_{r+1} = \ldots = \lambda_K = 0$. Hence if $r < K$ and $s = 0$, then $x \neq 0$ implies that $x'Ax \geq 0$. This explains why A is called positive *semi-definite* in this case.

Example 2.3

Consider the symmetric matrix

$$A = \begin{bmatrix} 1 & 1 & 0 \\ 1 & 1 & 0 \\ 0 & 0 & 0 \end{bmatrix}$$

with form $x_1^2 + 2x_1 x_2 + x_2^2$. Clearly the canonical form is

$$x'Ax = (x_1 + x_2)^2$$

so we should expect A to have a single non-zero eigenvalue. Indeed the characteristic equation is

$$(1 - \lambda)^2 - 1 = \lambda(\lambda - 2) = 0$$

and so

$$\lambda_1 = 2, \lambda_2 = \lambda_3 = 0$$

For $\lambda_1 = 2$, the eigenvector satisfies $x_1 + x_2 = 2x_1$ and $x_1 + x_2 = 2x_2$. Thus $v_1 = (1, 1, 0)$, or when normalised $q_1 = \dfrac{1}{\sqrt{2}}(1, 1, 0)$, is the first eigenvector.

For $\lambda_2 = 0$ we obtain $x_1 + x_2 = 0$, giving two eigenvectors $q_2 = \dfrac{1}{\sqrt{2}}(1, -1, 0)$ and $q_3 = (0, 0, 1)$. The orthogonal basis change matrix is

$$Q = \frac{1}{\sqrt{2}}\begin{bmatrix} 1 & 1 & 0 \\ 1 & -1 & 0 \\ 0 & 0 & \sqrt{2} \end{bmatrix}$$

It is a simple matter to verify that $Q'AQ = \wedge$ where $\wedge$ is the diagonal matrix with 2 in the top left-hand corner, and zero elsewhere. Now $z = Q'x$ and as a row vector z may be written

$$z' = \frac{1}{\sqrt{2}}(x_1 + x_2, x_1 - x_2, \sqrt{2}x_3)$$

Thus

$$x'Ax = 2z_1^2 + 0z_2^2 + 0z_3^2$$
$$= (x_1 + x_2)^2 + 0(x_1 - x_2)^2 + 0x_2^2$$

as expected. Suppose now that $x = (x_1, x_2, x_3)$ satisfies $x_1 + x_2 = 0$ even though $x \neq 0$. Clearly

$$x'Ax = 0$$

Hence while A is positive semi-definite (with rank 1) it is not positive definite. In the case that A is a $K \times K$ matrix that is *positive definite*, then we can show that there exists a matrix, called $A^{1/2}$, such that $A^{1/2}(A^{1/2})' = A$. To see this consider first of all $\wedge = QAQ'$, where Q is the orthogonal eigenvector matrix, and $\wedge$ is the diagonal eigenvalue matrix with λ_i in the ith diagonal position. Let $D = (\lambda_i^{-1/2})$ be the diagonal matrix with $1/\sqrt{\lambda_i}$ in the ith position. Since A is positive definite, no eigenvalue is zero, and so $D'\wedge D = I_K$, the identity $K \times K$ matrix. But then $D'Q'AQD = P'AP = I$ where $P = QD$ is a matrix of rank K. Then

$$A = (P')^{-1}P^{-1}$$

Moreover

$$(P')^{-1} = (D'Q')^{-1} = QD^{-1}$$

and

$$(P^{-1})' = (D^{-1}Q^{-1})' = QD^{-1}$$

Thus we may write

$$A = (P^{-1})'P^{-1}$$
$$= A^{1/2}(A^{1/2})'$$

where $A^{1/2} = (P^{-1})'$ is a non-singular matrix (of rank K).

In the next chapter we shall meet a symmetric matrix A such that $A^2 = A$. Clearly if x is an eigenvector of A with eigenvalue λ then

$$A^2(x) = A(Ax) = \lambda(Ax) = \lambda^2 x$$
$$= A(x) = \lambda x$$

Thus each eigenvalue of A is either 0 or 1. Consequently the trace of the eigenvalue matrix Λ for A is r, the rank of Λ, which is also equal to the rank of A. But as we have seen trace $(\Lambda) =$ trace (A), and so trace (A) = rank (A) for such a matrix.

We shall also be considering differentiation of vector expressions. It is convenient to briefly mention this procedure here. For example consider the expression

$$z = y'\beta = \sum_{i=1}^{K} y_i \beta_i$$

where both $y, \beta \in \mathbf{R}^K$ say.

Then $\dfrac{\partial z}{\partial \beta} = 0$ means $\dfrac{\partial z}{\partial \beta_i} = 0$ for $i = 1, \ldots, K$

or $y_1 = \ldots = y_K = 0$, so $y = 0$. On the other hand suppose $z = \beta' A \beta$ for a $K \times K$ matrix $A = (a_{ij})$.

Now

$$z = \sum_{i=1}^{K} \sum_{j=1}^{K} \beta_i a_{ij} \beta_j$$

Since $\dfrac{\partial z}{\partial \beta} = 0$ requires $\dfrac{\partial z}{\partial \beta_r} = 0$ for $r = 1, \ldots, K$ this means for each $r = 1, \ldots, K$

$$O = 2a_{rr}\beta_r + \beta_r \sum_{j \neq r} (a_{jr} + a_{rj}) = 0$$

In the case that A is symmetric, so $a_{jr} = a_{rj}$ we may write this as

$$2\left[\sum_{j=1}^{K} a_{rj}\beta_j \right] = 0$$

But these K equations can be represented by the matrix equation $2A\beta = 0$.

2.7 THE ORDINARY LEAST SQUARE ESTIMATORS

We consider the vector equation

$$Y = X\beta + U$$

where Y is a $T \times 1$ vector of observations $\{Y_1, \ldots, Y_t, \ldots, Y_T\}$ of the dependent variable, β is a $(K + 1) \times 1$ vector of coefficients, X is a $T \times (K + 1)$ matrix whose

$(j + 1)$st column is the vector of T observations of the jth variable $\{x_{ij}, \ldots, x_{tj}, \ldots, x_{Tj}\}$. Finally U is a $T \times 1$ vector of *disturbances* $\{U_1, \ldots, U_t\}$.

The task is to use the observations to compute the vector β.

Having selected an estimator $\hat{\beta}$ for β we may write

$$\hat{Y} = X\hat{\beta}$$

and

$$Y = \hat{Y} + e$$

where e is the 'error' vector $\{e_1, \ldots, e_t, \ldots, e_T\}$ which we may use to estimate the disturbance vector U.

As in the previous case with one or two independent variables, a choice b, say, for β defines the residual sum of squares

$$R(b) = \sum_{t=1}^{T} e_i^2 = e'e$$

where

$$e = Y - \hat{Y} = Y - Xb$$

Thus

$$R(b) = (Y - Xb)'(Y - Xb)$$
$$= Y'Y + (Xb)'Xb - (Xb)'Y - Y'(Xb)$$

Now $(Xb)'$ is a $1 \times T$ row vector and is equal to $b'X'$ while $(Xb)'Y$, since it is a real number, is equal to $Y'(Xb)$.

Hence

$$R(b) = Y'Y + b'X'Xb - 2Y'Xb$$

As we indicated in the previous section, the critical point with respect to b, of the expression $z = y'\beta$ is $y = 0$. Differentiating $R(b)$ with respect to b gives

$$\frac{\partial R}{\partial b} = 2(X'X)b - 2(Y'X)'$$

Thus the critical point of R satisfies

$$(X'X)b - X'Y = 0$$

Since $X'X$ is a $(K + 1) \times (K + 1)$ matrix, it may be non-singular, and have an inverse $(X'X)^{-1}$. Suppose therefore that $|X'X| \neq 0$. Then $\hat{\beta} = (X'X)^{-1}(X'Y)$ is the critical point for $R(b)$.

This estimator $\hat{\beta} = (X'X)^{-1}(X'Y)$ is called the *ordinary least square* (OLS) estimator for β, and is sometimes written $\hat{\beta}_{\text{OLS}}$.

Note that $(X'X) = (x_0 \ldots x_K)'(x_0 \ldots x_K)$ where x_j, $j \neq 0$, is the $T \times 1$ column vector given by the T observations $\{X_{1j} - \bar{X}_j, \ldots, X_{Tj} - \bar{X}_j\}$, while x_0 is the $T \times 1$

vector of 1's. As we showed in the previous section

$$X'X = \begin{bmatrix} T & 0 & . & 0 \\ 0 & S_{11} & . & S_{1K} \\ . & . & S_{ij} & . \\ 0 & S_{K1} & . & S_{KK} \end{bmatrix}$$

where $S_{ij} = \sum_{t=1}^{T} x_{ti}x_{tj} = x_i'x_j$ is the *co-variation* between the variables x_i and x_j. Now consider

$$X'Y = (x_0, \ldots, x_K)' \, Y = \begin{bmatrix} x_0'Y \\ x_1'Y \\ . \\ X_K'Y \end{bmatrix}$$

Clearly

$$x_0'Y = \sum_{t=1}^{T} Y_t = T\bar{Y}$$

while

$$x_j'Y = \sum_{t=1}^{T} x_{tj}Y_t = \sum_{t=1}^{T} x_{tj}(Y_t - \bar{Y}) \text{ since } \bar{Y} \sum_{t=1}^{T} x_{tj} = 0$$

Thus $x_j'Y = S_{jy}$, the covariation between the jth independent variable and the dependent variable Y.

Consider the case already examined with two independent variables $x_1 = x$ and $x_2 = z$. Then the covariation matrix is

$$X'X = \begin{bmatrix} T & 0 & 0 \\ 0 & S_{xx} & S_{xz} \\ 0 & S_{xz} & S_{zz} \end{bmatrix}$$

Suppose that $(X'X)^{-1}$ exists. Then, as we showed in the previous section,

$$(X'X)^{-1} = \frac{1}{D_{xz}} \begin{bmatrix} \frac{1}{T}D_{xz} & 0 & 0 \\ 0 & S_{zz} & -S_{xz} \\ 0 & -S_{xz} & S_{xx} \end{bmatrix}$$

where $D_{xz} = S_{xx}S_{zz} - S_{xz}^2$.

Since the OLS estimator $\hat{\beta} = (X'X)^{-1}(X'Y)$, we obtain

$$\begin{bmatrix} \hat{\beta}_0 \\ \hat{\beta}_1 \\ \hat{\beta}_2 \end{bmatrix} = \frac{1}{D_{xz}} \begin{bmatrix} \frac{1}{T}D_{xz} & 0 & 0 \\ 0 & S_{zz} & -S_{xz} \\ 0 & -S_{xz} & S_{xx} \end{bmatrix} \begin{bmatrix} T\bar{Y} \\ S_{xy} \\ S_{zy} \end{bmatrix}$$

Then

$$\hat{\beta}_0 = \bar{Y}$$

$$\hat{\beta}_1 = \frac{S_{zz}S_{xy} - S_{xz}S_{zy}}{D_{xz}}$$

$$\hat{\beta}_2 = \frac{S_{xx}S_{zy} - S_{xz}S_{xy}}{D_{xz}}$$

as we found in section 2.4.
Note that $\hat{\beta}_1$, for example, may be written

$$\hat{\beta}_1 = \sum_{t=1}^{T} d_t(Y_t - \bar{Y})$$

where

$$d_t = \frac{x_i S_{zz} - z_i S_{xz}}{D_{xz}}$$

Thus $\hat{\beta}_1$, and of course $\hat{\beta}_2$ are *linear* in the observations $\{Y_1, \ldots, Y_t, \ldots, Y_T\}$. In the case with K variables we obtain $\hat{\beta} = (X'X)^{-1}X'Y$ where $(X'X)^{-1}$ is a $(K+1) \times (K+1)$ matrix and X' is a $(K+1) \times T$ matrix. Clearly $(X'X)^{-1}X' = M(X)$ is a $(K+1) \times T$ matrix, whose entry in the (j,t)th position is m_{jt}, say. Thus the jth estimator is given by

$$\hat{\beta}_j = \sum_{t=1}^{T} m_{jt}Y_t$$

and so the OLS estimators are *linear* in the observations of the dependent variable.

Note that the term in the $(1,1)$st position in $X'X$ is always T, while the other terms S_{0j} or S_{j0} in the first row or column are zero, so the term in the $(1,1)$st position in $(X'X)^{-1}$ is $1/T$. Since the first term in the vector $X'Y$ is $T\bar{Y}$ this implies that the OLS estimator $\hat{\beta}_0 = \bar{Y}$. Clearly $\hat{\beta}_0$ is linear in the dependent variable. Moreover this suggests that we redefine the dependent variable, letting $y_t = Y_t - \bar{Y}$ for $t = 1, \ldots, T$. Let $X_* = (x_1, \ldots, x_K)$ be the $K \times K$ matrix of observations of the K independent variables, and let $\hat{\beta}_* = (\hat{\beta}_1, \ldots, \hat{\beta}_K)$ be the OLS estimator with no constant term. If we consider the vector equation

$$Y - \bar{Y} = y = X_*\beta_* + U$$

then the OLS estimator $\hat{\beta}_*$ may be written, in precisely the same way as before as

$$\hat{\beta}_* = (X_*'X_*)^{-1}(X_*'y)$$

Clearly

$$X_* y = \begin{bmatrix} S_{1_y} \\ \cdot \\ \cdot \\ \cdot \\ S_{K_y} \end{bmatrix}$$

as before.

Suppose that there are as many independent variables (K) as observation (T), and that the variables are themselves linearly independent, so that X_* has an inverse, X_*^{-1}.

In this case $(X_*' X_*)^{-1} = X_*^{-1} (X_*')^{-1}$ and so $\hat{\beta}_* = X_*^{-1} y$. But the original assumption is that $Y = X\beta + U$, or $y = X_* \beta_* + U$. In this case $y = X_* \hat{\beta}_*$ and so $\hat{\beta}_* = \beta$ and $U = 0$. In other words, we can *fit* the regression equation precisely. We shall suppose that $K < T$ from now on.

Although we have shown that the OLS estimator $\hat{\beta}$ is a critical point for the 'error' $R(b)$, in the sense that $\dfrac{\partial R}{\partial b} = 0$ at $R = R(\hat{\beta})$ we have not shown that $\hat{\beta}$ minimised $R(b)$.

As we have shown $\dfrac{\partial R}{\partial b} = 2(X'X)b - 2(X'Y)$. Now take the second derivative. Then $\dfrac{\partial^2 R}{\partial b^2} = 2(X'X)'$. The matrix $\dfrac{\partial^2 R}{\partial b^2}$ is known as the *hessian* of the function R, and by analogy with the calculus for a real variable, R is minimised at the vector $b = \hat{\beta}$ if $\dfrac{\partial^2 R}{\partial b^2}$ is *positive definite* (at $b = \hat{\beta}$). To see what this means in the case of two independent variables x, z, let $b' = (b_0, b_1, b_2)$. Then

$$(X'X)b = \begin{bmatrix} Tb_0 \\ b_1 S_{xx} + b_2 S_{xz} \\ b_1 S_{xz} + b_2 S_{zz} \end{bmatrix}$$

Hence

$$H = \frac{\partial^2 R}{\partial b^2} = \begin{bmatrix} T & 0 & 0 \\ 0 & S_{xx} & S_{xz} \\ 0 & S_{xz} & S_{zz} \end{bmatrix} = X'X$$

The Hessian, H, is positive definite iff its three eigenvalues $\lambda_0, \lambda_1, \lambda_2$, say, are strictly positive. Clearly T is positive, and so λ_0 must be positive. Thus H is positive definite iff the reduced covariation matrix

$$G = (X_*' X) = \begin{bmatrix} S_{xx} & S_{xz} \\ S_{xz} & S_{zz} \end{bmatrix}$$

is positive definite. Moreover the eigenvalues λ_1, λ_2 for H are also eigenvalues for G. But then as we have seen in the previous section, $\lambda_1 + \lambda_2 = \text{trace}(G)$, $\lambda_1 \lambda_2 = |G|$. Now $\text{trace}(G) = S_{xx} + S_{zz}$ is *positive*, since it is the sum of squares, while $|G| = D_{xz} = S_{xx} S_{zz} - S_{xz}^2$. To see that $|G|$ is positive, we note that the empirical correlation coefficient $r = r(x, z)$ between x and z satisfies $r(x, z) = \dfrac{S_{xz}}{\sqrt{S_{xx}S_{zz}}}$. Since $r^2 \leq$ I, $S_{xz}^2 \leq S_{xx}S_{zz}$. Certainly if x and z are linearly dependent as vectors, then $r^2 = 1$, and so $|G| = 0$. We have assumed however that $(X'X)^{-1}$ exists, and this is equivalent to requiring that $|X'X| \neq 0$. Hence $D_{xz} \neq 0$ and so $r(x, z)^2 < 1$. With this assumption, $|G|$ must be positive and so both eigenvalues λ_1, λ_2 must be positive. Hence G, and thus H, are positive definite and so $R(b)$ is minimised at the OLS estimator $\hat{\beta}$.

The same analysis may be developed for the general case of K independent variables. Proof that $R(b) = R(b_0, \ldots, b_K)$ is minimised at the OLS estimator $\hat{\beta}$ is then obtained by showing that $(X'X)$ is positive definite, when the regressors $x_1, \ldots, x_K$ are linearly independent. (See exercise 3 at the end of this chapter.)
Now

$$\frac{1}{T} x_i' x_j = \frac{1}{T} \sum_{t=1}^{T} x_{ti} x_{tj} = \sigma_{ij}$$

is an empirical estimate for the covariance σ_{ij} between the variables x_i and x_j. Hence

$$\frac{1}{T}(X'X) = \begin{bmatrix} 1 & 0 & . \\ 0 & \sigma_{11} & . \\ & . & . & . \\ 0 & \sigma_{K1} & . \end{bmatrix} = \begin{bmatrix} 1 & 0 \\ 0 & A \end{bmatrix}$$

Requiring H to be positive definite is equivalent to requiring the empirical covariance matrix A to be positive definite.

We shall show in the next chapter that for any choice $b_0, \ldots, b_K$ of coefficients, the residual sum of squares $R(b)$ may be written

$$R(b) = T(b_0 - \bar{Y})^2 + [Q(b - \hat{\beta})]' \wedge Q(b - \hat{\beta}) + a$$

where $\wedge$ may be interpreted as the eigenvalue matrix of the covariance matrix A, Q is an orthogonal basis change matrix and a is the residual sum of squares, $R(\hat{\beta})$, for the OLS estimator $\hat{\beta}$. Since we assume A is positive definite, so will be $\wedge$, and this implies that $R(b)$ is minimised at $b = \hat{\beta}$.

To extend the analysis, we now seek to compute the variances and covariances of the OLS coefficients $\hat{\beta}$. To do this of course we need to make assumptions about the underlying distribution from which the sample X, Y is drawn.

A first, standard assumption is the disturbance terms $\{U_1, \ldots, U_t, \ldots, U_T\}$ are independent with zero mean and identical variance σ^2. That is to say assume

1. $\qquad\qquad E(U_i) = 0 \qquad$ for all i
2. $\qquad\qquad E(U_i U_j) = \sigma^2 \qquad$ if $i = j$
     $\qquad\qquad\qquad\quad = 0 \qquad$ if $i \neq j$

The covariance matrix $E = (E(U_i U_j)) = \sigma^2 I$ where I is the $T \times T$ identity matrix. We shall sometimes write $V(U)$ for the (variance–covariance) matrix E, and also write

$$U \sim (0, \sigma^2 I) \quad \text{when} \quad V(U) = \sigma^2 I$$

Our assumption is that $Y = X\beta + U$, where β is the true coefficient vector whereas using the OLS estimator $\hat{Y} = X\hat{\beta} + e$ where e is the OLS estimator for the disturbance vector U.

Now

$$E(Y) = E(X\beta + U) = E(X\beta) \text{ since } E(U) = 0$$
$$= X\beta$$

Moreover

$$E(\hat{\beta}) = E((X'X)^{-1}(X'Y))$$
$$= E((X'X)^{-1}X'(X\beta + U))$$

To simplify this expression we may assume that the disturbance terms and the independent variables are independent. That is to say assume

$$E(X'U) = 0$$

Then the data matrix X may be treated as constant, and

$$E(\hat{\beta}) = (X'X)^{-1}X'X\beta$$

But we assume $(X'X)^{-1}$ exists, and so $(X'X)^{-1}X'X = I$. Thus $E(\hat{\beta}) = \beta$, and so $\hat{\beta}$ is unbiased. Note that if the disturbances and independent variables *are* correlated, then there is no guarantee that $\hat{\beta}$ will be unbiased. With these assumptions the covariance matrix for $\hat{\beta} - \beta$ is then

$$V(\hat{\beta}) = (E((\hat{\beta}_i - \beta_i)(\hat{\beta}_j - \beta_j)))$$

Another way of expressing this is to write $(\hat{\beta} - \beta)(\hat{\beta} - \beta)'$ for the $(K + 1) \times (K + 1)$ matrix $((\hat{\beta}_i - \beta_i)(\hat{\beta}_j - \beta_j))$. Then

$$V(\hat{\beta}) = E[(\hat{\beta} - \beta)(\hat{\beta} - \beta)']$$

Now

$$\hat{\beta} = (X'X)^{-1}X'Y = (X'X)^{-1}X'(X\beta + U)$$
$$= \beta + (X'X)^{-1}X'U$$

For convencience, in computing $V(\hat{\beta})$, let us define $B = (X'X)^{-1}$, so $\hat{\beta} - \beta = BX'U$. Then

$$V(\hat{\beta}) = E[BX'U(BX'U)']$$
$$= E[BX'UU'XB']$$

since

$$(BX'U)' = U'XB'$$

But X and U are assumed to be independent and the covariance matrix

$$V(U) = (E(U_iU_j))$$
$$= E(UU') = \sigma^2 I$$

Thus

$$V(\hat{\beta}) = BX'E(UU')XB'$$
$$= \sigma^2(BX'XB')$$

Now

$$B = (X'X)^{-1}$$

and so

$$V(\hat{\beta}) = \sigma^2 \, B' = \sigma^2 \, B = \sigma^2 (X'X)^{-1}$$

since B is symmetric.

In the case with two independent variables x, z, we have already shown that the $(1, 1)$st term B_{00} in $(X'X)^{-1}$ is $1/T$. Hence

$$\text{var}(\hat{\beta}_0) = E((\hat{\beta}_0 - \beta_0)^2) = \frac{\sigma^2}{T}$$

But also the term in the $(2,2)$ position, B_{11} is $\dfrac{S_{zz}}{D_{xz}}$ where $D_{xz} = S_{xx}S_{zz} - S_{xz}^2$. Thus

$$\text{var}(\hat{\beta}_1) = \frac{\sigma^2 S_{zz}}{D_{xz}}$$

and similarly

$$\text{var}(\hat{\beta}_2) = \frac{\sigma^2 S_{xx}}{D_{xz}}$$

as we guessed already in section 2.4. Note that this procedure also gives the covariance $B_{12} = \dfrac{-S_{xz}}{D_{xz}}$ between $\hat{\beta}_1$ and $\hat{\beta}_2$.

As we have already shown, the OLS estimator is linear and unbiased. With the assumptions that we have made we can show that it is BLUE, or has least variance among the linear unbiased estimators. More precisely, suppose b is another unbiased estimator for β, which is also linear in the dependent variable Y. This requirement of linearity implies that $b = AY$ for a $(K + 1) \times T$ matrix A. We shall say that $\hat{b}$ is BLUE if it linear, unbiased, and for any other linear, unbiased estimator b for β, the matrix $V(b) - V(\hat{b})$ is positive semi-definite. Let $\hat{\beta}$ be the OLS estimator and b any other linear unbiased estimator. Then we may write $b = \hat{\beta} + CY$ for some matrix C. But as we have seen

$$\hat{\beta} = \beta + BX'U \quad \text{where} \quad B = (X'X)^{-1}$$

Now

$$\begin{aligned}
E(b) &= E(\hat{\beta} + CY) \\
&= E(\beta + BX'U + C(X\beta + U)) \\
&= \beta + CX\beta \\
&= (I + CX)\beta
\end{aligned}$$

Thus $E(b) = \beta$ implies that $CX = 0$. Hence

$$b = \beta + BX'U + CU$$

Consequently

$$V(b) = E[(b - \beta)(b - \beta)']$$
$$= E[(BX' + C)U(BX' + C)'U']$$
$$= (BX' + C)E(UU')(BX' + C)'$$

Now $E(UU') = V(U)$ is the covariance matrix of the disturbances, which we assume to be $\sigma^2 I$. Thus

$$V(b) = \sigma^2(BX' + C)(BX' + C)'$$
$$= \sigma^2(BX' XB' + 2BX'C' + CC')$$

The covariance matrix for the OLS estimator is $V(\hat{\beta}) = \sigma^2 BX' XB'$. Moreover $CX = X'C' = 0$. Thus $V(b) = V(\hat{\beta}) + \sigma^2 CC'$. Clearly CC' is a symmetric $(K + 1) \times (K + 1)$ matrix whose diagonal entries are all non-negative. By Exercise 3 below CC' must be *positive semi-definite*. Thus the OLS estimator $\hat{\beta}$ is BLUE, under the conditions $E(X' U) = 0, E(UU') = \sigma^2 I$.

2.8 EXERCISES

1. Consider the symmetric matrix

$$A = \begin{bmatrix} 1 & 0 & 0 \\ 0 & 2 & 1 \\ 0 & 1 & 1 \end{bmatrix}$$

Show that A is positive definite by computing the three eigenvalues for A. Thus find three orthonormal eigenvectors (z_1, z_2, z_3) for A, and write down the orthogonal basis change matrix Q. Verify by computation that $\wedge = QAQ'$. Let $D = (\lambda_i^{-1/2})$ be the diagonal matrix. Compute $P = QD$, P^{-1} and $(P^{-1})'$. Thus show that $(P^{-1})'(P^{-1}) = A$.

2. Show, for any two vectors $x, z, \in \mathbf{R}^T$, that $x'z \leq ||x|| \, ||z||$, with an equality if and only if $x = \alpha z$. Thus show that if x, z are linearly independent then the reduced matrix

$$X'X = \begin{bmatrix} x'x & x'z \\ x'z & z'z \end{bmatrix}$$

is positive definite.

3. More generally show that if X is a $K \times T$ matrix of rank $K (\leq T)$ then the $K \times K$ matrix, $X'X$, is of rank K and is positive definite. Show that if X has rank $r(< K)$ then $X'X$ is positive semi-definite.

Hint: Let $X'X = (x_{ij})$ where $x_{ij} = x_i'x_j$. Show that

$$\beta'(X'X)\beta = \sum_{i,j=1}^{K} \beta_i \beta_j x_{ij}$$

$$= x_{11}\left(\beta_1 + \frac{x_{12}}{x_{11}}\beta_2 + \cdots\right)^2$$

$$+ \left[x_{22} - \frac{x_{12}^2}{x_{11}}\right](\beta_2 + \cdots)^2 + \cdots$$

$$= \sum_{i=1}^{K} y_i \alpha_i^2$$

where each y_i is positive (in the rank K case) and α_i is a linear function of $(\beta_i, \ldots, \beta_K)$. Show that this implies that $X'X$ is positive definite in the rank K case.

Chapter 3

General Regression Models

In the previous chapter we have developed the OLS regression model, under the assumption that the errors $\{U_t\}$ were uncorrelated with the data array X, and were themselves mutually independent with constant variance. With these assumptions the OLS estimators were shown to be unbiased. In this chapter we shall develop the model further.

We first of all introduce the correlation matrix R associated with the data array, and show the relationship between R and the correlation coefficient (the proportion of variance explained) in the case of OLS estimation, and then more generally. We shall then show how to construct confidence intervals for the estimators under the assumption that the errors are not only independently but also normally distributed. In a brief section we then outline the method of principal components as a procedure to deal with multicollinearity. We then introduce the general linear model, and show how we may deal with heteroscedasticity (changing variance in the errors) and autocorrelation (correlation between the errors).

3.1 THE CORRELATION COEFFICIENT AND CORRELATION MATRIX

In the case of one or two independent variables (or regressors) discussed previously, we defined the correlation coefficient r by

$$r^2 = \frac{\text{explained variation}}{\text{total variation}}$$

In the general multivariate case, with regressors $x_1, \ldots, x_K$, the variation unexplained by the regression model with OLS estimators $\hat{\beta}_0, \ldots, \hat{\beta}_K$ is

$$R(\hat{\beta}) = \sum_{t=1}^{T} (Y_t - \hat{Y}_t)^2, \quad \text{where} \quad \hat{Y}_t = \hat{\beta}_0 + \sum_{j=1}^{K} \hat{\beta}_j x_j$$

The total variation, on the other hand is $\sum_{t=1}^{T} (Y_t - \bar{Y})^2$. In vector notation these terms become

$$R(\hat{\beta}) = (Y - \hat{Y})'(Y - \hat{Y}) \quad \text{and} \quad (Y - \bar{Y})'(Y - \bar{Y}) = y'y$$

Now $R(\hat{\beta}) = (Y - X\hat{\beta})'(Y - X\hat{\beta})$ where $\hat{\beta}$ is the OLS estimator.

As we have seen $\hat{\beta}_0 = \bar{Y}$ while $\beta_* = (X_*'X_*)^{-1}X_*'Y$ gives the OLS coefficients $\hat{\beta}_1, \ldots, \hat{\beta}_K$. Here X_* is the reduced $(K \times K)$ data matrix $(x_1, \ldots, x_K)$. We may therefore decompose $R(\hat{\beta})$ by

$$R(\hat{\beta}) = (y - X_*\beta_*)'(y - X_*\beta_*)$$

where $y = Y - \hat{\beta}_0 = Y - \bar{Y}$ is the $T \times 1$ column vector of observations about the mean. Thus

$$R(\hat{\beta}) = y'y + (X_*\beta_*)'X_*\beta_* - 2y'X_*\beta_*$$

Note that this is precisely analogous to the original expression for the sum of squared residuals, except that we have required $\hat{\beta}_0 = \bar{Y}$. Substituting $\hat{\beta}_*$ in this expression gives

$$R(\hat{\beta}) = \beta_*'X_*'X_*\beta_* - 2y'X_*\beta_* + y'y$$

Now $\beta_*' = Y'X_*(X_*'X_*)^{-1}$ since $X_*'X_*$ is symmetric. Therefore

$$R(\hat{\beta}) = Y'X_*\beta_* - 2y'X_*\beta_* + y'y$$

Now consider the expression $\beta_*'X_*'y$. As we have seen the vector $X_*'y$ has the form

$$(x_1, \ldots, x_K)'y = \begin{bmatrix} x_1'y \\ . \\ . \\ . \\ x_K'y \end{bmatrix} = \begin{bmatrix} \sum_{t=1}^{T} x_{t1}(Y_t - \bar{Y}) \\ . \\ . \\ . \end{bmatrix} = \begin{bmatrix} S_{1y} \\ . \\ . \\ . \end{bmatrix}$$

where $S_{iy} = \sum_{t=1}^{T} x_{tj}(Y_t - \bar{Y}) = \sum_{t=1}^{T} x_{tj}Y_t$

Thus $\beta_*'X_*'y = \beta_*'X_*'Y$ and so we may write

$$R(\hat{\beta}) = y'y - \beta_*'(X_*'y)$$

Since the total variation is $y'y$, the *explained* variation is $\beta_*'(X_*'y)$ and so

$$r^2 = \frac{\beta_*'(X_*'y)}{y'y}$$

For example, in the case with two regressors, x and z, the numerator of this expression is

$$[\hat{\beta}_1, \hat{\beta}_2] \begin{bmatrix} S_{xy} \\ S_{zy} \end{bmatrix}$$

while the denominator is $y'y = S_{yy}$. Let us write $\sigma_e^2 = \dfrac{1}{T} R(\hat{\beta})$ and regard σ_e^2 as an estimate for the variance of the residuals. In the same way $\sigma_y^2 = \dfrac{1}{T} S_{yy}$ is an estimate for the variance in Y, while for each regressor $x_j, j = 1, \ldots, K$, $\sigma_j^2 = \dfrac{1}{T} S_{jj} = \dfrac{1}{T} \sum_{t=1}^{T} x_{tj}^2$ is an estimate of its variance. We now seek to normalise the variables, so as to obtain an expression for the correlation coefficient. First of all consider the case with two regressors x, z, in the regression equation for Y.

In the case of the regression between x and Y we have shown that $r_{xy} = \hat{\beta} \dfrac{\sigma_x}{\sigma_y}$ is the coefficient associated with the normalised variables $\dfrac{Y}{\sigma_y}$ and $\dfrac{X}{\sigma_x}$. This suggests that we consider normalised coefficients

$$\hat{\alpha}' = [\hat{\alpha}_0, \hat{\alpha}_1, \hat{\alpha}_2] = \left[\frac{\hat{\beta}_0}{\sigma_y}, \frac{\sigma_x}{\sigma_y}\hat{\beta}_1, \frac{\sigma_z}{\sigma_y}\hat{\beta}_2 \right]$$

In the same fashion, normalise the data arrays X, Y by writing

$$Z = \left[1, \frac{x}{\sigma_x}, \frac{z}{\sigma_z} \right]$$

and

$$Y_0 = \left[\frac{Y_1}{\sigma_y}, \ldots, \frac{Y_T}{\sigma_y} \right]$$

The general OLS equation $\hat{\beta} = (X'X)^{-1}X'Y$ can be written as $(X'X)\hat{\beta} = X'Y$, or in normalised form as $(Z'Z\hat{\alpha} = Z'Y_0$. To see this in the case of two regressors observe that

$$\begin{bmatrix} 1 & 0 & 0 \\ 0 & \dfrac{S_{xx}}{\sigma_x^2} & \dfrac{S_{xz}}{\sigma_x\sigma_z} \\ 0 & \dfrac{S_{xz}}{\sigma_x\sigma_z} & \dfrac{S_{zz}}{\sigma_z^2} \end{bmatrix} \begin{bmatrix} \dfrac{\hat{\beta}_0}{\sigma_y} \\ \dfrac{\sigma_x\hat{\beta}_1}{\sigma_y} \\ \dfrac{\sigma_z\hat{\beta}_2}{\sigma_y} \end{bmatrix} = \begin{bmatrix} \dfrac{T\bar{Y}}{\sigma_y} \\ \dfrac{S_{xy}}{\sigma_x\sigma_y} \\ \dfrac{S_{xy}}{\sigma_z\sigma_y} \end{bmatrix}$$

Moreover the empirical correlation coefficient

$$r_{xz} = \frac{S_{xz}}{\sqrt{S_{xx}S_{zz}}} = \frac{S_{xz}}{T\sigma_x\sigma_z}$$

and similarly for r_{xy}, r_{zy}. Dividing through by T gives

$$\begin{bmatrix} 1 & 0 & 0 \\ 0 & 1 & r_{xz} \\ 0 & r_{xz} & 1 \end{bmatrix} \begin{bmatrix} \dfrac{\beta_0}{\sigma_y} \\ \dfrac{\sigma_x\beta_1}{\sigma_y} \\ \dfrac{\sigma_z\beta_2}{\sigma_y} \end{bmatrix} = \begin{bmatrix} \dfrac{\bar{Y}}{\sigma_y} \\ r_{xy} \\ r_{zy} \end{bmatrix}$$

Clearly the first entry in this equation gives us no new information. However, the 2×2 matrix obtained by neglecting the first equation is called the *correlation matrix*, C, where

$$C = \begin{bmatrix} 1 & r_{xz} \\ r_{xz} & 1 \end{bmatrix}$$

We therefore obtain the matrix equation

$$C \begin{bmatrix} \hat{\alpha}_1 \\ \hat{\alpha}_2 \end{bmatrix} = \begin{bmatrix} r_{xy} \\ r_{zy} \end{bmatrix}$$

In this case the *correlation coefficient* r^2 is given by

$$r^2 = \frac{\hat{\beta}_1 S_{xy} + \hat{\beta}_2 S_{zy}}{S_{yy}}$$

But

$$\frac{\hat{\beta}_1 S_{xy}}{S_{yy}} = \frac{\sigma_y}{\sigma_x} \hat{\alpha}_1 \frac{S_{xy}}{S_{yy}} = \hat{\alpha}_1 r_{xy}$$

since

$$r_{xy} = \frac{S_{xy}}{\sqrt{S_{xx}S_{yy}}} = \frac{S_{xy}}{S_{yy}} \cdot \frac{\sigma_y}{\sigma_x}$$

Therefore

$$r^2 = [r_{xy}, r_{zy}] \begin{bmatrix} \hat{\alpha}_1 \\ \hat{\alpha}_2 \end{bmatrix}$$

But when $|r_{xz}| \neq 1$ (when x and z are independent) then $|C| \neq 0$ and so C^{-1} exists. In this case

$$\begin{bmatrix} \hat{\alpha}_1 \\ \hat{\alpha}_2 \end{bmatrix} = C^{-1} \begin{bmatrix} r_{xy} \\ r_{zy} \end{bmatrix}$$

and so

$$r^2 = (r_{xy}, r_{zy}) \begin{bmatrix} 1 & r_{xz} \\ r_{xz} & 1 \end{bmatrix}^{-1} \begin{bmatrix} r_{xy} \\ r_{zy} \end{bmatrix}$$

since $r_{xz} = r_{zx}$. Clearly

$$C^{-1} = \frac{1}{1 - r_{xz}^2} \begin{bmatrix} 1 & -r_{xz} \\ -r_{xz} & 1 \end{bmatrix}$$

and so

$$r^2 = \frac{r_{xy}^2 - 2r_{xz}r_{xy}r_{zy} + r_{zy}^2}{1 - r_{xz}^2}$$

which is the expression we obtained previously in section 2.4. To deal with the case of K regressors let

$$Z_* = \begin{bmatrix} \dfrac{x_1}{\sigma_1}, \dots, \dfrac{x_K}{\sigma_K} \end{bmatrix}$$

$$\hat{\alpha}_*' = \begin{bmatrix} \dfrac{\sigma_1}{\sigma_0} \hat{\beta}_1, \dots, \dfrac{\sigma_K}{\sigma_0} \hat{\beta}_K \end{bmatrix}$$

$$Y' = \begin{bmatrix} \dfrac{Y_1}{\sigma_0}, \dots, \dfrac{Y_K}{\sigma_0} \end{bmatrix}$$

where σ_0^2 is the empirical variance $\dfrac{1}{T}\sum^{T}(Y_i - \bar{Y})^2$ in Y. Let r_{ij}, for $i = 1, \dots, K$, $j = 1, \dots, K$ be the regression coefficients between the normalised variables. As in the simpler case we obtain the normalised OLS equation

$$(Z_*'Z_*)\hat{\alpha}_* = Z_*'Y_0$$

where

$$\frac{1}{T}(Z_*'Z_*) = \begin{bmatrix} 1 & r_{12} & \cdot & r_{1K} \\ & 1 & \cdot & \cdot \\ & & \cdot & r_{ij} \\ & & & \cdot \\ r_{K1} & & & 1 \end{bmatrix} = C$$

is the symmetric correlation matrix $C = C(1, \dots, K)$ for the independent variables. We may also write

$$\frac{1}{T}(Z_*'Y_0) = \begin{bmatrix} r_{01} \\ r_{0K} \end{bmatrix}$$

which is the column vector of correlations between Y and the regressors.

Letting $r_0 = (r_{0j})$ stand for this $K \times 1$ column vector we obtain the matrix equation.

$$C(\hat{\alpha}_*) = r_0$$

However, the correlation coefficient r^2 is

$$r^2 = r_0'\hat{\alpha}_* = \frac{1}{T}(\hat{\alpha}_*)'(Z_*'Y_0)$$

Thus

$$r^2 = r_0'[C^{-1}(r_0)]$$

Notice that C is a symmetric matrix, and so r^2 is a quadratic form in the vector of simple correlation coefficients r_0. Moreover the data array $Z_*'Z_*$ is positive definite and so C will be positive definite. Returning to the original matrix equation

$$Y = X\beta + U$$

this could be expressed in terms of normalised variables as

$$Y_0 = Z\alpha + U$$

The OLS estimator $\hat{\alpha}$ must then satisfy

$$(Z'Z)\hat{\alpha} = Z'Y_0$$

As we have seen this equation can be partitioned into

$$\hat{\alpha}_0 = \frac{\bar{Y}}{\sigma_y}$$

and

$$(Z_*'Z_*)\hat{\alpha}_* = Z_*'Y_0$$

or

$$C(\hat{\alpha}_*) = r_0$$

Clearly the residual sum of squares in the normalised equation is

$$e'e = (Y_0 - Z_*\hat{\alpha}_*)'(Y_0 - Z_*\hat{\alpha}_*)$$
$$= Y_0'Y_0 - Y_0'Z_*\hat{\alpha}_*$$

Now

$$Y_0'Y_0 = \frac{1}{\sigma_0^2}\sum(Y_t - \bar{Y})^2 = T$$

and so

$$\frac{e'e}{T} = 1 - \frac{1}{T}Y_0'Z_*\alpha_* = 1 - r^2 = 1 - r_0'\hat{\alpha}_*$$

As before, therefore, $r^2 = r_0'\hat{\alpha}_* = r_0'C^{-1}(r_0)$. Note also that $\frac{1}{T}e'e = 1 - r^2$ is an estimate for the variance of the residuals in the normalised equation.

The relationship between C, r_0 and r^2 can be explored further by considering the full correlation matrix.

In the case of two regressors x,z and independent variable y, define

$$D = \begin{bmatrix} 1 & r_{yx} & r_{yz} \\ r_{yx} & 1 & r_{xz} \\ r_{yz} & r_{xz} & 1 \end{bmatrix}$$

Clearly $|D| = |C| - |A|$ where C is the 2×2 correlation matrix for x,z, and $|A| = r_{yx}(r_{yx} - r_{yz}r_{xz}) - r_{yz}(r_{yx}r_{xz} - r_{yz})$. However, as we have already shown

$$r^2 = \frac{|A|}{|C|}$$

thus

$$r^2 = \frac{|C| - |D|}{|C|} = 1 - \frac{|D|}{|C|}$$

Note that

$$|A| = (r_{yx}, r_{yz}) \begin{bmatrix} 1 & -r_{xz} \\ -r_{xz} & 1 \end{bmatrix} \begin{bmatrix} r_{yx} \\ r_{yz} \end{bmatrix}$$

where the 2×2 matrix is the cofactor matrix of C. In the more general case of K regressors, let us write

$$D = \begin{bmatrix} 1 & r_{01} & . & r_{0K} \\ r_{01} & 1 & r_{ij} & . \\ . & . & . & . \\ r_{0K} & . & . & 1 \end{bmatrix}$$

for the full correlation matrix involving the 0th variable, Y, and the K regressors $x_1, \ldots, x_K$. Let C be the correlation matrix involving the K regressors. Then

$$D = \begin{bmatrix} 1 & r_0' \\ r_0 & C \end{bmatrix}$$

where $r_0' = (r_{01}, \ldots, r_{0K})$. Then as above $|D| = |C| - |A|$ where $|A| = r_0'(C_{ij})r_0$ and (C_{ij}) is the cofactor matrix of C. Again therefore

$$r^2 = r_0'C^{-1}r_0$$

$$= r_0' \frac{(C_{ij})}{|C|} r_0$$

$$= \frac{|A|}{|C|} = \frac{|C| - |D|}{|C|} = 1 - \frac{|D|}{|C|}$$

The full $(K + 1) \times (K + 1)$ covariance matrix D is frequently written R, while the matrix C, obtained from D by deleting the 0th row and column may also be written as R_{00}. Note that $|R_{00}|$ is the $(0,0)$ cofactor of D. From the expression

$$r^2 = \frac{|R_{00}| - |R|}{|R_{00}|}$$

we may interpret $|R_{00}|$ as a measure of the total variance in the dependent variable, while $|R|$ is a measure of the total unexplained variance. This formulation of the regression model allows us to give an interpretation of the normalised OLS coefficients $\hat{\alpha}$.

Since we have

$$\hat{\alpha}_* = C^{-1}(r_0)$$

$$= \frac{(C_{ij})}{|C|} r_0$$

we may express the jth coefficient as

$$\hat{\alpha}_j = \frac{1}{|C|} \sum_{i=1}^{K} C_{ij} r_{i0}$$

where C_{ij} is the (i,j) cofactor the matrix C. Now consider the $K \times K$ matrix $B = R_{0j}$ obtained from R by deleting the 0th row and jth column of R. By definition

$$|R_{0j}| = \sum_{i=1}^{K} r_{i0} B_{i0}$$

where B_{i0} is the determinant (up to sign) of the matrix obtained from R by deleting the 0th and ith row and the 0th and jth column of R. But this is precisely C_{ij}. Consequently, the numerator in the expression for $\hat{\alpha}_j$ is $(-1)^{j+1}|R_{0j}|$ and we may write

$$\hat{\alpha}_j = (-1)^{j+1} \frac{|R_{0j}|}{|R_{00}|}$$

For example, in the case of two regressors x, z we find that

$$\begin{bmatrix} \hat{\alpha}_1 \\ \hat{\alpha}_2 \end{bmatrix} = \frac{1}{1 - r_{xz}^2} \begin{bmatrix} r_{xy} - r_{xz}r_{zy} \\ r_{zy} - r_{xz}r_{xy} \end{bmatrix} = \frac{1}{|R_{00}|} \begin{bmatrix} |R_{01}| \\ -|R_{02}| \end{bmatrix}$$

In section 2.4 we showed that the partial correlation coefficient between x and y, holding z constant was

$$r_{yx,z} = \frac{r_{yx} - r_{xz}r_{yz}}{\sqrt{(1 - r_{yz}^2)(1 - r_{xz}^2)}}$$

Now $1 - r_{xz}^2 = |R_{00}|$ while $1 - r_{yz}^2 = |R_{11}|$, the determinant of the matrix obtained from R by deleting the (x,x) row and column. Thus

$$r_{yx,z} = \frac{|R_{01}|}{\sqrt{|R_{00}||R_{11}|}}$$

In identical fashion

$$r_{yz,x} = \frac{r_{yz} - r_{xz}r_{yx}}{\sqrt{(1 - r_{yx}^2)(1 - r_{zx}^2)}} = \frac{-|R_{02}|}{\sqrt{|R_{00}||R_{22}|}}$$

For K regressors, and one independent variable, x_0, the partial correlation coefficient between x_0 and x_j holding all other regressors constant is:

$$r_{0j,\bar{j}} = (-1)^{j+1} \frac{|R_{0j}|}{\sqrt{|R_{00}||R_{jj}|}}$$

In some cases we may choose to work directly with the *empirical* correlation matrix

$$R = \begin{bmatrix} & \cdot & \\ & \cdot & \\ & \cdot & \\ \cdots r_{ij} \cdots & \\ & \cdot & \\ & \cdot \quad \begin{matrix} i = 0,\ldots,K \\ j = 0,\ldots,K \end{matrix} \end{bmatrix}$$

and explore the extent to which variance in one variable x_i say is explained by the remaining variables

$$X_{\bar{i}} = (x_0,\ldots,x_{i-1}, x_{i+1},\ldots,x_K)$$

In this case the extent to which variance in x_i is explained is defined to be

$$r^2(i,\bar{i}) = \frac{|R_{ii}| - |r|}{|R_{ii}|}$$

The partial correlation of x_i on x_j, holding all others fixed is then

$$r_{ij,ij} = (-1)^{1+j+1} \frac{|R_{ij}|}{\sqrt{|R_{ii}||R_{jj}|}}$$

while the OLS estimator for the normalised coefficients of the regression equation of x_i on $X_{\bar{i}}$ is given by

$$\hat{\alpha}_* = (R_{\bar{i}\bar{i}})^{-1} r_{i\bar{i}}$$

Here R_{ii} is the $K \times K$ correlation matrix involving all variables other than x_i, and $r'_{i\bar{i}} = (r_{i0},\ldots,r_{iK})$ involves all terms r_{ij}, for $j \neq i$.

Note also athat the covariance between any two variables x_i, x_j is $\text{cov}(x_i,x_j) = \sigma_i\sigma_j r_{ij}$ where σ_i^2 is the variance in x_i. Given the observations $(x_0,\ldots,x_K)$, the *empirical* variance–covariance matrix $V = V(x_0,\ldots,x_K)$ is the symmetric $(K+1) \times (K+1)$

matrix

$$V = \begin{bmatrix} S_0^2 & r_{10}S_1S_0 & & & \\ r_{01}S_0S_1 & S_1^2 & . & & \\ & & . & & \\ & & & . & \\ & & & & S_K^2 \end{bmatrix}$$

which can also be written as

$$\begin{bmatrix} S_0 & . & 0 \\ & . & \\ 0 & . & S_K \end{bmatrix} \begin{bmatrix} 1 & r_{10} & . \\ r_{01} & 1 & . \\ . & . & 1 \end{bmatrix} \begin{bmatrix} S_0 & . & 0 \\ & . & \\ 0 & . & S_K \end{bmatrix}$$

$$= S(0,\ldots,K) \ RS(0,\ldots,K)$$

where $S_j = \dfrac{1}{T}\sum_{i=1}^{T} x_{tj}^2$ is an estimate for the variance in x_j.

Assuming that no two variables are perfectly correlated essentially implies that V has maximum rank $(K+1)$ and is therefore positive definite. The same conclusion therefore holds for the full correlation matrix R, and the correlation matrix R_{00} of the regressors. The quadratic form $r^2 = r_0' R_{00}^{-1} r_0$ is also positive definite, and so $r^2 > 0$ for the data array. Moreover the proportion of variance in x_i explained by $X_{\bar{i}} = (x_0,\ldots,x_{i-1},x_{i+1},\ldots,x_K)$ can also be written

$$r^2(i,\bar{i}) = r_{i\bar{i}}'(R_{ii})^{-1} r_{i\bar{i}}$$

where, as before, $r_{i\bar{i}}$ is the column of correlations between x_i and the other variables. Again R_{ii}^{-1} will be positive definite because R_{ii} is assumed to be positive definite. If however $X_{\bar{i}}$ includes highly correlated variables then R_i will be almost singular $(|R_{ii}| \simeq 0)$, and thus will distort the estimation procedure for $r^2(i,\bar{i})$. We shall refer to this problem of *multicollinearity* in a later section.

3.2 THE MULTIVARIATE NORMAL DISTRIBUTION

In deriving the OLS estimators we assumed that the errors were uncorrelated with zero mean and variance σ^2. Moreover, we assumed that the errors and the regressors $x_1,\ldots,x_K$ were uncorrelated. The first assumption implied that the covariance matrix of the errors could be written $V(U) = \sigma^2 I$, where I is the $T \times T$ identity matrix. Another notation for this is that $U \sim I(0,\sigma^2)$, meaning independently distributed with constant variance. If we wished to generalise the assumption and permit the error U_t in the tth observation to have variance σ_t^2 then we would write $U \sim I(0,\sigma_t^2)$. Furthermore, if we permit the errors to be correlated, with non-zero expected values, then we would write $U \sim (E(U), V)$ where $V = (\sigma_{ij})$ is the 'theoretical' covariance matrix for U. Here

$$\sigma_{ij} = E((U_i - E(U_i))(U_j - E(U_j)))$$
$$= \rho_{ij}\sigma_i\sigma_j$$

where σ_i^2, say, is the variance of the population from which U_i is drawn, and ρ_{ij} is the 'true' correlation coefficient between U_i and U_j. For $i = j$ we set $\sigma_{ii} = \sigma_i^2$, the variance in U_i. Note that

$$V = \begin{bmatrix} \sigma_{11} & \sigma_{12} & . \\ \sigma_{21} & \sigma_{22} & . \\ . & . & \sigma_{TT} \end{bmatrix} = \begin{bmatrix} \sigma_1^2 & \sigma_{12} & . \\ \sigma_{21} & \sigma_2^2 & . \\ . & . & \sigma_T^2 \end{bmatrix}$$

is a symmetric $T \times T$ matrix. A convenient vector expression for V is, of course,

$$E((U - E(U))(U - E(U))')$$

$$= E\begin{bmatrix} \begin{bmatrix} U_1 - E(U_1) \\ U_2 - E(U_2) \\ . \\ . \\ . \end{bmatrix} [U_1 - E(U_1) \ldots U_2 - E(U_2) \ldots] \end{bmatrix}$$

$$= E[(U_i - E(U_i))(U_j - E(U_j))]$$

Suppose that $U \sim I(0, \sigma^2)$, and moreover each error U_t has a normal probability distribution, with pdf

$$f(u_t) = \left[\frac{1}{\sigma\sqrt{2\pi}}\right] \exp\left(-\tfrac{1}{2}\left(\frac{\mu_t}{\sigma}\right)^2\right)$$

In this case we may write $U \sim N(0, \sigma^2 I)$ or sometimes $U \sim N_T(0, \sigma^2 I)$ to indicate that U is a T vector. Since the U_t's are independent, the pdf for U is

$$f(u) = \left[\frac{1}{\sigma\sqrt{2\pi}}\right]^T \exp\left[\frac{-1}{2\sigma^2}\sum_{t=1}^{T} u_t^2\right]$$

A more convenient expression for $\sum u_t^2$ is $u'u$, and so we obtain

$$f(u) = \left[\frac{1}{\sigma\sqrt{2\pi}}\right]^T \exp\left[-\frac{1}{2\sigma^2}u'u\right]$$

We now wish to construct the probability density function for a T vector U when $U \sim (0, V)$ and each U_t has a normal pdf. Such a vector is said to have a *multivariate normal distribution* and we write $U \sim N(0, V)$. We can show that the pdf for the multivariate normal distribution is given by

$$f(u) = \frac{|V|^{-1/2}}{(2\pi)^{T/2}} \exp[-\tfrac{1}{2}u'V^{-1}u]$$

Note that $u'V^{-1}u$ is a quadratic form in u, and thus a positive real number (when V is positive definite). In the case that $U \sim N(0, \sigma^2 I)$, clearly

$$V = \sigma^2 I \text{ and so } V^{-1} = \frac{1}{\sigma^2} I,$$

while

$$|V| = \sigma^{2T} \text{ so } |V|^{-1/2} = \frac{1}{\sigma^T}, \text{ as we know.}$$

The proof of the form of the pdf of the multivariate normal distribution is presented here for completeness. The reader may pass by the proof, or examine Maddala (1977, p. 453) for further details.

Lemma 3.1: Suppose that z is a random variable in $\mathbf{R}^n$, $z \sim N_n(0, I)$, and $u = C(z)$ is a random variable in $\mathbf{R}^T$, where C is a $T \times n$ matrix. If C has rank T, then u has a multivariate normal distribution

$$f(u) = \frac{|V|^{-1/2}}{(2\pi)^{T/2}} \exp(-\tfrac{1}{2}u'V^{-1}u)$$

where $V = CC'$, so that we may write $u \sim N_T(0, V)$.

Proof. Since C need not be square $(T < n)$ choose any $(n - T) \times n$ matrix D such that $B = \begin{bmatrix} C \\ D \end{bmatrix}$ is invertible. Define $x = D(z)$ so that $y = \begin{bmatrix} u \\ x \end{bmatrix} = B(z)$. Since $z \sim N_n(0, I)$, z has a normal distribution

$$f(z) = \frac{1}{(2\pi)^{n/2}} \exp(-\tfrac{1}{2}z'z)$$

Now

$$z'z = y'(B^{-1})'B^{-1}(y) = y'(BB')^{-1}y$$
$$= u'(CC')^{-1}u + x'(DD')^{-1}x$$

Moreover

$$z = B^{-1}y$$

and so the *Jacobian* of the transformation $y \to z$ is given by the matrix $dz = \begin{bmatrix} \dfrac{\partial z_j}{\partial y_i} \end{bmatrix} = B^{-1}$, with determinant $|B|^{-1}$. Hence

$$\int f(z)dz = \frac{1}{|B|} \int f(y)dy$$

where

$$f(y) = \frac{1}{(2\pi)^{n/2}} \exp -\tfrac{1}{2}(u'(CC')^{-1}u + x'(DD')^{-1}x)$$

Thus the joint pdf of u and x is given by

$$f(u,x) = f(u)f(x)$$

where

$$f(u) = \frac{1}{|CC'|^{1/2}} \frac{1}{(2\pi)^{T/2}} \exp(-\tfrac{1}{2}u'(CC')^{-1}u)$$

and

$$f(x) = \frac{1}{|DD'|^{1/2}} \frac{1}{(2\pi)^{(n-T)/2}} \exp(-\tfrac{1}{2}x'(CC')^{-1}x)$$

Moreover the covariance matrix of u is

$$E(uu') = E(Cz(Cz)') = E(Czz'C')$$
$$= E(CC')$$

since

$$E(zz') = I$$

Let

$$V = CC'$$

Then

$$f(u) = \frac{1}{|V|^{1/2}} \frac{1}{(2\pi)^{T/2}} \exp(-\tfrac{1}{2}u'V^{-1}u) \qquad\qquad \text{QED}$$

In the case that $E(u) = \mu$, but $u - \mu \sim N(0,V)$ then we write $u \sim N(\mu,V)$. Clearly the pdf for u is obtained by substituting $u - \mu$ for u in the expression for $f(u)$ presented above.

As an exercise the reader is asked at the end of this chapter to show that if $u \sim N_T(\mu,V)$ and $y = Bu$ where B is a $T \times T$ matrix of rank T then $y \sim N_T(B\mu, BVB')$.

We are now in a position to show the relationship between a variable distributed as $N(0,V)$ and the chi-square distribution. As we showed in a previous chapter, if $z \sim N_T(0,I)$ then $z'z = \sum_{}^{T} z_i^2$ is distributed as χ^2 with T degrees of freedom (i.e., $z'z \sim \chi^2(T)$).

Lemma 3.2: If $y \sim N_T(0,V)$ where V is a general covariance matrix for y (and therefore nonsingular, symmetric and positive definite) then $y'V^{-1}y \sim \chi^2(T)$.

Proof. Let $z = V^{-1/2}y$ where $V^{+1/2}$ is that $T \times T$ matrix which satisfies $(V^{1/2})(V^{1/2})' = V$, and $(V^{-1/2}) = (V^{1/2})^{-1}$. Now zz' is the covariance matrix for z and so

$zz' = V^{-1/2}yy'(V^{-1/2})' = V^{-1/2}V^{1/2}(V^{1/2})'(V^{-1/2})' = I$, where I is the identity $T \times T$ matrix. Since y is multivariate normal, the random variable $z = V^{-1/2}y$ is multivariate normal and thus $z \sim N_T(0,I)$. Consequently $z'z \sim \chi^2(T)$. However, $z'z = y'(V^{-1/2})'V^{-1/2}y \sim \chi^2(T)$. Since V is a covariance matrix, it is symmetric, and thus $(V^{-1/2})' = (V)^{-1/2}$. Hence $y'V^{-1}y \sim \chi^2(T)$.   QED

We have defined a matrix A to be *idempotent* iff it is square and satisfies $A^2 = A$. In this case the eigenvalues of A must be $+1$ or 0, and so trace $(A) = $ rank (A).

Lemma 3.3: If $y \sim N_T(0, I)$ and A is a $T \times T$ symmetric matrix of rank $k(< T)$ then $y'Ay \sim \chi^2(k)$ if and only if A is idempotent.

Proof. Since A is symmetric, all its eigenvalues are real. Let Q be the $T \times T$ orthogonal eigenvector matrix such that $\wedge = Q'AQ$ where $\wedge$ is the rank k eigenvalue matrix for A (see section 2.6). As we saw there, we may write $z = Q'y$ for the normal form of y, and

$$
\begin{aligned}
y'Ay &= y'Q\wedge Q'y \\
&= (Q'y)'\wedge(Q'y) \\
&= z'\wedge z \\
&= \sum_{i=1}^{k} \lambda_i z_i^2
\end{aligned}
$$

But since $y \sim N_T(0, I)$ and Q' is a square matrix of rank $T, z \sim N_T(0, Q'Q)$. Now $Q'Q = I$ since Q is orthogonal, and thus $z \sim N_T(0, I)$.

Suppose now that A is idempotent of rank k. Then $\lambda_i = 1$ for $i = 1, \ldots, k$ and so

$$
y'Ay = \sum_{i=1}^{k} z_i^2 \sim \chi^2(k)
$$

Conversely if $y'Ay \sim \chi^2(k)$ then $\lambda_i = 1$ for k eigenvalues and $\lambda_i = 0$ for $T - k$ eigenvalues and so A is idempotent.   QED

Lemma 3.4: If $y \sim N_T(0, V)$, then $y'Ay \sim \chi^2(T)$ if and only if $AVA = A$, where A is a rank T matrix.

Proof. As in lemma 3.2, if $z = V^{-1/2}y$ then $z \sim N_T(0, I)$. Now $y'Ay = (V^{1/2}z)'A(V^{1/2}z)$. By lemma 3.3 $y'Ay = z'(V^{1/2}AV^{1/2})z \sim \chi^2(T)$ if and only if $(V^{1/2}AV^{1/2})$ is idempotent. But this requirement is

$$
V^{1/2}AV^{1/2}V^{1/2}AV^{1/2} = V^{1/2}AV^{1/2}
$$

or

$$
AVA = A \qquad\qquad \text{QED}
$$

Suppose now that $y \sim N_T(0, I)$ and A,B are two symmetric $T \times T$ matrices. The covariance of $y'Ay$ and $y'By$ is $E(y'Ay \cdot y'By)$, while the covariance matrix for y is $E(yy')$. Consequently if $AB = 0$ then $y'Ay$ and $y'By$ are independent random variables. Thus we obtain the following.

Lemma 3.5: If $y \sim N_T(0, V)$, rank $V = T$ and A, B are $T \times T$ matrices of ranks a,b respectively then $y'Ay \sim \chi^2(a)$, $y'By \sim \chi^2(b)$ are independent random variables iff

1. $AVA = A$
2. $BVB = B$
3. $AVB = 0$

Proof. As in lemma 3.4, let $z = V^{-1/2} y$. Then $y'Ay \sim \chi^2(a)$ iff $V^{1/2} A V^{1/2}$ is an idempotent matrix of rank a, and so $AVA = A$. But in the same way $y'By \sim \chi^2(b)$ iff $BVB = B$. Finally, we require the independence of $z'(V^{1/2}AV^{1/2})z$ and $z'(V^{1/2}BV^{1/2})z$. Thus

$$V^{1/2} A V^{1/2} V^{1/2} B V^{1/2} = 0$$

or

$$AVB = 0 \qquad\qquad \text{QED}$$

3.3 SIGNIFICANCE TESTS AND ANALYSIS OF VARIANCE FOR THE OLS REGRESSION MODEL

In section 2.2, in the bivariate regression model, we argued that the OLS estimators $\dfrac{\hat{\beta}_0 - \beta_0}{\sigma/\sqrt{T}}$ and $\left[\dfrac{\hat{\beta}_1 - \beta_1}{\sigma}\right]\sqrt{S_{xx}}$ were normally and independently distributed as $N(0, 1)$, the case when the true errors were distributed as $N(0, \sigma^2 I)$. This permitted us to deduce that $\dfrac{1}{\sigma^2}\Sigma e_i^2$ was distributed as $\chi^2(T - 2)$. We shall now develop this argument formally for the multivariate OLS regression model. The OLS estimator $\hat{\beta}$ satisfies

$$\hat{\beta} = (X'X)^{-1} X'(X\beta + U)$$
$$= \beta + (X'X)^{-1} X' U$$

Thus

$$X(\hat{\beta} - \beta) = X(X'X)^{-1} X' U$$
$$= MU$$

where $M = X(X'X)^{-1} X'$ is a $T \times T$ matrix.

Now $(X'X)$ is a $(K + 1) \times (K + 1)$ matrix, where K is the number of regressors. We have also assumed that rank $(X'X) = K + 1$, since all regressors are linearly independent. Thus rank $(M) = K + 1$.

The vector of residuals is given by

$$e = Y - X\hat{\beta}$$

But our assumption is that $Y = X\beta + U$. Thus

$$e = X(\beta - \hat{\beta}) + U$$
$$= (I - M)U$$
$$= NU$$

where

$$N = I - M \text{ is a } (T - K - 1) \times (T - K - 1) \text{ matrix.}$$

Now

$$M^2 = X(X'X)^{-1}X'X(X'X)^{-1}X'$$
$$= X(X'X^{-1})X' = M$$

and

$$N^2 = (I - M)(I - M) = I - 2M + M^2$$
$$= I - M = N$$

Thus both N and M are idempotent. Moreover, $NM = (I - M)M = M - M^2 = 0$, the zero $T \times T$ matrix, while rank $(N) = T - K - 1$. Note that this result follows with no assumptions about the covariance matrix of (X, U) or of U. Suppose that $U \sim N_T(0, \sigma^2 I)$. By lemma 3.3,

$$\frac{1}{\sigma^2} U'MU \sim \chi^2(K+1)$$

$$\frac{1}{\sigma^2} U'NU \sim \chi^2(T - K - 1)$$

while $U'MU$ and $U'NU$ are independently distributed. Now

$$(\hat{\beta} - \beta)'X'X(\hat{\beta} - \beta) = U'M^2U = U'MU$$
$$(Y - X\hat{\beta})'(Y - X\hat{\beta}) = U'N^2U = U'NU$$

and these two variates are *independently distributed*. Note also that

$$U'U = U'(M + N)U$$
$$= (\hat{\beta} - \beta)'X'X(\hat{\beta} - \beta) + e'e$$

where $e'e$ is the residual sum of squares. Under our assumption M is idempotent of rank $(K + 1)$ and so

$$\frac{1}{\sigma^2} U'MU = \frac{1}{\sigma^2}(\hat{\beta} - \beta)'X'X(\hat{\beta} - \beta) \sim \chi^2(K+1)$$

while

$$\frac{1}{\sigma^2} U'NU = \frac{e'e}{\sigma^2} \sim \chi^2(T - K - 1)$$

This is essentially the full analysis of the representation of the quadratic form that we performed in section 2.2. Since the two variates have chi-square distribution, and are independent, the variate

$$F = \frac{(\hat{\beta} - \beta)'X'X(\hat{\beta} - \beta)}{e'e} \cdot \frac{T - K + 1}{K + 1}$$

has an F distribution with $(K + 1, T - K + 1)$ degrees of freedom. There are a number of further points to be made. Consider first of all $U'NU$. By our assumption

$\dfrac{U}{\sigma} \sim N_T(0, \mathrm{I})$ and so

$$\frac{1}{\sigma^2}(U'NU) = \sum_{i=1}^{T} \lambda_i z_i^2$$

where $\lambda_i = 1$ for $i = 1, \ldots, T - K - 1$, and $\lambda_i = 0$ otherwise. Here $T - K - 1$ is the rank of N (see lemma 3.3). Thus trace $N = T - K - 1$. Now

$$\frac{1}{\sigma^2} E(U'NU) = T - K - 1$$

since $z_i \sim N(0, 1)$. But the residual sum of squares e'e then satisfies $E(e'e) = (T - K - 1)\sigma^2$. Thus $\dfrac{e'e}{T - K - 1}$ is an unbiased estimator for the variance of the disturbance vector U. If we use $S^2 = \dfrac{e'e}{T - K - 1}$ as the estimator for the variance of the disturbance U then the F variate becomes

$$F = \frac{(\hat{\beta} - \beta)'X'X(\hat{\beta} - \beta)}{S^2(K + 1)}$$

The reader may wish to evaluate F in the two cases $K = 1$ and $K = 2$ that we developed in detail previously. As we have seen in section 2.2 in the case with one regressor $(K = 1)$

$$\frac{1}{\sigma^2}(\hat{\beta} - \beta)'X'X(\hat{\beta} - \beta)$$

$$= \frac{T}{\sigma^2}(\hat{\beta}_0 - \beta_0)^2 + \frac{S_{xx}}{\sigma^2}(\hat{\beta}_1 - \beta_1)^2$$

where

$$\mathrm{var}(\hat{\beta}_0) = \frac{\sigma^2}{T} \text{ and } \mathrm{var}(\hat{\beta}_1) = \frac{S_{xx}}{\sigma^2}$$

We argued in this case that $\sqrt{T}\dfrac{(\hat{\beta}_0 - \beta)}{\sigma}$ and $\sqrt{S_{xx}}\dfrac{(\hat{\beta}_1 - \beta_0)}{\sigma}$ were both distributed as $N(0, 1)$. We can obtain a similar result in the more general case with K regressors. As we have shown $\hat{\beta} - \beta = (X'X)^{-1}X'U$ where U is assumed to be distributed as $N_T(0, \sigma^2 \mathrm{I})$.

By lemma 3.1, $(\hat{\beta} - \beta) \sim N_{K+1}(0, \sigma^2 \mathrm{V}(\hat{\beta} - \beta))$ where $\sigma^2 \mathrm{V}(\hat{\beta} - \beta)$ is the covariance matrix of $(\hat{\beta} - \beta)$. But as we have shown

$$\mathrm{V}(\hat{\beta} - \beta) = [(X'X)^{-1}X'][(X'X)^{-1}X']' = (X'X)^{-1}$$

which is a $(K + 1) \times (K + 1)$ matrix of rank $(K + 1)$ by assumption.

As we did in section 2.6, let $B = (X'X')^{-1}$ be this symmetric $(K + 1) \times (K + 1)$ matrix, with term (b_{ij}) in the (i, j) position. As we have seen $b_{00} = \dfrac{1}{T}$

and so $\sigma^2 V(\hat{\beta}_0) = \dfrac{\sigma^2}{T}$ as we earlier obtained. Since $(\hat{\beta} - \beta)$ has a multivariate normal distribution, we may deduce that each $(\hat{\beta}_i - \beta_i)$ is itself normally distributed.

More precisely, let $(\hat{\beta} - \beta)_I$ be the vector associated with a subset I of $|I|$ coefficients, and let J be the subset of the remaining coefficients. The matrix $\sigma^2 V \hat{\beta}$ may be partitioned as

$$\sigma^2 \begin{bmatrix} \mathbf{B}_{II} & \mathbf{B}_{IJ} \\ \mathbf{B}_{IJ} & \mathbf{B}_{JJ} \end{bmatrix}$$

where $\mathbf{B}_{II}$ is the covariance matrix of $(\hat{\beta} - \beta)_I$. The probability density function of $(\hat{\beta} - \beta)$ may then be written

$$f(\hat{\beta} - \beta) = f((\hat{\beta} - \beta)_I/(\hat{\beta} - \beta)_J)$$

where

$$f((\hat{\beta} - \beta)_I/(\hat{\beta} - \beta)_J)$$

is the conditional probability density of $(\hat{\beta} - \beta)_I$, given $(\hat{\beta} - \beta)_J$ and

$$f((\hat{\beta} - \beta)_I) = \frac{1}{|\mathbf{B}_{II}|(2\pi\sigma^2)^{1/2}} \exp\left(\frac{-1}{2\sigma^2} (\hat{\beta} - \beta)'_I \, \mathbf{B}_{II}^{-1} \, (\hat{\beta} - \beta)_I \right)$$

In other words the variate $(\hat{\beta} - \beta)_I$ itself has a normal distribution $N_{|I|}(0, \sigma^2 \mathbf{B}_{II})$. Consider the case of a single coefficient $i = I$, and let $\mathbf{B} = (b_{ij})$. Then the pdf of $(\hat{\beta}_i - \beta_i)$ is

$$\frac{1}{b_{ii}(2\pi\sigma^2)^{1/2}} \exp\left[\frac{-1}{2\sigma^2} \frac{(\hat{\beta}_i - \beta_i)^2}{b_{ii}} \right]$$

and so

$$(\hat{\beta}_i - \beta_i) \sim N(0, b_{ii}\sigma^2)$$

But we also know that the residual sum of squares $\dfrac{e'e}{\sigma^2} \sim \chi^2(T - K - 1)$. Thus

$$\frac{(\hat{\beta}_i - \beta_i)^2}{b_{ii}\sigma^2} \frac{(T - K + 1)\sigma^2}{e'e} = \frac{(\hat{\beta}_i - \beta_i)^2}{b_{ii}} \frac{1}{S^2}$$

is an F variate with $(1, T - K - 1)$ degrees of freedom. Consequently

$$t = \frac{(\hat{\beta}_i - \beta_i)}{S\sqrt{b_{ii}}}$$

is a t-variate with $(T - K - 1)$ degrees of freedom. Here, as before, $S^2 = \dfrac{e'e}{T - K - 1} =$

$\dfrac{R(\hat{\beta})}{T - K - 1}$ is the estimator for the variance σ^2 of the disturbance. Just as in the single regressor case the 95 per cent confidence interval for the true coefficient β_i is

$$(\hat{\beta}_i - t \cdot S\sqrt{b_{ii}}, \ \hat{\beta}_i + t \cdot S\sqrt{b_{ii}})$$

where t is the value of the t-variate with $T - K - 1$ dof such that $P(x < t) = 0.975$.
Again $S \sqrt{b_{ii}} = S_i$ is an estimate for the standard deviation in β_i. If $\left| \dfrac{\hat{\beta}_i}{S_i} \right| = t_i < t$ then
the 95 per cent confidence interval for β_i includes 0, and so the hypothesis that $\delta_i = 0$
cannot be rejected at the 5 per cent significance level. Of course in the case of a single
regressor, $K = 1$, and

$$X'X = \begin{bmatrix} T & 0 \\ 0 & S_{xx} \end{bmatrix}$$

so that

$$B = (X'X)^{-1} = \begin{bmatrix} \dfrac{1}{T} & 0 \\ 0 & \dfrac{1}{S_{xx}} \end{bmatrix}$$

Thus $S_1 = S \sqrt{b_{ii}} = \dfrac{S}{\sqrt{S_{xx}}}$ as we obtained before.

We can use this procedure to construct a test for a subset of the coefficients in the
following way. We know that $(\hat{\beta} - \beta) \sim N_{K+1}(0, \sigma^2 B)$. In lemma 3.2 we showed in
such a case how to construct normal, and independent, variates from a normal
multivariate. In the same way therefore define

$$\hat{\gamma} = W^{-1}\hat{\beta} \text{ and } \gamma = W^{-1}\beta$$

where

$$WW' = B = (XX')^{-1}$$

Then

$$(\hat{\gamma} - \gamma)(\hat{\gamma} - \gamma)' = W^{-1}(\hat{\beta} - \beta)(\hat{\beta} - \beta)'(W^{-1})'$$
$$= \sigma^2 W^{-1}WW'(W^{-1})' = \sigma^2 I$$

since $(\hat{\beta} - \beta)(\hat{\beta} - \beta)' = \sigma^2 B$ is the covariance matrix of the coefficients. Thus
$\hat{\gamma} - \gamma \sim N_{K+1}(0, \sigma^2 I)$, and the new coefficients $\hat{\gamma}_0, \ldots, \hat{\gamma}_K$ are mutually independent.
Now

$$\hat{\gamma} = W^{-1}\hat{\beta} = W^{-1}(X'X)^{-1}X'Y = Z'Y$$

where

$$Z' = W^{-1}(X'X)^{-1}X'$$

But

$$(X'X)^{-1} = B = WW'$$

and so

$$Z' = W^{-1}WW'X' = W'X' \text{ or } Z = XW$$

As a consequence $Z'Z = W'X'XW$ where $X'X = B^{-1} = (W')^{-1} W^{-1}$, and so $Z'Z = I$, the $(K + 1) \times (K + 1)$ identity matrix. Suppose, therefore, that we transform the data matrix X to $Z = XW$. Then the regression equation becomes

$$Y = X\hat{\beta} + e$$
$$= XW\hat{\gamma} + e$$
$$= Z\hat{\gamma} + e$$

Moreover, $\hat{\gamma} = Z'Y = (Z'Z)^{-1}Z'Y$ since $Z'Z$ is the $(K + 1) \times (K + 1)$ identity matrix. Thus $\hat{\gamma}$ is precisely the OLS estimator for the regression equation $Y = Z\gamma + U$. Note that

$$(\hat{\beta} - \beta)'X'X(\hat{\beta} - \beta)$$
$$= (\hat{\gamma} - \gamma)'W'(X'X)W(\hat{\gamma} - \gamma) = (\hat{\gamma} - \gamma)'(\hat{\gamma} - \gamma)$$

and so

$$F = \frac{(\hat{\gamma} - \gamma)'(\hat{\gamma} - \gamma)}{S^2(K + 1)}$$

is an F-variate with $(K + 1, T - K - 1)$ degree of freedom.

As we know already, the term in the $(0, 0)$ position in XX' is T, while terms in the $(0, j)$ or $(j, 0)$ position, for $j \neq 0$, are zero. Thus $b_{00} = 1/T$ while $b_{0j} = b_{j0} = 0$ for $j \neq 0$. As a result the matrix W may be factored as

$$\begin{bmatrix} \dfrac{1}{\sqrt{T}} & 0 \\ 0 & W_* \end{bmatrix}$$

where W_* is a $K \times K$ matrix such that $W_* W_*' = (X_* X_*')^{-1}$ is the $K \times K$ symmetric covariation matrix considered in section 2.7. Consequently $\hat{\gamma}_0 = \sqrt{T}\beta_0$ with variance $T \operatorname{var}(\beta_0) = \sigma^2$ as expected.

If we let $y = Y - \bar{Y}$ as before then we obtain the reduced form of the regression equation

$$y = Z_*\hat{\gamma}_* + e$$

where $\hat{\gamma}_* = W_*^{-1}\beta_*$ and $Z_* = X_*W_*$ is a $T \times K$ data matrix. In the same way

$$F = \frac{(\hat{\gamma}_* - \gamma_*)'(\hat{\gamma}_* - \gamma_*)}{K \cdot S^2}$$

is an F-variate with $(K, T - K - 1)$ degrees of freedom, and can be used to test the significance of $(\hat{\gamma}_1, \ldots, \hat{\gamma}_K)$. However, as we showed in section 2.7, the sum of squared residuals is given by

$$R(\hat{\beta}) = \hat{\beta}_*'X_*'X_*\hat{\beta}_* + y'y = \hat{\gamma}_*\hat{\gamma}_* + y'y = R(\hat{\gamma})$$

Moreover the ratio of explained variation to total variation is given by

$$r^2 = \frac{y'y - R(\hat{\beta})}{y'y}$$

Therefore explained variation is equal to $\hat{\gamma}_*\hat{\gamma}$ and

$$\frac{r^2}{1 - r^2} = \frac{\hat{\gamma}_*\hat{\gamma}_*}{R(\hat{\gamma})}$$

Now $R(\hat{\gamma}) = e'e$ since this is simply the sum of squared residuals, and so

$$\frac{r^2}{1 - r^2} = \frac{\hat{\gamma}_*\hat{\gamma}}{e'e}$$

On the other hand $S^2 = \dfrac{e'e}{T - K - 1}$ is the estimator for the disturbance variance σ^2. If we adopt the hypothesis that $\beta_1 = \ldots = \beta_K = 0$ (i.e., that $\gamma_1 = \ldots = \gamma_K = 0$) then

$$F = \frac{\hat{\gamma}'_*\hat{\gamma}_*}{KS^2} = \frac{r^2}{1 - r^2}\left[\frac{T - K - 1}{K}\right]$$

and so the F test gives a test on the significance of the statistic r^2. We may also use the F test to examine the significance of a set of coefficients $\hat{\beta}_i$ for $i \in I$.

We may choose the $K \times K$ matrix W_* to have the triangular form

$$\begin{bmatrix} w_{11} & \cdot & w_{1K} \\ & \cdot & \\ & & \cdot \\ & \cdot & \\ 0 & & w_{KK} \end{bmatrix}$$

where all terms below the diagonal are zero. In this case we may write

$$z_j = \sum_{r=1}^{j} w_{rj}x_r$$

so that each vector z_j is a linear combination of $\{x_1, \ldots, x_j\}$. We now show that we can indeed write $Z_* = X_*W_*$, where Z_* is an orthogonal matrix whose column vectors $\{z_1, \ldots, z_K\}$ satisfy

$$z'_i z_j = \begin{matrix} 0 & \text{if } i \neq j \\ 1 & \text{if } i = j \end{matrix}$$

and W_* is a triangular $K \times K$ matrix. We make use of the following Gram–Schmidt orthogonalisation process.

Lemma 3.6: If X is a $K \times K$ matrix of rank K, then there exists a triangular $K \times K$ matrix W such that $Z = XW$ is an orthogonal matrix of rank K.

Proof. As before for a vector $z \in \mathbf{R}^K$ we use the notation $||z||^2 = z'z$. Proceed inductively on $j = 1, \ldots, K$ by defining $z_1 = w_{11}x_1$ where $w_{11} = \dfrac{1}{||x_1||}$. Now define

$$z_2 = c_{11}z_1 + c_{21}x_2$$

where

$$c_{11} = -c_{21}(z_1' x_2)$$
$$c_{21} = ||x_2 - (z_1' x_2)z_1||^{-1}$$

Then

$$z_2 = c_{21}(x_2 - (z_1' x_2)z_1)$$

Clearly

$$z_1' z_2 = c_{21}((z_1' x_2) - (z_1' x_2)1) = 0$$

while

$$z_2' z_2 = c_{21}^2 ||x_2 - (z_1' x_2)z_1||^2 = 1$$

We therefore obtain

$$z_2 = w_{12}x_1 + w_{22}x_2$$

where

$$w_{12} = -c_{21}(z_1' x_2)w_{11}$$

and

$$w_{22} = c_{21}$$

Proceed inductively in this way by defining $s_j = x_j - \sum_{r=1}^{j-1} (z_r' x_j)z_r$, and $z_j = \dfrac{s_j}{||s||}$, for $j = 2, \ldots, K$. By the induction procedure, $z_a' z_b = 0$ for all $a \neq b$, $a, b < j$. Moreover

$$z_b' z_j = (z_b' x_j) - \sum_{r=1}^{j-1} (z_r' x_j)(z_b' z_r)$$
$$= (z_b' x_j) - (z_b' x_j) = 0$$

since $z_b' z_r = 0$ if $b \neq r$ and $z_b' z_r = 1$ if $b = r$. Thus if $\{z_1, \ldots, z_{j-1}\}$ is an orthonormal set of vectors then so is $\{z_1, \ldots, z_j\}$. By induction $\{z_1, \ldots, z_K\}$ is an orthonormal set of vectors and the matrix $Z = (z_1, \ldots, z_K)$ satisfies the conditions of the lemma. By the method of construction, W has rank K and so is a basis change matrix. Since X has rank K, its column vectors form a basis for $\mathbf{R}^K$, and so, therefore, do the column vectors of Z. Thus rank $(Z) = K$. QED

We may therefore proceed as before to construct a new set of regressors $\{z_1, \ldots, z_K\}$ where z_j is a linear combination of $x_1, \ldots, x_j$. Moreover $\hat{\gamma}_* = Z_*' y$ is the OLS estimator for the regression equation $y = Z_* \gamma + U$. Since $Z_* = (z_1, \ldots, z_K)$ is an orthogonal matrix, $\sum_{r=1}^{j} \hat{\gamma}_r^2$ gives an expression for the variation explained by the new regressors $\{z_1, \ldots, z_j\}$. Since z_j is a linear combination only of $\{x_1, \ldots, x_j\}$, $\sum_{r=1}^{j} \hat{\gamma}_r^2$ gives the variation explained by $\{x_1, \ldots, x_j\}$. In particular $\hat{\gamma}_{j+1}^2$ is a measure of the increase in the explained variation as a result of adding the regressor z_{j+1} to the regression equation. Thus $\dfrac{\hat{\gamma}_{j+1}^2}{S^2}$ gives the proportion of variation explained by adding z_{j+1} (or

x_{j+1}) to the regression equation. For example consider the case $j + 1 = K$. The matrix W satisfies $WW' = B$. Thus the term w_{KK} in the (k, k) position in W satisfies $w_{KK}^2 = b_{KK}$.

But $\hat{\beta} = W\hat{\gamma}$ and so $\hat{\beta}_K = w_{KK}\hat{\gamma}_K$. As we have seen $\dfrac{\hat{\beta}_K - \beta_K}{S\sqrt{b_{KK}}}$ is a t-variate, and so

$$F = \frac{(\hat{\beta}_K - \beta_K)^2}{S^2\sqrt{b_{KK}}}$$

$$= \frac{(\hat{\beta}_K - \beta_K)^2}{S^2 w_{KK}} = \frac{(\hat{\gamma}_K - \gamma_K)^2}{S^2}$$

Hence the t-test on $\hat{\beta}_K$ may be interpreted as a test on the increased variance explained by adding x_K to the list $\{x_1, \ldots, x_{K-1}\}$ of regressors.

More generally, to analyse the increment of variance explained by adding a list $\{x_i : i \in I\}$ to the regression equation, partition the matrix B in the form

$$\begin{bmatrix} B_{II} & B_{IJ} \\ B_{IJ} & B_{JJ} \end{bmatrix}$$

and let $\hat{\beta} = (\hat{\beta}_I, \hat{\beta}_J)$. This of course may involve a permutation of the names of the regressors. Proceed as before to find a triangular matrix W such that $WW' = B$ and let $\hat{\gamma} = (\hat{\gamma}_I, \hat{\gamma}_J) = W^{-1}\beta$. Since W is a matrix with zeros below the diagonal, W^{-1} is a matrix with zeros above the diagonal. As a result $\hat{\gamma}_I$ is a linear function only of $\hat{\beta}_I$, while $\hat{\gamma}_J$ is a linear function of $\{\hat{\beta}_1, \ldots, \hat{\beta}_K\}$.

Consequently $\sum_{j \in J} \hat{\gamma}_j^2 = \hat{\gamma}_J'\hat{\gamma}_J$ gives the incremental variation explained by adding

$\{x_j : j \in J\}$ to the list of regressors, and so

$$F = \frac{\hat{\gamma}_J'\hat{\gamma}_J}{|J|S^2}$$

is an F-variate with $(|J|, T - K - 1)$ degrees of freedom and can be used to test the significance of the added variance explained by $\{x_j : j \in J\}$. This procedure suggests that we devise a procedure to add regressors in such a way as to maximise the incremental variance explained. We turn to this method of *principal components* in the next section.

3.4 PRINCIPAL COMPONENTS ANALYSIS

In section 3.1 we normalised the set of regressors and wrote $Z_* = \begin{bmatrix} \dfrac{x_1}{\sigma_1}, \ldots, \dfrac{x_K}{\sigma_K} \end{bmatrix}$ for the

normalised $T \times K$ data matrix. As we saw

$$\frac{1}{T}(Z_*'Z_*) = R_{00}$$

was the $K \times K$ correlation matrix for the regressors. In the case of two regressors x, z we have seen that $|R_{00}| = 1 - r_{xz}^2$, so that if x and z were highly correlated ($r_{xz} \simeq 1$), the correlation matrix was almost singular. The same is true in the more general case if one of the regressors is linearly dependent on the others. This problem of *multicollinearity* gives rise to large variances for the coefficient estimators, and thus to problems of interpretation. For example suppose the data matrix $X'X$ for two regressors is given by

$$X'X = \begin{bmatrix} 1 & r \\ r & 1 \end{bmatrix}$$

Then

$$(X'X)^{-1} = \frac{1}{1 - r^2} \begin{bmatrix} 1 & -r \\ -r & 1 \end{bmatrix}$$

and so the variance of $\hat{\beta}_1$ is $\dfrac{\sigma^2}{1 - r^2}$. The t value for $\hat{\beta}_1$ is then $\dfrac{|\hat{\beta}_1|}{|S_{\beta_1}|}$ where $S_{\beta_1} = \dfrac{S}{\sqrt{1 - r^2}}$ is the empirical estimate for the standard deviation in β_1. Clearly if r is close to unity, then S_{β_1} will be large, and the t-value small.

One method of analysing the relationship between the regressors, is to transform the data matrix by constructing a new set of regressors in a stepwise fashion so as to maximise the variation explained by each new regressor.

We may either use the procedure on the set $\{x_1, \ldots, x_K\}$ of regressors, or add the dependent variable y to the set. Therefore let

$$\begin{bmatrix} 1 & r_2 & & \\ r_1 & 1 & & \\ & & \ddots & \\ & & & r_{KK} \end{bmatrix}$$

be the symmetric full $K \times K$ correlation matrix, involving all variables under consideration, and let $X = (x_1, \ldots, x_K)$ be the $T \times K$ matrix of normalised variables, so that

$$x_i' x_j = \begin{matrix} 1 & \text{if } i = j \\ r_{ij} & \text{if } i \neq j \end{matrix}$$

That is to say if X_{tj} is the tth observation of the jth variable then

$$x_{tj} = \frac{1}{\sqrt{T}} \left[\frac{X_{tj} - \bar{X}_{tj}}{\sigma_j} \right]$$

where σ_j^2 is the variance of x_j, and $X'X = R$. We now seek a $K \times K$ orthogonal basis change matrix $B = (b_{ij})$ such that

$$Z = XB$$

where Z is a $T \times K$ matrix such that $Z'Z = \Lambda$ is a diagonal eigenvalue matrix whose diagonal entries are ordered by size. For the first column z_1 of Z and b_1 of B we may write

$$z_1 = Xb_1$$

Now

$$\text{var}(z_1) = z_1' z_1 = b_1'(X'X)b_1 = b_1' R b_1$$

To maximise $\text{var}(z_1)$ subject to $b_1' b_1 = 1$ construct the Lagrangian

$$\phi_1 = b_1' R b_1 - \lambda_1(b_1' b_1 - 1)$$

Then

$$\frac{d\phi_1}{db_1} = 2R b_1 - 2\lambda_1 b_1 \text{ or } (R - \lambda_1 I)b_1 = 0$$

Thus b_1 satisfies the conditions if b_1 is an eigenvector of R corresponding to the eigenvalue λ_1. Moreover

$$\text{var}(z_1) = b_1' R(b_1) = b_1'(\lambda_1 b_1) = \lambda_1$$

since

$$b_1' b_1 = 1$$

Thus the variance, σ_1^2, of z_1 is λ_1.

If $|R| \neq 0$ then R will have K non-zero roots to the characteristic equation. Indeed since R will be positive definite, the eigenvalues $\lambda_1, \ldots, \lambda_K$ will all be positive. As we know from Chapter 2, we may find K linearly independent, and orthonormal eigenvectors $b_1, \ldots, b_K$, forming a basis for $\mathbf{R}^K$. Rank their eigenvalues, so that $\lambda_1 \geq \lambda_2 \geq \ldots \geq \lambda_K$. Now

$$z_i' z_j = b_i' R(b_j) = \lambda_j b_i' b_j = 0 \quad \text{if } i \neq j$$
$$= \lambda_j \quad \text{if } i = j$$

Thus the covariance matrix of $\{z_1, \ldots, z_K\}$ may be written $\Lambda = (\lambda_i)$ and so $Z'Z = \Lambda$. Moreover $Z'Z = B'X'XB = B'RB = \Lambda$. However, B is an orthogonal matrix, and so $B^{-1} = B'$. Thus $R = B\Lambda B'$. The diagonal terms of $B\Lambda B'$ are of the form

$$a_{jj} = \sum_{i=1}^{K} b_{ji}^2 \lambda_i = 1, \text{ since } r_{jj} = 1. \text{ But from the matrix expression } Z = XB \text{ we see that}$$

$$z_i = \sum_{j=1}^{K} x_j b_{ji} \text{ and so } r_{ji}^2 \text{ (the proportion of the variation in } x_j \text{ explained by } z_i\text{) is } \lambda_i b_{ji}^2.$$

Thus the variables $z_1, \ldots, z_K$ explain the variation in x_j, according to the ratios

$$r_{j1}^2 = \lambda_1 b_{j1}^2, \ r_{j2}^2 = \lambda_2 b_{j2}^2, \ldots, r_{jK}^2 = \lambda_K b_{jK}^2$$

A set $\{z_1, \ldots, z_p\}$ of principal components explains a proportion $\sum_{i=1}^{p} r_{ji}^2 = \sum_{i=1}^{p} \lambda_i b_{ji}^2$ of the proportion of the variance in the original variable x_j. Now

$$\text{trace } (XX') = K$$
$$= \text{trace } (Z'Z)$$
$$= \text{trace } (\Lambda) = \sum_{i=1}^{K} \lambda_i$$

Hence $\dfrac{\lambda_i}{K}$ is the proportion of total variation explained by the variable z_i, and so

$\dfrac{1}{K} \sum\limits_{i=1}^{p} \lambda_i$ gives the proportion of total variation in $\{x_1, \ldots, x_K\}$ explained by

$\{z_1, \ldots, z_p\}$. The principal components $\{z_1, \ldots, z_p\}$ will of course be normally and independently distributed. Having selected an appropriate subset of such principal components, explaining a large proportion of total variation in the regressors, one could then proceed to a regression model of involving a dependent variable and the principal components.

3.5 GENERALISED LEAST SQUARES ESTIMATORS

In section 2.7, we made the assumption that the residual vector U was distributed as $(0, \sigma^2 I)$, and was uncorrelated with the independent variables given in the data matrix X.

On this basis we were able to show that the vector $\hat{\beta}$ of OLS estimators was unbiased, and had a covariance matrix $V(\hat{\beta}) = \sigma^2 (X'X)^{-1}$ such that $V(b) - V(\hat{\beta})$ was a semi-positive definite matrix, for any other linear unbiased estimator b. In other words we showed that $\hat{\beta}$ was BLUE.

In this section we shall consider the situation where the covariance matrix

$$E(UU') = V$$

for V a general symmetric, positive definite matrix. Clearly, if $U \sim (0, V)$ then the random variable $U_* = V^{-1/2} U$ is distributed as $(0, I)$, where I is the $T \times T$ identity matrix. If we transform the regression model

$$Y = X\beta + U$$

by premultiplying by $V^{-1/2}$ then we obtain $Y_* = X_* \beta + U_*$ where $U_* \sim (0, I)$. The OLS estimator, $\hat{\alpha}$, for this model is then

$$\begin{aligned}
\hat{\alpha} &= (X'_* X_*)^{-1} X'_* Y_* \\
&= [(V^{-1/2} X)' (V^{-1/2} X)]^{-1} (V^{-1/2} X)' V^{-1/2} Y \\
&= (X' V^{-1} X)^{-1} X' V^{-1} Y
\end{aligned}$$

This estimator $\hat{\alpha}$ for β is called the GLS (or generalised least squares estimator) and sometimes written $\hat{\beta}_{GLS}$. Proceeding as in section 2.7, we find that

$$E(\hat{\alpha}) = E((X'V^{-1}X)^{-1} X'V^{-1} (X\beta + U)) = \beta$$

under the assumption that $E(X'U) = 0$ (i.e., X and U are uncorrelated), and so the GLS estimator is unbiased. As we have seen the OLS estimator $\hat{\beta}$ has expected value $E(\hat{\beta}) = E((X'X)^{-1} X'(X\beta + U))$. However, since we assume $U \sim (0, V)$, $E(U) = 0$, and (X, U) are uncorrelated, we still find that $E(\hat{\beta}) = \beta$, so $\hat{\beta}$ is also unbiased. However, the covariance matrix for $\hat{\beta} = \hat{\beta}_{OLS}$ is now given by

$$V(\hat{\beta}) = E((\hat{\beta} - \beta)(\hat{\beta} - \beta)')$$
$$= AX' E(UU')XA'$$

where $A = (X'X)^{-1}$ as before, but now $E(UU') = V$. Thus

$$V(\hat{\beta}) = AX'VXA'$$

On the other hand the GLS estimator $\hat{\alpha}$ has covariance matrix

$$V(\hat{\alpha}) = (X'_* X_*)^{-1} = [X'(V^{-1/2})' V^{-1/2}X]^{-1}$$
$$= (X'V^{-1}X)^{-1}$$

Just as we showed that the OLS estimator was BLUE when $V = \sigma^2 I$, we can show that the GLS estimator $\hat{\alpha}$ is BLUE in the more general case. If we let $B = (X'V^{-1}X)^{-1}$ then $\hat{\alpha} = BX'V^{-1}Y$ or $\hat{\alpha} = \beta + BX'V^{-1}U$ and

$$V(\hat{\alpha}) = BX'V^{-1}E(UU')(BX'V^{-1})'$$
$$= BX'(BX'V^{-1})'$$

If we consider any other linear unbiased estimator, b, then we may write $b = \hat{\alpha} + CY$. Unbiasedness implies that $CX = 0$. Hence $b = \beta + BX'V^{-1}U + CU$. Thus

$$V(b) = E((b - \beta)(b - \beta)')$$
$$= E((BX'V^{-1} + C)UU'(BX'V^{-1} + C)')$$
$$= V(\hat{\alpha}) + CVC'$$

Since V is positive definite, we may write $V = V^{1/2}(V^{1/2})'$ and so $CV^{1/2}(CV^{1/2})'$ is a positive semi-definite matrix. Thus the GLS estimator $\hat{\alpha} = \hat{\beta}_{GLS}$ is BLUE. In particular since the OLS estimator $\hat{\beta}_{OLS}$ is linear we find that

$$V(\hat{\beta}_{OLS}) - V(\hat{\beta}_{GLS}) = CVC'$$

is a positive semi-definite matrix. Note that the matrix need not be positive definite since C may have non-maximal rank. For example, if $V = \sigma^2 I$ then $C = 0$. We say that the GLS estimator is more *efficient* than $\hat{\beta}_{OLS}$.

In Chapter 1 we defined the *risk* associated with a single sample estimator $\hat{\theta}$ for θ to be $R(\hat{\theta}, \theta) = E((\hat{\theta} - \theta)^2)$. In the more general case we may define the *risk matrix* associated with a multivariate estimator $\hat{\beta}$ for β to be $R(\hat{\beta}, \beta) = E((\hat{\beta} - \beta)(\hat{\beta} - \beta)')$. In the case we are considering, the GLS estimator is unbiased and so $R(\hat{\beta}_{GLS}, \beta) = V(\hat{\beta}_{GLS})$. To interpret the risk matrix, we may assign a vector of cost weights $w' = (w_0, \ldots, w_K)$ to errors in the kth coefficient and define a cost function

$$C(\hat{\beta}) = w'R(\hat{\beta}, \beta)w$$

Since $R(\hat{\beta}_{OLS}, \beta) - R(\hat{\beta}_{GLS}, \beta)$ is a positive semi-definite matrix, this implies that $C(\hat{\beta}_{OLS}) \geq C(\hat{\beta}_{GLS})$ for any vector of cost weights. If all weights are positive, then $C(\hat{\beta}_{OLS}) > C(\hat{\beta}_{GLS})$.

A further point worth making is that the GLS estimator $\hat{\alpha} = \hat{\beta}_{GLS}$ minimises the variance, and risk, in each coefficient $\hat{\alpha}_j$, for $j = 1, \ldots, K$.

In other words the GLS estimator $\hat{\alpha}$ is a *solution* to the set of problems: for each $j = 1, \ldots, K$ minimise $E((\hat{\beta}_j - \beta_j)^2)$ subject to $E(\hat{\beta}_j) = \beta_j$ and $\hat{\beta}_j = k_j' Y$ where $k_j \in \mathbf{R}^T$. The result which we have obtained here is known as the Gauss–Markov theorem.

The Gauss–Markov theorem

If $Y = X\beta + U$ where $E(X', U) = 0$, $E(U) = 0$ and $E(UU') = V$ is a positive definite matrix then the GLS estimator $\hat{\alpha} = (X'V^{-1}X)^{-1}X'V^{-1}Y$ for β is linear, unbiased and has *minimum variance*, in the sense that, for each j, $\mathrm{var}(\hat{\alpha}_j) \leq \mathrm{var}(\hat{\beta}_j)$ for any other estimator $\hat{\beta}' = (\ldots \hat{\beta}_j \ldots)$ which is both an unbiased estimator for β, and is linear in Y.

Since the risk matrix $R(\hat{\beta}, \beta)$ is a $(K + 1) \times (K + 1)$ matrix for any estimator β in the general regression model, we may write $R_T(\hat{\beta}, \beta)$ for the risk of the estimation procedure involving T observations of the variables, and inquire how $R_T(\hat{\beta}, \beta)$ behaves as T approaches infinity. Say that the procedure is *risk consistent* if $R_T(\hat{\beta}, \beta)$ approaches zero as T approaches infinity. Intuitively this means that the covariation matrix $(X'X)$ dominates the covariance matrix V in the limit. We shall return to consistency properties later when dealing with the situation where the data array X and disturbance vector U are correlated.

3.6   MAXIMUM LIKELIHOOD ESTIMATION

We can give another interpretation of the GLS estimator when the disturbances are in fact normally distributed. Suppose that U has a multivariate normal distribution $N(0, V)$. As we saw in section 3.2, the pdf for U is then

$$f(u) = \frac{1}{|V|^{1/2}} \frac{1}{(2\pi)^{T/2}} \exp(-\tfrac{1}{2}u'V^{-1}u)$$

When the coefficient b is used in the regression equation the estimator $e(b)$ for the disturbance is then given by $e(b) = Y - Xb$. Thus, given the data (Y, X) the likelihood function for the estimator b is

$$L(b) = \frac{1}{|V|^{1/2}} \frac{1}{(2\pi)^{T/2}} \exp(-\tfrac{1}{2}e(b)'V^{-1}e(b))$$

The MLE (maximum likelihood estimator) for the estimator is that value $\hat{\beta}$ for b such that $L(b)$ is maximised. Clearly $L(b)$ is maximised when $e(b)'V^{-1}e(b) = e(b, V)$ is minimised. To illustrate, suppose that $V = \sigma^2 I$. Then $V^{-1} = \sigma^{-2}I$ and so $e(b, V) = \frac{1}{\sigma^2}e(b)'e(b) = \frac{1}{\sigma^2}R(b)$, where $R(b)$ is the sum of residual squares associated with the coefficient b. Thus the MLE b is that vector of coefficients such that $R(b) = e(b)'e(b) = (Y - Xb)'(Y - Xb)$ is minimised. But this was precisely the condition for the OLS estimator $\hat{\beta}$, and so $\hat{\beta}$ is also an MLE.

It is useful to show that $\hat{\beta}$ is an MLE without using calculus, in the case $V = \sigma^2 I$. To see that this is so, note that for any coefficient vector b,

$$R(b) = Y'Y + b'X'Xb - 2b'X'Y$$

Because $X'X$ is symmetric we may write

$$(b - \hat{\beta})(X'X)(b - \hat{\beta})$$
$$= b'(X'X)b - 2b'(X'X)\hat{\beta} + \hat{\beta}'(X'X)\hat{\beta}$$

However, the OLS estimator $\hat{\beta} = (X'X)^{-1}X'Y$ and so the right-hand side becomes

$$b'(X'X)b - 2b'X'Y + \hat{\beta}'(X'X)\hat{\beta}$$
$$= R(b) - Y'Y + \hat{\beta}'(X'X)\hat{\beta}$$

On the other hand

$$R(\hat{\beta}) = e(\hat{\beta})'e(\hat{\beta}) = Y'Y - \hat{\beta}'(X'X)\hat{\beta}$$

Thus

$$(b - \hat{\beta})'(X'X)(b - \hat{\beta}) = e(b)'e(b) - e(\hat{\beta})'e(\hat{\beta})$$
$$= R(b) - R(\hat{\beta})$$

If we let $b = (b_0, \ldots, b_K)$, and note that the top-left term in $X'X$ is T, then

$$R(b) = T(b_0 - \bar{Y})^2 + A + R(\hat{\beta})$$

where

$$A = (b_* - \hat{\beta}_*)'(X_*'X_*)(b_* - \hat{\beta}_*)$$

is a quadratic form associated with the vector

$$(b_* - \hat{\beta}_*) = (b_1 - \hat{\beta}_1, \ldots, b_K - \hat{\beta}_K)$$

But since $X_*'X_*$ is a positive definite symmetric matrix there exists an orthogonal basis change matrix Q such that $(X_*'X_*) = Q'\wedge Q$. We can therefore write

$$R(b) = T(b_0 - \bar{Y})^2 + [Q(b_* - \hat{\beta}_*)]'\wedge [Q(b_* - \hat{\beta}_*)] + R(\hat{\beta}).$$

Since $\wedge$ is positive definite, A is strictly positive for all $b \neq \hat{\beta}$. Thus $R(b) > R(\hat{\beta})$ for all $b \neq \hat{\beta}$, and so $R(b)$ is minimised at $b = \hat{\beta}$.

On the other hand consider the more general case with a disturbance covariance matrix V. As we have seen the MLE estimator is that vector b which minimises $e(b, V) = e(b)'V^{-1}e(b)$. For any two estimators b_1, b_2 we can show in the same way that

$$e(b_1)'V^{-1}e(b_1) - e(b_2)'V^{-1}e(b_2)$$
$$= (b_1 - b_2)(X'V^{-1}X)(b_1 - b_2) + [b_2'X'V^{-1}Y - b_2'X'V^{-1}Xb_2]$$

Suppose now we let $b_2 = (X'V^{-1}X)^{-1}X'V^{-1}Y$, the GLS estimator. Then the second term on the right-hand side becomes

$$b_2'X'V^{-1}Y - b_2'(X'V^{-1}X)(X'V^{-1}X)^{-1}X'V^{-1}Y = 0$$

Since the first term on the right-hand side is a quadratic form involving $X'V^{-1}X$, and both $(X'X)$ and V^{-1} are positive definite, $X'V^{-1}X$ will be positive definite. Hence, $e(b_1)'V^{-1}e(b_1) > e(b_2)'V^{-1}e(b_2)$ for all $b_1 \neq b_2$, and so $e(b,V)$ is minimised at the GLS estimator. Consequently, the GLS estimator $\hat{\alpha}$ is the maximum likelihood estimator.

We can also use the results of section 3.2 to obtain statistical tests on the GLS estimators when the disturbances are normally distributed. Suppose, therefore, that $U \sim N(0, V)$, and consider the GLS estimator $\hat{\alpha}$ for the model $Y = X\beta + U$. As we have seen

$$\hat{\alpha} = \beta + BX'V^{-1}U \text{ where } B = (X'V^{-1}X)^{-1}$$

and
$$V(\hat{\alpha}) = B$$

Now let $V = SS'$ where $S = V^{1/2}$ as in Section 3.2. Then

$$z = S^{-1}X(\hat{\alpha} - \beta)$$
$$= mU$$

where

$$m = V^{-1/2}XBX'V^{-1}$$

We wish to show that $z'z$ is a χ^2 variate. First of all

$$z'z = U'm'mU$$

while

$$m'm = V^{-1}XBX'(S')^{-1}S^{-1}XBX'V^{-1}$$
$$= V^{-1}XBX'V^{-1}$$
$$= (S')^{-1}m$$

By lemma 3.4 of section 3.2, $z'z = U'(m'm)U$ is a χ^2 variate if and only if $(m'm)V(m'm) = (m'm)$. But the left-hand side is

$$(S')^{-1}mV(S')^{-1}m = (S')^{-1}m = (m'm)$$

Moreover, rank $(m'm) = K + 1$ and so

$$z'z = (\hat{\alpha} - \beta)'X'V^{-1}X(\hat{\alpha} - \beta) = (\hat{\alpha} - \beta)'[V(\hat{\alpha})]^{-1}(\hat{\alpha} - \beta)$$

is a χ^2 variable, with $K + 1$ degrees of freedom.

In a similar fashion, the vector of residuals is given by

$$e = e(\hat{\alpha}) = Y - X\hat{\alpha} = X(\beta - \hat{\alpha}) + U$$
$$= [I - XBX'V^{-1}]U$$

Now let

$$w'w = e'V^{-1}e,$$

so that

$$w = V^{-1/2}e = nU$$

where

$$n = S^{-1}(I - XBX'V^{-1})$$

We wish to show that $w'w$ is a χ^2 variate. But $w'w = U'n'nU$ is a χ^2 variate if and only if $n'nVn'n = n'n$. Now $n = S^{-1} - m$ where $m = S^{-1}XBX'V^{-1}$ as before. But then

$$n'n = (S^{-1} - m)'(S^{-1} - m)$$
$$= V^{-1} - 2(S')^{-1}m + m'm$$
$$= V^{-1} - m'm$$

since we showed that $m'm = (S')^{-1}m$. Thus

$$n'nVn'n = (V^{-1} - m'm)V(V^{-1} - m'm)$$
$$= (I - m'mV)(V^{-1} - m'm)$$
$$= V^{-1} - 2m'm + m'mVm'm$$
$$= V^{-1} - m'm = n'n$$

Now $m'm$ is a $T \times T$ matrix with rank $K + 1$, and so $n'n$ will be a $T \times T$ matrix of rank $T - (K + 1)$. By lemma 3.4 of section 3.2, $w'w$ is a χ^2 variate with $T - (K + 1)$ degrees of freedom.

The final task is to show that $z'z$ and $w'w$ are independent. By lemma 3.5 of section 3.2, if $m'mVn'n = 0$ then the two chi square variables are independent. But

$$m'mVn'n$$
$$= m'mV(V^{-1} - m'm)$$
$$= m'm - m'mVm'm = 0$$

Thus

$$z'z = (\hat{\alpha} - \beta)'X'V^{-1}X(\hat{\alpha} - \beta)$$

and

$$w'w = e'V^{-1}e$$

are independent χ^2 variates with $(K + 1)$, $(T - K - 1)$ degrees of freedom respectively. As in the case of the OLS estimator, the variate

$$F = \frac{(\hat{\alpha} - \beta)'V(\hat{\alpha})^{-1}(\hat{\alpha} - \beta)}{K + 1} \Bigg/ \frac{e(\hat{\alpha})'V^{-1}e(\hat{\alpha})}{T - K - 1}$$

is F-distributed with $(K + 1, T - K - 1)$ degrees of freedom.

The term $e(\hat{\alpha})'V^{-1}e(\hat{\alpha})$ is minimised at the GLS estimator $\hat{\alpha}$, while the denominator has expected value 1.

As an illustration of a situation where the covariance matrix V has a general but tractable form, suppose that

$$V = E(U_iU_j) = \begin{matrix} \sigma_i^2 & \text{if } i = j \\ 0 & \text{if } i \neq j \end{matrix}$$

Then V^{-1} has $\dfrac{1}{\sigma_t^2}$ in the (t, t) position and zero terms off the diagonal. In this case of

heteroscedastic disturbances, where V^{-1} has only diagonal elements of the form $\dfrac{1}{\sigma_t^2}$ the

GLS estimator can be found by minimising $\displaystyle\sum_{t=1}^{T} \dfrac{\left(Y_t - b_0 - \displaystyle\sum_{k=1}^{K} b_k x_{tK}\right)^2}{\sigma_t^2}$ with respect to $b = (b_0, \ldots, b_K)$.

In time series analysis, particularly, the disturbances are likely to be correlated so that the covariance matrix V has off diagonal terms. However, the method of generalised least squares can be used in this case to factor out this autocorrelation. The next section focuses on this problem and also on autoregressive processes (where the dependent variable y_t is correlated with y_{t-1}).

3.7   TIME SERIES ANALYSIS

Consider the case where the disturbances, U, are not independent, but are in fact, *weakly stationary* in the sense that $E(U_t) = 0$ and $E(U_t U_s)$ depends only on $|t - s|$ and not on t and s themselves.

A particular instance of such a case is when the disturbances are *autocorrelated* and satisfy $U_t = \rho U_{t-1} + V_t$, $V_t \sim I(0, \sigma^2)$ and $|\rho| < 1$. Expanding the series into the far past we obtain

$$U_t = \rho(\rho U_{t-2} + V_{t-1}) + V_t$$

$$= \rho^2(\rho U_{t-3} + V_{t-2}) + \rho V_{t-1} + V_t$$

$$= \sum_{r=0}^{\infty} \rho^r V_{t-r}$$

Thus

$$E(U_t) - \sum \rho^r E(V_{t-r}) = 0$$

Moreover

$$E(U_t^2) = \operatorname{var}(U_t)$$

$$= E\left(\left(\sum_{r=0}^{\infty} \rho^r V_{t-r}\right)^2\right)$$

$$= E\left(\sum_{r=0}^{\infty} \rho^{2r} V_{t-r}^2 + \sum_{r \neq s} \rho^{r+s} V_{t-r} V_{t-s}\right)$$

$$= E\left(\sum_{r=0}^{\infty} \rho^{2r}\right) \sigma^2, \text{ since } E(V_r V_s) = 0 \text{ if } r \neq s$$

$$= \frac{\sigma^2}{1 - \rho^2} = \sigma_u^2$$

since $\sum_{r=0}^{\infty} \rho^{2r} = \frac{1}{1 - \rho^2}$ when $|\rho| < 1$. Moreover

$$E(U_t U_{t-1}) = E((\rho U_{t-1} + V_t)U_{t-1})$$

$$= \rho \ \text{var}(U_{t-1}) + E(V_t U_{t-1})$$

Now U_{t-1} can be expanded in terms involving V_{t-1}, V_{t-2} etc. Since the covariance terms of $\{V_t\}$ are zero, $E(V_t U_{t-1}) = 0$ and so

$$E(U_t U_{t-1}) = \frac{\rho \cdot \sigma^2}{1 - \rho^2}$$

In the same way $E(U_t U_{t-s}) = \rho^s \ \text{var}(U_t)$

$$= \rho^s \frac{\sigma^2}{1 - \rho^2} = \rho^s \ \text{var}(U_t)$$

Thus $E(U_t U_{t-s})$ is a function only of $|t - (t - s)| = s$ rather than t and $t - s$ and so the disturbances are *weakly stationary*. As a test on the existence of *autocorrelation*, for a sample of size T, let

$$\delta^2 = \frac{1}{T-1} \sum_{t=1}^{T-1} (U_{t+1} - U_t)^2$$

$$= \frac{1}{T-1} \sum_{t=1}^{T-1} (U_{t+1}^2 + U_t^2 - 2U_t U_{t+1})$$

But

$$E(U_{t+1}^2) = E(U_t^2) = \sigma_u^2$$

and

$$E(U_{t+1} U_t) = \rho \sigma_u^2$$

Thus

$$E(\delta^2) = 2\sigma_u^2(1 - \rho)$$

Moreover

$$s^2 = \frac{1}{T-1} \sum_{t=1}^{T} U_t^2 \ \text{has} \ E(s^2) = \sigma_u^2$$

The empirical ratio $\frac{\sigma^2}{s^2} = d$ is called the *Durbin–Watson Statistic* and is of the order of magnitude of $2(1 - \rho)$. If $d \ll 2$ then autocorrelation between the errors is likely. To correct for autocorrelation we may use the method of generalised least squares. As we have seen the covariance matrix V of the disturbances is

$$V = \frac{\sigma^2}{1-\rho^2}\begin{bmatrix} 1 & \rho & \rho^2 & \cdot & \cdot & \cdot \\ \rho & 1 & \rho & \cdot & \cdot & \cdot \\ \cdot & & \cdot & & \cdot \\ \cdot & & & \cdot & \\ \cdot & & & & \cdot \end{bmatrix}$$

with inverse

$$V^{-1} = \frac{1}{\sigma^2}\begin{bmatrix} 1 & -\rho & & \cdot & & \\ -\rho & 1+\rho^2 & -\rho & & & \\ & -\rho & 1+\rho^2 & & & \\ & & & & \cdot & \\ & & & & & \cdot \\ & & & & & & 1 \end{bmatrix}$$

Now define

$$D = \begin{bmatrix} \sqrt{1-\rho^2} & 0 & & \\ -\rho & 1 & & \\ & -\rho & 1 & \\ & & -\rho & 1 \end{bmatrix}$$

Then

$$D'D = \begin{bmatrix} \sqrt{1-\rho^2} & -\rho & & & \\ 0 & 1 & -\rho & & \\ & 0 & 1 & & \\ & & & -\rho & \\ & & & & 1 \end{bmatrix}\begin{bmatrix} \sqrt{1-\rho^2} & 0 & & & \\ -\rho & 1 & & & \\ & -\rho & 1 & & \\ & & & 1 & \\ & & & -\rho & 1 \end{bmatrix}$$

$$= \begin{bmatrix} 1 & -\rho & & & & \\ -\rho & 1+\rho^2 & -\rho & & & \\ & -\rho & 1+\rho^2 & & & \\ & & -\rho & \cdot & & \\ & & & \cdot & & \\ & & & & \cdot & -\rho \\ & & & & -\rho & 1 \end{bmatrix}$$

Consequently $D'D = \sigma^2 V^{-1}$. Now we have seen that the estimator for $\hat{\beta}$, by the method of generalised least squares is:

$$\hat{\beta} = (X'V^{-1}X)^{-1}X'V^{-1}Y$$

$$= \left[\frac{X'D'DX}{\sigma^2}\right]^{-1}\left[\frac{X'D'D}{\sigma^2}\right]Y$$

$$= ((DX)'DX)^{-1}(DX)'DY$$

In other words if we transform X and Y to DX and DY and then perform OLS regression we obtain a better estimate of $\hat{\beta}$. Now let $a = \sqrt{1 - \rho^2}$ for convenience and note that

$$DY = \begin{bmatrix} aY_1 \\ Y_2 - \rho Y_1 \\ . \\ . \\ . \\ Y_T - \rho Y_{T-1} \end{bmatrix} \quad \text{and} \quad DX = \begin{bmatrix} a & ax_{11} & \ldots ax_{1K} \\ 1-\rho & x_{21} - \rho x_{11} & \\ . & . & \\ . & . & \\ . & . & \end{bmatrix}$$

To obtain an estimate of ρ proceed as follows:

Take

$$\hat{\beta} = (X'X)^{-1}X'Y$$

and

$$\hat{Y} = X\hat{\beta}$$

From this regression obtain estimates for the residuals $\hat{e}_t = Y_t - \hat{Y}_t$. Then regress $\hat{e}_t$ on $\hat{e}_{t-1}$ to obtain $\hat{e}_t = \hat{\rho}e_{t-1} + v_t$. Define new variables $DY, Dx_1, \ldots, Dx_K$ by

$$DY_t = Y_1\sqrt{1 - \hat{\rho}^2} \quad \text{if } t = 1$$

$$= Y_t - \hat{\rho}Y_{t-1} \quad \text{if } t > 1$$

and

$$Dx_{tj} = x_{ij}\sqrt{1 - \hat{\rho}^2} \quad \text{if } t = 1$$

$$= x_{tj} - \hat{\rho}x_{t-1,j} \quad \text{if } t > 1$$

In the regression of DY on $Dx_1, \ldots, Dx_K$ the error terms DU_t are given by

$$DU_t = 1 - \hat{\rho}^2 U_1 = V_1 \quad \text{if } t = 1$$

$$= U_t - \hat{\rho}U_{t-1} = V_t \quad \text{if } t > 1$$

Moreover, the covariance matrix $V(DU)$ of DU is

$$V(DU) = E((DU)(DU)') = DVD'$$

$$= \sigma^2 D(D'D)^{-1}D' = \sigma^2 I$$

By use of the linear transformations D on Y and X we have effectively removed the influence of the autoregressive errors.

In a similar fashion we may consider an autoregressive process of the form

$$y_t = \alpha y_{t-1} + U_t \text{ where } U_t \sim I(0, \sigma^2)$$

Then just as in the case of autocorrelated disturbances, we may write

$$y_t = \sum_{r=0}^{\infty} \alpha^r U_{t-r}$$

and so

$$\mathrm{var}(y_t) = \sigma_y^2 = \frac{\sigma^2}{1 - \alpha^2}$$

and

$$E(y_t y_{t-s}) = \alpha^s \sigma_y^2$$

Again the process $\{y_t\}$ is weakly stationary.

As with autocorrelated errors, a test on the occurrence of autoregression is given by the von Neumann ratio $\dfrac{\delta^2}{S^2}$ where

$$\delta^2 = \frac{1}{T-1} \sum_{t=1}^{T-1} (y_{t+1} - y_t)^2$$

and

$$S^2 = \frac{1}{T-1} \sum_{t=1}^{T} y_t^2$$

If $\dfrac{\delta^2}{S^2} \ll 2$, then ρ is likely to be greater than 0.

General autoregressive processes may involve quite complex *lag structures*. If we write $L(y_t) = y_{t-1}$ for the *lag operator*, then the autoregressive process just considered may be written $\alpha(L) y_t = U_t$ where

$$\alpha(L)(y_t) = (1 - \alpha L)(y_t) = y_t - \alpha L(y_t)$$

$$= y_t - \alpha y_{t-1}$$

and $\alpha(L)$ is a polynomial of degree 1 in the lag operator.

The autocorrelated disturbance system $U_t = \rho U_{t-1} + V_t$ which we have just considered can be written

$$\rho(L) = (1 - \rho L) U_t$$

$$= U_t - \rho U_{t-1} = V_t$$

in this notation.

A general procedure for an autoregressive system $\{y_t, U_t\}$ is to find lag operators

$\alpha(L), \rho(L)$ such that $\{\alpha(L)y_t, \rho(L)U_t\}$ are *weakly stationary* that is to say that $E(\alpha(L)y_t)$ is independent of t, and

$$\text{cov}(\alpha(L)y_t, \alpha(L)y_s)$$

$$\text{cov}(\rho(L)U_t, \rho(L)U_s)$$

are only dependent on $|t - s|$. The autoregressive model can then be written in the form

$$\alpha(L)y_t = \rho(L)U_t$$

We shall discuss this procedure, together with a number of examples in Chapter 6.

A second procedure for analysing general autoregressive processes is to analyse the *autocovariance* $\gamma_\theta = \text{cov}(y_t, y_{t+\theta})$ at a lag θ. We define the autocorrelation coefficient, r_θ, at lag θ, by

$$\gamma_\theta = r_\theta \gamma_0 \text{ where } \gamma_0 = \text{var}(y_t) = \sigma_y^2$$

For example in the autoregressive process

$$\alpha(L)(y_t) = (1 - \alpha(L))(y_t) = y_t - \alpha y_{t-1} = U_t$$

which we have just considered

$$\gamma_0 = \sigma_y^2 = \frac{\sigma^2}{1 - \alpha^2}, \gamma_\theta = \alpha^\theta \gamma_0 \text{ and so } r_\theta = \alpha^\theta$$

Since $|\alpha| < 1$, the autocorrelation coefficient approaches zero as θ approaches infinity.

For a general process, r_θ need not decrease (monotonically) with θ, but might oscillate because of inherent periodicities in the process. An empirical estimate $\hat{r}_\theta$ of the autocorrelation coefficient can, of course, be determined. Let

$$C_\theta = \frac{1}{T} \sum_{t=1}^{t-\theta} y_t y_{t+\theta}$$

be the *empirical autocovariance* and

$$C_0 = \frac{1}{T} \sum_{t=1}^{T} y_t^2$$

be an estimate for the variance. The estimator for the correlation coefficient between y_t and $y_{t+\theta}$ is

$$\hat{r}_\theta = \frac{\sum_{t=1}^{T-\theta} y_t y_{t+\theta}}{\sqrt{\sum_{t=1}^{T} y_t^2 \sum_{t+\theta=1}^{t+\theta=T} y_{t+\theta}^2}} = \frac{C_\theta}{C_0}$$

We would expect the 'empirical' autocorrelation coefficient $\hat{r}_\theta$ to approach zero as θ approaches infinity.

The graph of $\hat{r}_\theta$ against θ is called the *correlogram* of the process, and might, for example, resemble Figure 3.1.

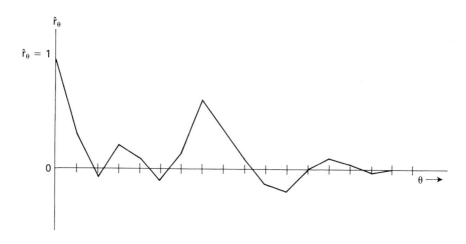

Figure 3.1 *A typical correlogram*

3.8 CONSISTENCY OF ESTIMATORS

The crucial assumption used to justify the GLS estimator in section 3.6 was that X and U were uncorrelated. In cross-sectional analyses, particularly, this property might well be violated and we give a brief outline of the consequences in this section, with more details in the next chapter.

If $E(X'U) \neq 0$ then neither the OLS nor GLS need be unbiased. In this case, however, we may enquire whether the estimation procedure $\hat{\beta}_T$, now regarded as dependent on the number of observations, *converges* to the true parameter β.

To generalise the definition of Chapter 1, say an estimation procedure $\{\hat{\beta}_T : \hat{\beta}_T \in \mathbf{R}^K, T = K + 1, \ldots\}$ converges to $b \in \mathbf{R}^K$ if

$$\lim_{T \to \infty} P(\|\hat{\beta}_T - b\| < \varepsilon) = 1$$

for all $\varepsilon > 0$. The limit, b, is also called the probability limit or plim of $\hat{\beta}$, and we write $b = \text{plim}\,\hat{\beta}_T$.

In the case that the estimation procedure $\{\hat{\beta}_T\}$ converges to the true vector parameter β we shall say that the estimation procedure is *p-consistent* (or consistent in probability).

Previously, in section 1.6, we defined the risk $R(\hat{\beta}, \beta)$ associated with a real valued estimator $\hat{\beta}$ for β, and said that an estimation procedure $\{\hat{\beta}_T\}$ was consistent if

$\lim_{T \to \infty} R(\hat{\beta}_T, \beta) = 0$. To distinguish this form of consistency from *p*-consistency we shall now call it *r*-consistency. As in section 3.5, if β is a parameter, in $\mathbf{R}^K$, then an estimation procedure $\{\hat{\beta}_T\}$ for β is *r*-consistent if the risk matrix $R(\hat{\beta}_T, \beta) = E((\hat{\beta}_T - \beta)(\hat{\beta}_T - \beta)')$ is *asymptotically zero* (i.e. zero is the limit). Now

$$R(\hat{\beta}_T, \beta) = V(\hat{\beta}_T) + B(\hat{\beta}_T, \beta)$$

where $B(\hat{\beta}_T, \beta)$ is the *bias matrix*. If $\{\hat{\beta}_T\}$ is r-consistent then both the covariance matrix $V(\hat{\beta}_T)$ and bias matrix are asymptotically zero. Since the diagonal terms of the bias matrix will then be zero in the limit, this implies that the asymptotic bias $\lim_{T \to \infty} E(\hat{\beta}_T) - \beta$, will be zero, and so the asymptotic expectation

$$\lim_{T \to \infty} E(\hat{\beta}_T) = \beta$$

As we shall show in the next chapter, r-consistency of an estimation procedure implies p-consistency and in this case the asymptotic expectation and plim will both equal the true parameter. Note that asymptotic unbiasedness alone is not sufficient for p-consistency, as the following example from Maddala (1977, p. 150) illustrates.

Suppose that $\{x_1, \ldots, x_T\}$ is a sample of size T from a normal distribution $N(\mu, 1)$. Consider the estimator $\hat{\mu}_T = \dfrac{x_1}{2} + \dfrac{1}{2T} \sum_{t=2}^{T} x_i$. Clearly $E(\hat{\mu}_T) = \dfrac{\mu}{2} + \dfrac{T-1}{T}\mu$ and so the asymptotic bias, $\lim_{T \to \infty} E(\hat{\mu}_T) - \mu$, is 0. However

$$V(\hat{\mu}_T) = \frac{1}{4} + \frac{T-1}{4T^2} \to \frac{1}{4} \text{ as } T \to \infty$$

Thus $\{\hat{\mu}_T\}$ is not r-consistent. Moreover plim $(\hat{\mu}_T) = \dfrac{x_1}{2} + \dfrac{\mu}{2}$ and so $\{\hat{\mu}_T\}$ is not p-consistent either. It is possible also for a procedure $\{\hat{\beta}_T\}$ to be p-consistent, even though the asymptotic bias, and thus the asymptotic risk, are non-zero, and the asymptotic expectation $\lim_{T \to \infty} E(\hat{\beta}_T)$ does not equal the true parameter β (see Johnston, 1972, p. 272 for discussion).

Another difficulty arises since asymptotic variance and expectation may also be interpreted as the variance and expectation of the limiting distribution of the estimator. In this context if an estimation procedure is p-consistent and has a limiting normal distribution, then it will be asymptotically unbiased. (The interested reader is referred to the discussion in Maddala, 1977, section 9.4.)

To return to the OLS estimator in the regression model, suppose that the regressors, X, are *stochastic* and $E(X'U) \neq 0$. As we have seen

$$\hat{\beta}_T = (X'X)^{-1} X'Y$$
$$= (X'X)^{-1}X'(X\beta + U)$$
$$= \beta + (X'X)^{-1}(X'U)$$
$$= \beta + \left[\frac{X'X}{T}\right]^{-1}\left[\frac{X'U}{T}\right]$$

Since, for all T, $(X'X)$ and $(X'U)$ are respectively a $(K+1) \times (K+1)$ matrix and $(K+1)$ vector we may determine their asymptotic behaviour. Suppose, therefore, that plim $\left[\dfrac{X'X}{T}\right]$ is a positive definite matrix and plim $\left[\dfrac{X'U}{T}\right] = 0$. As we shall see in the next chapter this implies that $\text{plim}\,\hat{\beta}_T = \beta$, so that the estimation procedure is p-consistent.

On the other hand if $\text{plim}\left[\dfrac{X'U}{T}\right] \neq 0$ then the OLS estimation procedure need not be p-consistent. For example, consider one regressor, x, and suppose that for each t

$$\begin{bmatrix} x_t \\ U_t \end{bmatrix} \sim \left[\begin{bmatrix} 0 \\ 0 \end{bmatrix},\; E(x_t\,U_t)\right]$$

where $E(x_t\,U_t)$ is the covariance matrix

$$\begin{bmatrix} \sigma_x^2 & \rho\sigma_x\sigma \\ \rho\sigma_x\sigma & \sigma^2 \end{bmatrix}$$

As we shall discuss in the next chapter, under certain conditions $\text{plim}\left[\dfrac{x'U}{T}\right] = \rho\sigma_x\sigma$ while

$$\text{plim}\left[\frac{X'X}{T}\right] = \sigma_x^2$$

Thus

$$\text{plim}\,(\hat{\beta} - \beta) = \text{plim}\left[\frac{X'U}{T}\right] \Big/ \text{plim}\left[\frac{X'X}{T}\right]$$

$$= \frac{\rho\sigma_x\sigma}{\sigma_x^2} = \frac{\rho\sigma}{\sigma_x} \neq 0$$

Hence $\{\hat{\beta}_T\}$ will not be a p-consistent estimation procedure. We shall call the term, $\text{plim}\,(\hat{\beta} - \beta)$, the *asymptotic inconsistency* of the procedure $\{\hat{\beta}_T\}$. Intuitively, $\left[\dfrac{X'U}{T}\right]$ will be a p-consistent estimator for $\rho\sigma_x\sigma$ when $\text{var}\left[\dfrac{X'U}{T}\right] \to 0$ as $T \to \infty$ and this will be the case when the fourth moments $E((x'U)(x'U)')$ are bounded.

Finally if (x, U) have a limiting normal distribution, then we may identify the asymptotic inconsistency of $\{\hat{\beta}_T\}$ with the asymptotic bias.

Because it is generally easier to use the properties of plim rather than analyse asymptotic bias and variance, we shall use consistency to refer to p-consistency in discussing these questions more fully in the next chapter.

3.9 EXERCISES

1. Show that if $u \sim N_T(\mu, V)$ and $y = Bu$, where B is a $T \times T$ matrix of rank T, then $y \sim N_T(B\mu, BVB')$. Thus show that if C is a $K \times T$ matrix of rank K then

$$Cu \sim N_K(C\mu, CVC')$$

Hint: Using lemma 3.1, substitute $u = B^{-1} y$ into the expression for the pdf of u, to obtain

$$f(y) = \frac{1}{(2\pi)^{T/2}} \frac{|V|^{1/2}}{|B|} \exp\left[-\tfrac{1}{2}(B^{-1} y - \mu)' V^{-1}(B^{-1} y - \mu)\right]$$

Then rearrange terms to obtain

$$f(y) = \frac{1}{(2\pi)^{T/2}} |C|^{-1} \exp\left[-\tfrac{1}{2}(y - B\mu)' C^{-1}(y - B\mu)\right]$$

where $C = BVB'$.

2. More generally, show that if $u \sim (\mu, V)$ i.e., u has expectation $\mu \in \mathbf{R}^T$ with covariance matrix V, then $Bu \sim (B\mu, BVB')$ for any $K \times T$ matrix B of rank K.

FURTHER READING FOR PART I

Probability theory

Probability itself is a subtle concept and opinions vary as to how it should best be defined. One procedure, the frequency *experimentalist* method, is to assume that the probability of an event is defined in terms of limit of a sequence of replications of an appropriate sampling experiment. See

van Mises, R. (1939) *Probability, Statistics and Truth* (trans. Neyman, J., Sholl, D., and Rabinovitch, E.), New York: Macmillan.

van Mises, R. (1964) *Mathematical Theory of Probability and Statistics*, New York: Academic Press.

The *subjectivist* position might be summed up by the remark that probability is a 'degree of belief, that belongs to a body of beliefs, from which most inconsistencies have been removed by means of detached judgments'. See, for example,

Good, I. J. (1959) 'Kinds of Probability,' *Science* 129:443–447.

'Subjectivist' probability theory is related both to utility theory and decision theory, See, for example,

Marschak, J. (1954) 'Probability in the Social Sciences.' In P. F. Lazarfeld (ed.), *Mathematical Thinking in the Social Sciences*, pp. 166–215, New York: The Free Press. Reprinted in Marschak, J. (1974) *Economic Information, Decision and Prediction, Part I*, Reidel, Dordrecht, Holland.

Another, and possibly fruitful, procedure is to regard probability as encoding information that an individual has about an uncertain environment. For example, if the individual has no prior information then the prior probability distribution should reflect this, in the sense of having maximum entropy. See for example

Jaynes, E. T. (1968) 'Prior Probabilities', *IEEE Transactions on Systems Science and Cybernetics*, pp. 227–241.

Statistical theory and econometrics

The field of statistical theory and econometrics is immense. Some of the standard textbooks are:

Hogg, R. V. and Craig, A. T. (1970) *Introduction to Mathematical Statistics*, London: Macmillan.

Johnston, J. (1972) *Econometric Methods* (second edition), New York: McGraw Hill.

Maddala, G. S. (1977) *Econometrics*, New York: McGraw Hill.

Malinvand, E. (1970) *Statistical Methods of Econometrics*, Amsterdam: North-Holland.

Mood, A. M., and Graybill, F. A. (1963) *Introduction to the Theory of Statistics*, New York: McGraw Hill.

Rao, P., and Miller, R. (1971) *Applied Econometrics*, London: Wadsworth.

Wonnacott, T. H., and Wonnacott, R. J. (1970) *Econometrics*, London: Wiley.

Part II

Econometric Principles and Applications in Economics

Chapter 4

Econometric Principles

In this chapter we utilise the statistical theory presented in the previous chapters to develop the fundamental basis of econometrics. This is a subject which is primarily concerned with the quantitative and empirical analysis of economic problems. It can, however, be equally applied in other social sciences where controlled experiment is not possible. We develop the econometric tools that are necessary for serious investigation of economic problems, and then in the following chapter these tools are applied to the analysis of a classic paper in macroeconomics.

4.1 MODELS IN ECONOMETRICS

The fundamental tool in quantitative economics is a mathematical model. The philosophy underlying model-building is fairly deep and for our purposes only the briefest, most simplified sketch is required. Mathematical models typically consist of a set of equations which show the relationship between sets of variables. In economic theory the variables are typically deterministic. That is, the variables in the equations are not stochastic or random. The addition of a stochastic (random) component is usually the way by which economic models are converted into econometric models. (For a fuller discussion see Stewart and Wallis (1980), chapter 2.)

In what follows we discuss different forms of common econometric models without attempting to be exhaustive.

Single equation models: linear models

We shall start our discussion with the consumption function. We know that

$$C_t = f(I_t) + U_t \qquad \qquad \textbf{4.1}$$

where C_t is aggregate nominal consumption, I_t is aggregate nominal income and simplistically we think I_t is exogenous. Since we do not know the functional form of f, we assume that U_t, the error, is an unobserved random variable with mean 0, variance σ^2, i.e. $U_t \sim (0, \sigma^2)$, and $E(U_t U_s) = 0$, $t \neq s$. For simplicity of estimation, interpretation and aggregation, we let $f(I_t) = \alpha + \beta I_t$ where α and β are unknown parameters. The statistical problem is, given $(C_t, I_t, t = 1, \ldots, T)$, estimate α, β and σ^2. This is under the maintained hypothesis that we have outlined above. We describe the above model as being linear in variables (endogenous and exogenous) and linear in parameters. We now generalise it for a single endogenous variable, which we call Y_t, and K exogenous variables $X_{t1}, \ldots, X_{tK}, t = 1, \ldots, T$. Our general relationship is

$$Y_t = \sum_{j=1}^{K} X_{tj}\beta_j + U_t \qquad t = 1, \ldots, T \qquad \textbf{4.1(a)}$$

We can write this in matrix notation as

$$Y = X\beta + U \qquad \textbf{4.2}$$

where Y is a $T \times 1$ vector with tth element Y_t
$\quad\quad\,\, X$ is a $T \times K$ matrix with $(t, j$th$)$ element X_{tj}
$\quad\quad\,\, \beta$ is a $K \times 1$ vector with jth element j
$\quad\quad\,\, U$ is a $T \times 1$ vector with tth element U_t

We also note that we can express the distributional properties of U in an obvious extension of our previous notation as $U \sim (0, \sigma^2 I_T)$, where 0 is a $T \times 1$ vector of zeros corresponding to the mean of U and $\sigma^2 I_T$ is σ^2 times a $T \times T$ identity matrix which corresponds to the covariance matrix of U. The estimation problem for this model is, given $(Y$ and $X)$ estimate β and σ^2.

Single equation models: non-linear models and non-linearity in variables

Suppose for our consumption function in 4.1, we choose to measure C_t and I_t in real terms, that is, we divide by P_t, where P_t is some form of price index, then our model would be

$$\frac{C_t}{P_t} = \frac{I_t}{P_t} + U_t \qquad \textbf{4.3}$$

and we have an equation which is non-linear in the variables (C_t, I_t, P_t), although linear in $\dfrac{C_t}{P_t}, \dfrac{I_t}{P_t}$. If P_t is exogenous this new model presents no serious problem but if P_t is endogenous then for the model to determine the endogenous variables we would need another equation. Essentially non-linearity in exogenous variables presents no problems, it is only non-linearity in endogenous variables that is awkward.

Non-linearity in parameters

We consider the usual Cobb–Douglas production function where Q_t is output, K_t is capital, and L_t is labour

$$Q_t = AL_t^\alpha K_t^\beta + U_t \qquad \textbf{4.4}$$

Note that (Q_t, K_t, L_t) are the variables and we have to estimate A, α, β and σ^2. Equation 4.4 is non-linear in both variables and parameters. The way economists get out of this problem is to assume a different maintained hypothesis

$$Q_t = AL_t^\alpha K_t^\beta \exp(U_t) \qquad \textbf{4.4a}$$

and take logarithms to base e. Equation 4.4a becomes

$$\log Q_t = \log A + \alpha \log L_t + \beta \log K_t + U_t$$

which is linear in $(\log A, \alpha, \beta)$ and $(\log Q_t, \log L_t,$ and $\log K_t)$. It is clear that there is no simple transformation to linearise 4.4. Since linearity in parameters plus an additive error is a desired aim in model-building, the usual procedure for a non-trivial, non-linear model is to approximate it linearly by taking a Taylor's series expansion around the means of the variables (see Exercise 1 to this section). The alternative is to estimate directly, which is both complicated and computationally expensive.

Cross-section models

All the previous models have been subscripted by t and have implicitly referred to the behaviour of an agent or market at consecutive points in time. However, a great deal of economic analysis refers to a collection of agents or firms or even markets at a point in time and here we shall use the index i. If we consider a group of N consumers in an economy, each of whom has a linear expenditure function for the one good in the economy, then $C_i = \alpha_i + \beta_i I_i + U_i$ where C_i and I_i are the consumption and income of the ith consumer, $i = 1, \ldots, N$. The parameters for each consumer are α_i, β_i and σ_i^2 and U_i is an error $\sim (0, \sigma_i^2)$. If we had several years of census data so that we could observe these expenditure functions through time, then we would have

$$C_{ti} = \alpha_i + \beta_i I_{ti} + U_{ti} \quad i = 1, \ldots, N, t = 1, \ldots, T \qquad \textbf{4.5}$$

Aggregation

It is clear too that there must be some connection with our model in 4.1 and our model in 4.5. Now

$$C_t = \sum_{i=1}^{N} C_{ti}, I_t = \sum_{i=1}^{N} I_{ti}$$

but the relationship between the parameters is less obvious. If $\alpha_i = \alpha_0$ for all i and

$\beta_i = \beta_0$ for all i, then $\alpha = N\alpha_0$, $\beta = N\beta_0$, $U_t = \sum_{i=1}^{N} U_{ti}$, $\sigma^2 = \sum_{i=1}^{N} \sigma_i^2$, if we assume that the U_{ti}'s are uncorrelated with respect to i. Notice that if we do not assume that each consumer has identical expenditure functions the problem becomes rather intractable. (See Exercise 2 to this section.)

We write our general cross-section model to take into account the possibility that the dependent variable will have both temporal and cross-sectional components

$$Y_{ti} = \alpha + \beta_i + \gamma_t + X_{ti}$$

Box–Jenkins models

This is a class of models in which economic theory plays no role. Instead of attempting to build an econometric model in which economics guides the choice of variables, one could attempt to predict some variable y_t by nothing but past values of y_t. To do this we investigate the class of weakly stationary processes. We assume y_t is a sequence of random variables such that $E(y_t)$ is the same for all t and $E(y_t y_s)$ depends only upon $|t - s|$, i.e. $E(y_{t+k}, y_{s+k})$ is the same for all integer k. This means that y will have the same first and second moments when observed in 1900 as in 1960 or 1980. Clearly these assumptions are a bit unrealistic and in practice what one does it to transform the series until it is stationary. There are several simple ways of doing this. Firstly we can take logarithms, because $\log(y_t)$ tends to have less heteroscedasticity than y_t. Another method is to difference y_t to remove trends, i.e. if $y_t = a + bt + U_t$ where $U_t \sim (0, \sigma^2)$.

$$E(y_t) = a + bt \qquad \text{and } U_t \text{ independent,}$$
$$y_t - y_{t-1} = b + U_t - U_{t-1} \qquad (U \sim I(0, \sigma^2)),$$
$$E(y_t - y_{t-1}) = b$$

It may be necessary to difference a number of times to achieve this. (See Exercise 3 to this section.)

Having made y_t stationary, we now propose a model of the following form. Let y_t^* be the transformed series which is stationary. Then

$$y_t^* = \gamma(L)y_t \quad \text{and} \quad \alpha(L)y_t^* = b + \beta(L)U_t \qquad \qquad \textbf{4.6}$$

where $U_t \sim I(0, \sigma^2)$ and $\alpha(L)$, $\beta(L)$, $\gamma(L)$ are polynomials in the lag operator L, where $Ly_t^* = y_{t-1}^*$.

Example: If $\alpha(L) = 1 - L$, $\gamma(L) = 1$
$$\beta(L) = 1 + \beta_1 L + \beta_2 L^2$$

then our model would be

$$y_t - y_{t-1} = b + U_t + \beta_1 U_{t-1} + \beta_2 U_{t-2}$$

Because this model is not based on economic theory we have no maintained hypothesis about $\alpha(L)$ or $\beta(L)$. We let the data choose $\alpha(L)$ and $\beta(L)$ by use of various diagnostics arising in estimation, such as significant t statistics, high r^2, etc. These sorts of procedures tend to predict rather well although they tend not to give us any insight at all into why things are happening. An equation of the form $\alpha(L)C_t^* = U_t$ is called an autoregressive (AR) model, an equation of the form $C_t^* = \beta(L)U_t$ is called a moving average (MA) model, and the combination is called an autoregressive moving average model (ARMA).

Recently attempts have been made to combine Box–Jenkins type models with econometric models. Typically, such models are of the form $\alpha(L)y_t = \beta(L)x_t + \phi(L)U_t$ where x_t is exogenous. As with Box–Jenkins procedures the data are allowed to choose $\alpha(L)$ and $\beta(L)$ and $\phi(L)$ but a maintained hypothesis about the long-run effect of x on y, i.e. $\dfrac{\beta(1)}{\alpha(1)}$ is sometimes imposed. (See Exercise 4 to this section.)

Exercises to section 4.1

1. Show that the non-linear model (4.4) can be approximately linearised as

$$\frac{Q_t}{\bar{Q}} - 1 = \alpha \left[\frac{L_t}{\bar{L}} - 1 \right] + \beta \left[\frac{K_t}{\bar{K}} - 1 \right] + v_t$$

   where $\bar{X}$ is the mean value of $X, X = Q, L, K$.
   Discuss the nature of the approximation and the properties of the error term.
2. Show that if $\beta_i \neq \beta_0$ for all i, then the linear cross-section consumption model cannot be converted into a linear aggregate consumption model. Why is the assumption $\alpha_i = \alpha_0$ for all i less critical?
3. Show that if $y_t = a + bt + U_t$ where $U_t \sim I(0, \sigma^2)$ then $\Delta y_t = y_t - y_{t-1}$ is a weakly stationary process.
4. For the model
   $\alpha(L)y_t = \beta(L)x_t + \phi(L)u_t$ show that the long-run multiplier of x on y is given (for stationary equilibria) by $\dfrac{\beta(1)}{\alpha(1)}$.
   Hint: Write out $\beta(L)$ and $\alpha(L)$ in full as polynomials in L of order r and s respectively. Then compute the stationary equilibrium effect by setting $x_t = x_{t-s} = x$ and $y_t = y_{t-s} = y$ for all s.

4.2 SIMULTANEOUS EQUATION MODELS

We now proceed to a discussion of simultaneous equation models (SEMs). These are of great importance as they are used to explain the simultaneous determination of a set of endogenous variables given another set of exogenous variables. Again these models can be linear or non-linear in variables and parameters. We shall concentrate on the linear model as it is easiest to work with and it is a natural generalisation of the single-equation multiple-regression model. (See Theil, 1971, section 9.3.)

We first consider a simple example of a simultaneous equation model. We return to the consumption function of the previous section, where $C_t = I_t \beta + U_t$. We now assume an income identity $I_t = C_t + G_t$ where G_t is nominal governmental expenditure in time t and is assumed exogenous. By substitution, we see that

$$I_t = \frac{G_t}{1 - \beta} + U_t$$

and

$$C_t = \frac{\beta G_t}{1 - \beta} + \frac{U_t}{1 - \beta}$$

We see that *both* I_t and C_t are simultaneously determined, given values of (exogenous) G_t. (See Exercises 2 and 3.) This also raises new issues of identification and estimation than those covered in the regression model. These will be discussed at a later point.

Notation for the system

We consider a complete linear system in G jointly dependent variables and K predetermined variables.

We write y_{tg} for the tth value of the gth dependent variable and x_{tk} for the corresponding value of the kth predetermined variable. The number of observations is T, each consisting of $K + G$ values:

$$(y_{t1} \dots y_G \; x_{t1} \; x_{t2} \cdots x_{tK}) \; t = 1, \dots, T \qquad \textbf{4.7}$$

The x, y notation suggests that the predetermined variables are the extensions of the explanatory variables of the standard linear model and that the jointly dependent variables are the extensions of the single dependent variable of that model.

The system consists of G structural equations, and can be written as follows:

$$\sum_{g=1}^{G} \alpha_{gj} y_{tg} + \sum_{k=1}^{K} \beta_{kj} x_{tk} = u_{tj} \qquad \begin{matrix} t = 1, \dots, T \\ j = 1, \dots, G \end{matrix} \qquad \textbf{4.8}$$

where u_{tj} is the disturbance of the tth observation, and the jth equation and the β's and α's are parameters to be estimated. We introduce the $T \times K$ matrix X and the $T \times G$ matrix Y of, respectively, the values taken by the predetermined variables and those taken by the jointly dependent variables:

$$X = [x_{tk}] = \begin{bmatrix} x_{11} & x_{12} \dots x_{1K} \\ x_{21} & x_{22} \dots x_{2K} \\ \cdot & \cdot \quad\cdot \\ \cdot & \cdot \quad\cdot \\ \cdot & \cdot \quad\cdot \\ x_{T1} & x_{T2} \dots x_{TK} \end{bmatrix} \qquad Y = [y_{tg}] = \begin{bmatrix} y_{11} & y_{12} \dots y_{1G} \\ y_{21} & y_{22} \dots y_{2G} \\ \cdot & \cdot \quad\cdot \\ \cdot & \cdot \quad\cdot \\ \cdot & \cdot \quad\cdot \\ y_{T1} & y_{T2} \dots y_{TG} \end{bmatrix} \qquad \textbf{4.9}$$

Comparing this notation with 4.7 we see that the T observations consist of the successive rows of $[Y\,X]$. Furthermore, we introduce the $T \times G$ matrix U of disturbances:

$$U = [u_{tj}] = \begin{bmatrix} u_{11} & u_{12} \cdots u_{1G} \\ u_{21} & u_{22} \cdots u_{2G} \\ \cdot & \cdot \\ \cdot & \cdot \\ \cdot & \cdot \\ u_{T1} & u_{T2} \cdots u_{TG} \end{bmatrix} = [U_1\ U_2 \cdots U_G] \qquad \textbf{4.10}$$

where U_j is the jth column of U (corresponding to the jth equation). Finally, consider the $K \times G$ matrix B and the $G \times G$ matrix A of parameters:

$$B = [\beta_{kj}] = \begin{bmatrix} \beta_{11} & \beta_{12} \cdots \beta_{1G} \\ \beta_{21} & \beta_{22} & \beta_{2G} \\ \cdot & \cdot & \cdot \\ \cdot & \cdot & \cdot \\ \cdot & \cdot & \cdot \\ \beta_{K1} & \beta_{K2} & \beta_{KG} \end{bmatrix} \quad A = [a_{gj}] \begin{bmatrix} a_{11} & a_{12} \cdots a_{1G} \\ a_{21} & a_{22} \cdots a_{2G} \\ \cdot & \cdot & \cdot \\ \cdot & \cdot & \cdot \\ \cdot & \cdot & \cdot \\ a_{G1} & a_{G2} & a_{GG} \end{bmatrix} \qquad \textbf{4.11}$$

Note that A is square and that Y and U are of the same order $(T \times G)$ because of the completeness of the system.

Using these matrices, we can write equation 4.8 for all pairs (g, j) in the following compact form:

$$YA + XB = U \qquad \textbf{4.12}$$

For example, the simple model becomes

$$\begin{bmatrix} C_1 & I_1 \\ C_2 & I_2 \\ \cdot & \cdot \\ \cdot & \cdot \\ \cdot & \cdot \\ C_T & I_T \end{bmatrix} \begin{bmatrix} 1 & 1 \\ -\beta & -1 \end{bmatrix} + \begin{bmatrix} G_1 \\ G_2 \\ \cdot \\ \cdot \\ \cdot \\ G_T \end{bmatrix} [0\ 1] = \begin{bmatrix} U_1 & 0 \\ U_2 & 0 \\ \cdot & \cdot \\ \cdot & \cdot \\ \cdot & \cdot \\ U_T & 0 \end{bmatrix} \qquad \textbf{4.13}$$

If we take any row (say, the tth) of such a matrix equation, we obtain all G structural equations corresponding to the tth observation. In the general case 4.12 we then have on the left:

$$[y_{t1} \cdots y_{tG}] \begin{bmatrix} \alpha_{11} & \cdots \alpha_{1G} \\ \cdot & \cdot \\ \cdot & \cdot \\ \cdot & \cdot \\ \alpha_{G1} & \alpha_{GG} \end{bmatrix} + [x_{t1} \cdots x_{tK}] \begin{bmatrix} \beta_{11} & \cdots \beta_{1G} \\ \cdot & \cdot \\ \cdot & \cdot \\ \cdot & \cdot \\ \beta_{K1} & \beta_{KG} \end{bmatrix}$$

and on the right $[u_{t_1} \cdots u_{tG}]$. Note that the second subscript of the elements of B, A, and U is the number of the structural equation. Similarly, if we take any column (say, the jth) of the matrix equation 4.12, we obtain the jth structural equation for all T observations:

$$
\begin{bmatrix} y_{11} \cdots y_{1G} \\ \cdot \quad \cdot \\ \cdot \quad \cdot \\ \cdot \quad \cdot \\ y_{T1} \cdots y_{TG} \end{bmatrix}
\begin{bmatrix} a_{1j} \\ \cdot \\ \cdot \\ \cdot \\ a_{Gj} \end{bmatrix}
+
\begin{bmatrix} x_{11} \cdots x_{1K} \\ \cdot \quad \cdot \\ \cdot \quad \cdot \\ \cdot \quad \cdot \\ x_{T1} \quad x_{TK} \end{bmatrix}
\begin{bmatrix} \beta_{ij} \\ \cdot \\ \cdot \\ \cdot \\ \beta_{Kj} \end{bmatrix}
=
\begin{bmatrix} u_{ij} \\ \cdot \\ \cdot \\ \cdot \\ u_{Tj} \end{bmatrix}
$$

The matrix A is square because there are as many equations as jointly dependent variables. It is assumed to be non-singular, so that the system can be solved for these variables:

$$ Y = -XBA^{-1} + UA^{-1} \qquad\qquad 4.14 $$

This is the reduced form for all T observations and all G jointly dependent variables.

Means, variances, and covariances of disturbances

The assumptions on the disturbance moments of the first and second order are now discussed. The expectations are supposed to vanish:

$$ E(U_j) = 0 \qquad j = 1, \ldots, G \qquad\qquad 4.15 $$

where U_j is the jth column of the disturbance matrix U or, equivalently, the T-element disturbance vector of the jth structural equation. All lagged covariances, $E(U_{\alpha j}U_{tg})$ for $\alpha \neq t$ are assumed to vanish and all contemporaneous covariances, $E(U_{\alpha j}U_{\alpha g})$, are supposed to be constant in the sense of being independent of α. We will write σ_{jg} for the covariance of $U_{\alpha j}$ and $U_{\alpha g}$, so that the disturbance variance of the jth structural equation is written σ_{jj}. The assumption on the second moments can then be compactly written as

$$ E(U_j U_g') = \sigma_{jg} I_T \qquad j, g = 1, \ldots, G \qquad\qquad 4.16 $$

The left-hand side contains the contemporaneous covariances $E(U_{\alpha j}U_{\alpha g})$ on the diagonal and the right-hand side indicates that these are all equal to σ_{jg}. The off-diagonal elements on the left are all covariances which are not contemporaneous and, therefore, are equal to zero as $\sigma_{jg}I$ on the right confirms.

The σ's defined in 4.10 can be arranged in matrix form:

$$ V = [\sigma_{jg}] = \begin{bmatrix} \sigma_{11} & \sigma_{12} \cdots \sigma_{1G} \\ \sigma_{21} & \sigma_{22} & \sigma_{2G} \\ \cdot & \cdot & \cdot \\ \cdot & \cdot & \cdot \\ \cdot & \cdot & \cdot \\ \sigma_{G1} & \sigma_{G2} & \sigma_{GG} \end{bmatrix} \qquad\qquad 4.17 $$

which is the covariance matrix of $[U_{\alpha 1} \ldots U_{\alpha G}]$ for any value of α, as is easily verified. Therefore, V is symmetric and positive semi-definite. Notice that if we include an identity as in our example V would be singular.

Exercises to section 4.2

1. Let $[U_{t1}, \ldots, U_{tG}]$ be the error corresponding to the tth observations. What is its mean and covariance matrix? If we considered the error of the reduced-form corresponding to the tth observations $[U'_{t1}, \ldots, U'_{tG}]$, what would be its mean and covariance matrix?
2. We are given the model $C_t = \beta_1 + \beta_2 I_t + U_{t1}, I_t = \alpha_1 + \alpha_2 C_{t-1} + U_{t2}$, where C_t and I_t are defined in the text:
   (a) Write this model in the notation of the section;
   (b) Find the reduced form.
3. In the example in the section find the reduced form if I_t is exogenous.

4.3   THE NORMAL DISTRIBUTION

This distribution is of fundamental importance in econometric theory, and is constantly used by economists to model stochastic behaviour because of its mathematical tractability.

The distribution is characterised by two sets of parameters, the mean vector, which we shall denote by μ, and the covariance matrix for which we shall use the symbol V. We shall use the notation $y \sim N(\mu, V)$ to mean that the vector of random variables y is normally distributed with mean μ and covariance matrix V.

The multivariate normal distribution

The density function of $y \sim N(\mu, V)$ is defined to be $f(y)$ where

$$f(y) = \left(\frac{1}{2\pi}\right)^{T/2} \frac{1}{|V|^{1/2}} [\exp(-\tfrac{1}{2}(y - \mu)' V^{-1}(y - \mu))] \qquad \textbf{4.18}$$

The parameters are T, μ, and V, where T is the sample size or number of observations. We can see from 4.18 that knowledge of μ and V is equivalent to knowing $f(y)$.

We can prove using multivariate integration that any subset of y will also be multivariate normal. Let $y = \begin{pmatrix} y_1 \\ y_2 \end{pmatrix}$ where y_1 is the subset of interest. We partition $E(y) = \begin{pmatrix} \mu_1 \\ \mu_2 \end{pmatrix}$ and partition $\text{cov}(Y)$ as

$$\text{cov}(y) = \begin{bmatrix} V_{11} & V_{12} \\ V_{21} & V_{22} \end{bmatrix} = V$$

conformably. Then the marginal distribution of $y_1 \sim N(\mu_1, V_{11})$, from this we can deduce the following result.

Theorem 4.1

A linear combination of normal variables is itself normal.

Proof. We wish to show that $Z_1 = a_1 y_1 + a_2 y_2 + \ldots + a_T y_T$ is normally distributed. We write this in vector notation as $Z_1 = a' y$, where

$$a = \begin{pmatrix} a_1 \\ \cdot \\ \cdot \\ \cdot \\ a_T \end{pmatrix} \quad y = \begin{pmatrix} y_1 \\ \cdot \\ \cdot \\ \cdot \\ y_T \end{pmatrix}$$

and a_i are all constants.

Consider any $T \times (T-1)$ matrix A such that $B = [a, A]$ is non-singular. Let $Z = By$ then $y = B^{-1} Z$ and substituting into 4.18 gives us $f(Z)$ as

$$f(Z) = \left(\frac{1}{2\pi}\right)^{T/2} \frac{|V|^{-1/2}}{|B|} \exp[-\tfrac{1}{2}(B^{-1} Z - \mu)' V^{-1}(B^{-1} Z - \mu)] \qquad 4.19$$

As in the exercise to Chapter 3, we can arrange this to obtain

$$f(Z) = \left(\frac{1}{2\pi}\right)^{T/2} |BVB'|^{-1/2} \exp[-\tfrac{1}{2}(Z - B\mu)'(BVB')^{-1}(Z - B\mu)] \qquad 4.20$$

Thus we see that

$$Z \sim N(B\mu, BVB') \qquad\qquad \text{QED}$$

From the previous paragraph we see that the marginal distribution of Z_1 is normal. Further, $E(Z_1) = a'\mu$, $\text{cov}(Z_1) = a'Va$, This generalises to the following result.

Let C be an $r \times T$ matrix. Then

$$Cy \sim N(C\mu, CVC') \qquad\qquad 4.21$$

The bivariate normal distribution

It is easier to understand the properties of the normal distribution if we consider the special case of two variables, y_1 and y_2. Then $\mu = \begin{bmatrix} \mu_1 \\ \mu_2 \end{bmatrix}$ and $V = \begin{bmatrix} \sigma_{11} & \sigma_{12} \\ \sigma_{12} & \sigma_{22} \end{bmatrix}$. It is convenient to reparametrise V. Since we define the correlation coefficient ρ by

$$\rho^2 = \frac{\sigma_{12}^2}{\sigma_{11}\sigma_{22}}, \text{we replace } \sigma_{12} \text{ by } \rho\sqrt{\sigma_{11}}\sqrt{\sigma_{22}}. \text{ Note that } |\rho| \le 1. \text{ Using our formula for 4.18,}$$

we see that

$$f(y_1, y_2) = \frac{\xi}{2\pi\sqrt{(1-\rho^2)}\sigma_{11}\sigma_{22}}$$

$$\text{4.22}$$

$$\xi = \exp\left\{-\tfrac{1}{2}\left[\frac{\sigma_{22}(y_1-\mu_1)^2 - 2\rho\sigma_{11}\sigma_{22}(y_1-\mu_1)(y_2-\mu_2) + \sigma_{11}(y_2-\mu_2)^2}{(1-\rho^2)\sigma_{11}\sigma_{22}}\right]\right\}$$

The Conditional Density of y_1 given y_2

Since

$$f(y_2) = \frac{1}{\sqrt{2\pi}\sqrt{\sigma_{22}}}\exp\{-\tfrac{1}{2}(y_2-\mu_2)^2/\sigma_{22}\} \qquad \text{4.23}$$

we can derive the conditional density of y_1 given y_2 using 4.22 and 4.23.

Now
$$f(y_1/y_2) = f(y_1, y_2)/f(y_2)$$

$$= \frac{1}{\sqrt{2\pi}\sqrt{1-\rho^2}\sqrt{\sigma_{11}}}\exp\left(-\tfrac{1}{2}\frac{1}{\sigma_{11}(1-\rho^2)}\left(y_1-\mu_1-\frac{\rho\sigma_{11}}{\sigma_{22}}(y_2-\mu_2)\right)^2\right) \quad \text{4.24}$$

(See Exercise 1 to this section.)
We see that 4.24 is of the same form as 4.18 so that we have shown that

$$y_1(\text{given } y_2) \sim N\left(\mu_1 + \rho\frac{\sqrt{\sigma_{11}}}{\sqrt{\sigma_{22}}}(y_2-\mu_2), \sigma_{11}(1-\rho^2)\right)$$

This formula is full of intuitive content, that is, if $\rho = 0$, $y_1 \sim N(\mu_1, \sigma_{11})$ hence $f(y_1/y_2) = f(y_1)$ and y_1 and y_2 are independent. Also as ρ increases $\sigma_{11}(1-\rho^2)$ decreases; that is, the more dependent y_1 is on y_2 the more y_1 will be fixed if y_2 is fixed so that the variance of y_1 will decrease.

The regression model

We consider the familiar multivariate regression model

$$y = X\beta + U \qquad \text{4.25}$$

where X is a $T \times K$ matrix of fixed (non-stochastic) numbers of rank K and β is a $K \times 1$ vector of parameters. We assume that $U \sim N(0, \sigma^2 I_T)$ where I_T is the $T \times T$ diagonal matrix, so $y \sim N(X\beta, \sigma^2 I_T)$ and we could write down the density function of y.

An alternative weaker assumption about the model 4.25 is that X and U are jointly normal and independent; we shall illustrate this for $K = 1$. We assume

$$\begin{pmatrix} x_t \\ U_t \end{pmatrix} \sim N\left(\begin{pmatrix} \mu_x \\ 0 \end{pmatrix}, \begin{bmatrix} \sigma_x^2 & 0 \\ 0 & \sigma^2 \end{bmatrix} \right)$$

If each observation is independent of the other, then,

$$\text{cov}(y_t, x_t) = \sigma_x^2 \qquad\qquad \textbf{4.26}$$

(See Exercise 8 to this section.)

Moreover
$$E(y_t/x_t) = \mu\beta + \frac{\sigma_x \cdot \sigma \beta (x_t - \mu)}{\sigma_x \cdot \sigma}$$

$$= x_t \beta$$

Thus the model 4.25 can be interpreted as $y_t = E(y_t/x_t) + U_t$.

Likelihood function

Given the model 4.25, it is often of interest to write down the joint density of $(y_1, \ldots, y_T)'$.
This becomes

$$f(y) = \left(\frac{1}{2\pi\sigma^2} \right)^{T/2} \exp\left[-\left(\frac{(y - X\beta)'(y - X\beta)}{2\sigma^2} \right) \right] \qquad\qquad \textbf{4.27}$$

upon simplification. We can give 4.27 a different interpretation. Let us fix y and X (if X is not already fixed) and regard $f(y)$ as a function of β and σ^2. We shall then write it as $L = f(y, \beta, \sigma^2)$. This function is called the *likelihood function*. Intuitively the value of β and σ^2 that maximises L should be a good choice as an estimate of β and σ^2 since it is the 'most likely' in some vague sense. However, the value of $\theta = (\beta, \sigma^2)'$ that maximises L will be the same value θ that maximises $\log L$ (see Exercise 9) so that we choose θ to maximise

$$\log L = -\frac{T}{2} \log(2\pi\sigma^2) - \frac{(y - X\beta)'(y - X\beta)}{2\sigma^2}$$

We differentiate with respect to β and σ^2,

$$\frac{\partial \log L}{\partial \sigma^2} = -\frac{T}{\sigma^2} + \frac{(y - X\beta)'(y - X\beta)}{2\sigma^4}$$

$$\textbf{4.28}$$

$$\frac{\partial \log L}{\partial \beta} = \frac{X'(y - X\beta)X}{\sigma^2}$$

We set 4.28 equal to zero and denote the solutions by $\hat{\theta} = (\hat{\beta}, \hat{\sigma}^2)'$. Then

$$X'y = X'X\hat{\beta}$$

$$T = (y - X\hat{\beta})'(y - X\hat{\beta})/\hat{\sigma}^2$$

so that

$$\hat{\beta} = (X'X)^{-1}X'y$$

and

$$\hat{\sigma}^2 = (y - X\hat{\beta})'(y - X\hat{\beta})/T \qquad \textbf{4.29}$$

are the maximum likelihood estimators (MLEs) of θ. Note that $\hat{\beta}$ is the same as the OLS estimator of β.

Identification of parameters

We say that a parameter is identified if it can be deduced uniquely from the likelihood function. In the case of the model $N(\mu, V)$, knowledge of L implies knowledge of μ and V. However, for the regression model, knowledge of $N(X\beta, \sigma^2 I_T)$ implies that we can deduce σ^2 uniquely and $E(y) = X\beta$. However, we will not be able to deduce β uniquely unless the column rank of X is K and $T \geq K$. These are the conditions for identification. As an example consider

$$y_t = X_{t1}\beta_1 + X_{t2}\beta_2 + U_t$$

where $X_{t1} = X_{t2}, t = 1, \ldots, T$.
Then $y_t = X_{t1}(\beta_1 + \beta_2) + U_t$. Knowledge of $E(y_t)$ will allow us to deduce $\beta_1 + \beta_2$ but not β_1 and β_2 individually.

Exercises to section 4.3

1. Prove formula 4.24 in the text.
2. In 4.29 we showed that $\hat{\beta} = (X'X)^{-1}X'y$ is the MLE of β. Find the density function of $\hat{\beta}$. (Hint, use the result 4.21.)
3. How does 4.18 reduce if:
   (a) y_t are independent $N(\mu, \sigma^2)$;
   (b) y_t are independent $N(0, \sigma^2)$?
4. Show 4.22 to be true using 4.18.

5. Calculate $E(y/x)$ where $\begin{pmatrix} y \\ x \end{pmatrix} \sim N\left(\begin{pmatrix} 2 \\ 3 \end{pmatrix}, \begin{bmatrix} 5 & 2 \\ 2 & 4 \end{bmatrix} \right)$.

6. Find the distribution of $4y_1 - 3y_2$ if $\begin{pmatrix} y_1 \\ y_2 \end{pmatrix} \sim N\left(\begin{pmatrix} 0 \\ 1 \end{pmatrix}, \begin{pmatrix} 2 & 1 \\ 1 & 2 \end{pmatrix} \right)$.

7. Prove that

$$E(y_t) = E_x(E_y(y_t/x_t))$$

(where E_y means expectation with respect to y etc.) for the regression model $y_t = x_t\beta + U_t$.
8. Prove the result in 4.26.
9. Show that if x maximises $L(x)$, then it maximises $\log L(x)$ and conversely.

4.4 EXPECTATIONS IN ECONOMICS

Frequently in economic models terms occur that are equal to the expectations of random variables. For instance the so-called 'classical' aggregate supply function states that the deviation from normal output y_t depends upon the difference between the actual price p_t and the price expected to occur at time t, given the information up to and including period $t - 1$. We write this as

$$y_t = \alpha(p_t - p^*_{t,t-1}) + \mu_t$$

We can model $p^*_{t,t-1}$ in various ways. One is to assume that price expectations are *adaptive*. That is, we weight our current expectation by a linear combination of last period's price plus the error made in the last period. We write this as

$$p^*_{t,t-1} = (1 - \theta)p_{t-1} + \theta(p_{t-1} - p^*_{t-1,t-2}), \text{ for } \theta \in [0, 1] \qquad \textbf{4.30}$$

This is one approach to the problem of specifying a behavioural relationship which allows us to substitute for an unobservable variable such as $p_{t,t-1}$. If we write 4.30 in lag notation,

$$(1 - \theta L)p^*_{t,t-1} = p_{t-1}$$

so that

$$p^*_{t,t-1} = \frac{1}{1 - \theta L}(p_{t-1})$$

$$p^*_{t,t-1} = \sum_{i=0}^{\infty} \theta^i p_{t-1-i} \qquad \textbf{4.31}$$

An alternative approach is to assume that p_t is generated by some ARMA process, say $a(L)p_t = b(L)v_t$, and then assume that $p^*_{t,t-1} = E(p_t/p_{t-1}, p_{t-2}, \ldots)$. In this approach favoured by the rational expectations school of macro-economists, we set our expectation equal to the conditional expectation of the full model. This need not differ from adaptive expectations since adaptive expectations could be rational under some circumstances.

In our model we now assume that

$$p_t = \gamma p_{t-1} + v_t$$

where $v_t \sim I(0, \sigma_v^2)$ and u_t and v_s are independent for all t and s. Since p_{t-1} is independent of v_t, $E(p_t/p_{t-1}, p_{t-2}, \ldots) = \gamma p_{t-1}$. So that if we set $E(p_t/p_{t-1}, p_{t-2}, \ldots) = p^*_{t,t-1}$ which is the rational expectations hypothesis, we see that our supply function becomes, in terms of observable variables,

$$y_t = \alpha(p_t - \gamma p_{t-1}) + u_t$$
$$= \alpha p_t - \alpha\gamma p_{t-1} + u_t \qquad \textbf{4.32}$$

Thus α and γ can be estimated.

A question of interest is the following. Can we assume a certain data-generating process for p_t that guarantees that the adaptive expectations mechanism of 4.30 is rational? This is equivalent to the condition

$$E(p_t/p_{t-1}, p_{t-2}, \ldots) = \frac{1}{1 - \theta L} p_{t-1} \qquad \textbf{4.33}$$

This condition will be satisfied by a variety of models, including for example

$$p_t = \frac{1}{1 - \theta L} p_{t-1} + u_t$$

This can be written as

$$p_t - \theta p_{t-1} = p_{t-1} + u_t - \theta u_{t-1}$$
$$p_t = (1 - \theta) p_{t-1} + u_t - \theta u_{t-1}$$

Exercises to section 4.4

1. Suppose that

$$\log\left(\frac{M}{P}\right)_t = \alpha + \beta \pi_t + V_t \qquad \textbf{4.34}$$

where M is demand for nominal money balances, P is the price level, π_t is expected inflation at time t, and $\beta < 0$. This is Cagan's (1956) demand function for real money balances. Cagan assumed that

$$\pi_t = \frac{(1 - \lambda)}{(1 - \lambda L)} X_t \qquad \textbf{4.35}$$

where $0 \leq \lambda < 1$ and X_t is equal to $\log(P_t) - \log(P_{t-1})$, the actual rate of inflation. Show that 4.35 is an adaptive expectations mechanism. Rewrite 4.34 in terms of observable variables.
2. Take first differences of 4.34 in Exercise 1. Let $\mu_t = \log M_t - \log M_{t-1}$, the growth rate of money. Derive an expression for X_t in terms of μ_t and V_t.

4.5 SIMULTANEOUS EQUATION MODELS AND CONDITIONAL EXPECTATIONS

Introduction

Previously in the multivariate linear regression model, we noted that $y_t = x_t \beta + U_t$ can be estimated by least squares and that the estimators are unbiased. We also in section 4.3 gave an interpretation of this for the case where x_t and U_t are bivariate independent normal, and $E(y_t/x_t) = x_t\beta$. We now examine the general case where U_t and x_t are bivariate normal. For simplicity

$$\begin{pmatrix} x_t \\ U_t \end{pmatrix} \sim N\left[\begin{pmatrix} 0 \\ 0 \end{pmatrix}, \begin{pmatrix} \sigma_x^2 & \rho\sigma_x\sigma_u \\ \rho\sigma_x\sigma_u & \sigma_u^2 \end{pmatrix} \right]$$

Then we see that $E(y_t/x_t) = (\beta + \rho\sigma_u/\sigma_x)x_t$. We can use this result to determine the expected value of

$$\hat{\beta} = \frac{\sum x_t y_t}{\sum x_t^2}$$

the OLS estimator of β. We do this by using the formula $E(\theta) = E_x E(\hat{\theta}/x)$. (See Exercise 7, in section 4.3.) Firstly,

$$E(\hat{\beta}/x_1, \ldots, x_T) = \frac{\sum x_t \left(\beta + \frac{\rho\sigma_u}{\sigma_x} \right) x_t}{\sum x_t^2}$$

and so

$$E(\hat{\beta}/x_1, \ldots, x_T) = \beta + \frac{\rho\sigma_u}{\sigma_x}$$

Therefore,

$$E(\hat{\beta}) = E(E(\hat{\beta}/x_1, \ldots, x_T))$$

$$= \beta + \frac{\rho\sigma_u}{\sigma_x}$$

so that $\hat{\beta}$ is an unbiased estimator if $\rho = 0$, that is, if x_t and U_t are independent. In the simultaneous equation model the right-hand side variables are correlated with the error term and hence with the left-hand side variable. This suggests that OLS will give biased estimators in SEM models and that this should occur when the right-hand side cannot be interpreted as a conditional expectation. We should be careful in extending this argument to the case $y_t = \alpha y_{t-1} + U_t$. In this case if y_0 is known y_{t-1} is determined completely by previous values of the error term so that it is not meaningful to consider a bivariate distribution. The other assumption that is violated in this context is serial independence. We assumed in our argument that $\begin{pmatrix} x_t \\ U_t \end{pmatrix}$ is a serially independent vector. Clearly y_{t-1} is not independent of y_{t-2}.

Identification in the simultaneous equation model

We previously defined a parameter of a model as being identified if we could deduce it uniquely from a knowledge of the likelihood function of the model. We consider a linear model like that described in section 4.2 and first calculate its likelihood function assuming normality.

Theorem 4.2

The likelihood function of the model YA + XB = U is

$$(2\pi)^{-GT/2}|V|^{-T/2}||A||^T \exp(-\tfrac{1}{2}(\text{trace }[V^{-1}(YA + XB)'(YA + XB)]))$$

i.e.

$$(2\pi)^{-GT/2}|\Omega|^{-T/2} \exp(-\tfrac{1}{2}(\text{trace}[\Omega^{-1}(Y - X\Pi)'(Y - X\Pi)]))$$

where $\Omega = A^{-1}{'}\wedge A^{-1}$ and $\Pi = -BA^{-1}$. (Note that $||A||$ means the absolute value of the determinant of A.)

Proof. Consider the tth observation of the model, $Y_tA + X_tB = U_t$. (Here we use Y_t, X_t to refer to the tth row of the Y, X matrices.) Since U_t' is distributed as $N(0, V)$, its likelihood function is

$$(2\pi)^{-G/2}|V|^{-1/2} \exp(-\tfrac{1}{2}U_t.V^{-1}U_t'.)$$

Now in order to make the transformation from $U_t.$ to $Y_t.$, note that

$$\frac{\partial U_{ti}}{\partial Y_{tj}} = A_{ji}$$

in light of the fact that $U_t = -Y_tA - X_tB$. Therefore the absolute value of the determinant of Jacobian of the transformation is

$$\left|\left|\frac{\partial U_{ti}}{\partial Y_{tj}} i,j = 1,2,\ldots,G\right|\right| = ||-A'|| = ||A||$$

Therefore the likelihood function associated with the tth observation can be written

$$(2\pi)^{-G/2}|V|^{-1/2}||A|| \exp(-\tfrac{1}{2}(Y_tA + X_tB)V^{-1}(Y_tA + X_tB)')$$

For all T observations on the model, the likelihood function is just the product of these 'individual' likelihood functions, assuming serial independence, that is:

$$(2\pi)^{-GT/2}|V|^{-T/2}||A||^T \exp\left(-\tfrac{1}{2}\sum_{t=1}^{T}(Y_tA + X_tB)V^{-1}(Y_tA + X_tB)'\right)$$

$$= (2\pi)^{-GT/2}|V|^{-T/2}||A||^T \exp(-\tfrac{1}{2}\text{trace }[(YA + XB)V^{-1}YA + XB)'])$$

$$= (2\pi)^{-GT/2}|V|^{-T/2}||A||^T \exp(-\tfrac{1}{2}\text{trace}[V^{-1}(YA + XB)'(YA + XB)])$$

This proves the first part of the theorem.

To show that the second expression in the statement of the theorem is indeed equivalent to the first, note that

$$|\Omega| = |(A^{-1})'VA^{-1}| = |V|||A||^{-2}$$

so that

$$|\Omega|^{-T/2} = |V|^{-T/2}||A||^T$$

or

trace $(\Omega^{-1}(Y - X\Pi)'(Y - X\Pi))$

$\quad = $ trace $((Y - X\Pi)\Omega^{-1}(Y - X\Pi)')$

$\quad = $ trace $((Y + XBA^{-1})(AV^{-1}A')(Y + XBA^{-1})')$

$\quad = $ trace $((YA + XB)V^{-1}(YA + XB)')$

$\quad = $ trace $(V^{-1}(YA + XB)'(YA + XB))$.

From these substitutions, the two expressions in the statement of the theorem are seen to be equivalent.   QED

From the model of the theorem we see immediately that Π and Ω are identified and so the identification problem is based upon whether we can deduce A, B, and V from Π and Ω. Since $\Pi = -BA'$ and $\Omega = (A^{-1})'VA^{-1}$, we see that if we can deduce B and A from Π then V will be automatically identified so that we concentrate on the first of these problems and do not discuss the second. Our interest, however, is really with the identification of the parameters of a single equation, in the next section we discuss why this is important.

The economics of identification

Historically, single-equation identification grew out of a single market problem. Suppose we have a single market in equilibrium where quantity supplied equals quantity demanded and both are a function of price only, then can the observations of annual prices and quantities give us any information about our demand and supply curves? The answer is no! Our system is

$$p_t = a_1 + b_1 q_{dt} + u_{1t_1}$$

$$p_t = a_2 + b_2 q_{st} + u_{2t_2}$$

$$q_{dt} = q_{st} = \bar{q}_t$$

where the notation is obvious. In our terminology p_t, q_{dt} and q_{st} are endogenous variables, $\bar{q}_t = q_{dt} = q_{st}$ is an identity reducing the number to 2 and the constant term is

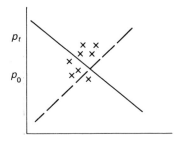

Figure 4.1

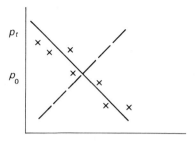

Figure 4.2

a single exogenous variable. The pairs $(p_t, \bar{q}_t)$ represent points around the deterministic equilibrium (p_0, q_0). (See Figure 4.1.)

If we now assume that q_{st} depends upon weather forecasts w_t, whilst q_{dt} does not, then our new system will be, after eliminating the identity,

$$p_t = a_1 + b_1 \bar{q}_t + u_{1t}$$

$$p_t = a_2 + b_2 \bar{q}_t + b_3 w_t + u_{2t}.$$

Assuming variation in weather forecasts, the new equilibria $(p_t, \bar{q}_t)$ will trace out a curve as w_t varies. (See Figure 4.2.) Thus we see that the presence of extra information in the supply curve allows us to plot out our demand curve. We can put this another way. If we know constraints on the demand curve, such as that the coefficient of weather in the demand function is zero, then these constraints will lead to the identi-fication of the demand function.

Single-equation identification

We consider the ith equation which without loss of generality can be the first.

We define the matrix $\theta = \begin{pmatrix} A \\ B \end{pmatrix}$, the parameters of the first equation are where given by the column $\theta_{.1}$. We can write $Z = (Y, X)$, then a notation for the first equation is $Z\theta_{.1} = U_{.1}$ where Z is $T \times (G + K)$. The parameters for the first equation may be subject to R linear homogeneous restrictions, of the form $\phi\theta_{.1} = 0$ where ϕ is an $R \times (G + K)$ matrix of known constants.

Example 4.1

If $G = 3$ and $K = 2$, suppose the first equation is $y_{t1} = a_{21}(y_{t2} - y_{t3}) + B_{11}x_{t1} + u_{t1}$. Then the restrictions are

$$a_{11} = -1, B_{21} = 0$$

$$a_{21} + a_{31} = 0$$

The first restriction is the normalisation which we shall temporarily ignore. The other two restrictions can be written as

$$
\begin{bmatrix} 0 & 1 & 1 & 0 & 0 \\ 0 & 0 & 0 & 0 & 1 \end{bmatrix}
\begin{bmatrix} a_{11} \\ a_{21} \\ a_{31} \\ B_{11} \\ B_{21} \end{bmatrix}
=
\begin{bmatrix} 0 \\ 0 \end{bmatrix}
$$

where ϕ is 2×5 matrix

$$
\begin{bmatrix} 0 & 1 & 1 & 0 & 0 \\ 0 & 0 & 0 & 0 & 1 \end{bmatrix}
$$

Theorem 4.3

A necessary and sufficient condition for the identification of the first equation under the restrictions $\phi \theta_{.1} = 0$ is

$$
\text{rank} \begin{bmatrix} \pi, I_K \\ \phi \end{bmatrix} = G + K - 1
$$

Proof. All possible observational information is contained in the reduced-form parameters. Since we are assuming that there is no *a priori* knowledge of V, all that is available is the knowledge that $\Pi A = -B$ or $(\Pi, I)\theta = 0$ and that $\phi \theta_{.1} = 0$. That is, the available information — both *a priori* and observational — on $\theta_{.1}$ is that

$$
\begin{bmatrix} \Pi, I \\ \phi \end{bmatrix} (\theta_{.1}) = 0
$$

Hence the first equation is identified if and only if this equation can be solved for $\theta_{.1}$, and if the solution is unique up to scalar multiplication. But since $\theta_{.1}$ is of dimension $G + K$, this can be done if and only if

$$
\text{rank} \begin{pmatrix} \Pi, I \\ \phi \end{pmatrix} = G + K - 1 \qquad\qquad \text{QED}
$$

It is useful to have a simple necessary condition for identification, this is contained in the following corollary.

Corollary 4.1

Note that since the matrix

$$
\begin{bmatrix} \Pi, I \\ \phi \end{bmatrix}
$$

is of dimension $(R + K) \times (G + K)$, a necessary condition for identification is that $R \geq G - 1$.

We now prove a somewhat technical lemma

Lemma 4.1

$$\mathrm{rank}\begin{bmatrix} \Pi, \mathrm{I} \\ \phi \end{bmatrix} = \mathrm{rank}\,(\phi\theta) + K$$

Proof. We will use the fact that the rank of a matrix is not changed when the matrix is multiplied by a non-singular matrix.

$$\mathrm{rank}\begin{bmatrix} \Pi, \mathrm{I}_K \\ \phi \end{bmatrix} = \mathrm{rank}\begin{bmatrix} \Pi, \mathrm{I}_K \\ \phi \end{bmatrix}\begin{bmatrix} \mathrm{A} & 0 \\ \mathrm{B} & \mathrm{I}_K \end{bmatrix}$$

$$= \mathrm{rank}\begin{bmatrix} 0 & \mathrm{I}_K \\ \phi\theta & \mathrm{N} \end{bmatrix} \text{(where N is made up of the last } K \text{ columns of } \phi)$$

$$= \mathrm{rank}\left[\begin{pmatrix} \mathrm{I}_K & 0 \\ -\mathrm{N} & \mathrm{I}_R \end{pmatrix}\begin{pmatrix} 0 & \mathrm{I}_K \\ \phi\theta & \mathrm{N} \end{pmatrix}\right]$$

$$= \mathrm{rank}\begin{bmatrix} 0 & \mathrm{I}_K \\ \phi\theta & 0 \end{bmatrix}$$

$$= \mathrm{rank}(\phi\theta) + K \qquad\qquad \text{QED}$$

We can combine the lemma with theorem 4.3 to arrive at a more useful set of necessary and sufficient conditions. These are the following:

The first equation is identified under the restriction $\phi\theta_{.1} = 0$ if and only if

$$\mathrm{rank}(\phi\theta) = G - 1$$

We now apply our last result to the supply and demand examples. For the first case $G = 2$, $K = 1$ and there are no restrictions so that $\mathrm{rank}(\phi\theta) = 0$ but $G - 1 = 1$. For the second case with weather, our model is $p_t - a_1 - b_1\bar{q}_t = u_{t1}$

$$p_t - a_2 - b_2\bar{q}_t - b_3 w_t = u_{t2}$$

We can rewrite this system for $G = 2$ and $K = 2$. Letting $y_{.t} = (p_t, q_t)$, $x_{.t} = (1, w_t)$, we see that there are no restrictions on the second equation, the supply function, but there is one restriction on the demand function of the form $\phi = (0 \ 0 \ 0 \ 1)$ and $\phi\theta = [0, -b_3]$. The rank of $\phi\theta$ is 1 if b_3 is not equal to zero so that the demand function is identified.

Lastly we should define three terms frequently used to describe linear economic models. We say that an equation is *over-identified* if $\mathrm{rank}(\phi\theta) = G - 1$ and $\mathrm{rank}(\phi) > G - 1$. We say it is *just identified* if $\mathrm{rank}(\phi\theta) = G - 1$ and $\mathrm{rank}(\phi) = G - 1$ and if $\mathrm{rank}\,(\phi\theta) < G - 1$ we say that the equation is *under-identified*.

Exercises to section 4.5

1. Check the identification of the model in Chapter 5, particularly equations 22', 15', and 27'.
2. Give an example of an equation which is not identified but satisfies the order condition given in corollary 4.1.
3. If

$$A = \begin{pmatrix} a_{11} & 0 & 0 \\ a_{21} & a_{22} & 0 \\ a_{31} & a_{32} & a_{33} \end{pmatrix}, \quad B = \begin{pmatrix} b_{11} & 0 & b_{31} \\ b_{21} & b_{22} & b_{32} \end{pmatrix},$$

describe the system being discussed. Also discuss whether the equations in this system are over, under, or just identified.

4.6   ESTIMATION

We now consider the case of estimation in the single-equation model $y_{t1} = Y_{t1}\alpha + X_{t1}\beta + U_{t1}$ where we have imposed the identifying restrictions and Y_{t1} and X_{t1} refer to the g_1 endogenous and K_1 exogenous variables in the first equation. The procedure is described in many texts and so our treatment is fairly cursory. We note from the previous sections that $E(y_{t1}/Y_{t1}, X_{t1}) \neq Y_{t1}\alpha + X_{t1}\beta$ so that OLS will not lead to unbiased estimation. In fact for this model we cannot hope to achieve unbiased estimators, the best we can hope for is consistent estimators. We shall digress to discuss consistency.

Consistency

We define $\hat{\theta}_T$ to be a *consistent* estimator of θ if, given $\varepsilon > 0$, $\lim_{T \to \infty} P\{|\hat{\theta}_T - \theta| < \varepsilon\} = 1$.

As the number of observations increases the probability that our estimator is 'very close' to the true parameter value tends to 1. See the discussion in section 3.8 of the previous chapter. We now show that *r-consistency* implies consistency (in probability) by using the following inequality due to Chebyshev (see section 1.8 of Chapter 1).

Theorem 4.4 (Chebyshev's theorem)

If $x \sim (\mu, \sigma)$ then $P\{|x - \mu| \geq k\sigma\} \leq \dfrac{1}{k^2}$.

Proof. This argument can be generalised.

$$\sigma^2 = \int_{-\infty}^{\infty} (x - \mu)^2 \, \partial F(x) \quad \text{by definition.}$$

$$= \int_{(x-\mu) \geq k\sigma} (x - \mu)^2 \, \partial F(x) + \int_{(x-\mu) < k\sigma} (x - \mu)^2 \, \partial F$$

$$\geq \int_{(x-\mu) \geq k\sigma} (x - \mu)^2 \, \partial F(x)$$

$$\geq k^2 \sigma^2 \int_{|x-\mu| \geq k\sigma} \partial F(x)$$

$$\therefore \mathrm{P}\{|x - \mu| \geq k\sigma\} \leq \sigma^2 / k^2 \sigma^2 = \frac{1}{k^2} \qquad \text{QED}$$

Theorem 4.5

If $\hat{\theta}_T$ is an estimator of θ such that $\mathrm{E}(\hat{\theta}_T) = \theta$ *and* $\lim_{T \to \infty} \mathrm{V}(\hat{\theta}_T) = 0$ then $\hat{\theta}_T$ is a consistent estimator of θ.

Proof. By Chebyshev's inequality, putting $\theta = \mathrm{E}(\hat{\theta}_T)$ and $\varepsilon = k\sqrt{\mathrm{V}(\hat{\theta}_T)}$,

$$\mathrm{P}\{|\hat{\theta}_T - \theta| \geq \varepsilon\} \leq \frac{1}{k^2} = \frac{\mathrm{V}(\hat{\theta}_T)}{\varepsilon^2}$$

so that $\lim_{T \to \infty} \mathrm{P}\{|\hat{\theta}_T - \theta| > \varepsilon\} \leq \lim_{T \to \infty} \mathrm{V}(\hat{\theta}_T)/\varepsilon^2 = 0.$

Hence $\lim_{T \to \infty} \mathrm{P}\{|\hat{\theta}_T - \theta| < \varepsilon\} = 1$ and $\hat{\theta}_T$ is a consistent estimator of θ.

Example 4.2. In the regression $y_t = \beta + U_t$, $U_t \sim \mathrm{I}(0, \sigma^2)$ $\hat{\beta}_{\mathrm{OLS}} = \sum_{t=1}^{T} y_t/T$ and $\mathrm{E}(\hat{\beta}) =$ $\beta, \mathrm{V}(\hat{\beta}) = \sigma^2/T$ so that the conditions of theorem 4.5 are satisfied and $\hat{\beta}$ is a consistent estimator of β.

As before write plim $\hat{\beta} = \beta$ if $\hat{\beta}$ is a consistent estimator of β. We shall now prove that the plim of a *continuous* function is a continuous function of the plim.

Theorem 4.6

If $\hat{\theta}_T$ is a vector estimator such that plim $\hat{\theta}_T = \theta$, then plim $g(\hat{\theta}_T) = g(\theta)$ where g is a real-valued function continuous in the neighbourhood of θ.

Proof plim $\hat{\theta}_T = \theta$ implies that given $\varepsilon > 0$ $\lim_{T \to \infty} P\{||\hat{\theta}_T - \theta|| < \varepsilon\} = 1$ where $||..||$

is the vector distance. Also $g(\theta_T)$ is continuous at θ if given $\varepsilon > 0$ we can find $\delta > 0$ such that $||\hat{\theta}_T - \theta|| < \delta$ implies that $|g(\hat{\theta}_T) - g(\theta)| < \varepsilon$. Therefore $P\{|g(\hat{\theta}_T) - g(\theta)| < \varepsilon\} \geq P\{||\hat{\theta}_T - \theta|| < \delta\}$ if g is continuous at θ. Then $\lim_{T \to \infty} P\{|g(\hat{\theta}_T) - g(\theta)| < \varepsilon\} \geq$

$\lim_{T \to \infty} P\{||\hat{\theta}_T - \theta|| < \delta = 1$ since $\hat{\theta}_T$ is consistent. We have shown that plim $g(\hat{\theta}_T) = g(\theta)$.

$P\{||\hat{\theta}_T - \theta|| < \delta\} = 1$ since $\hat{\theta}_T$ is consistent. We have shown that plim $g(\hat{\theta}_T) = g(\theta)$.
                                                                                                    QED

This theorem has important corrolaries, since we can choose g to be any suitable

function. Let $\hat{\theta} = \begin{pmatrix} \hat{\theta}_1 \\ \hat{\theta}_2 \end{pmatrix}$ and choose $g(\hat{\theta})$ to be either $= \hat{\theta}_1 + \hat{\theta}_2, \hat{\theta}_1 - \hat{\theta}_2, \hat{\theta}_1\hat{\theta}_2, \hat{\theta}_1/\hat{\theta}_2$. We

have shown the following result.

Corollary 4.2

The plim of the sum, difference, product or quotient is the sum, difference, product or quotient of the plims. (We need to assume that the true value of θ_2 is non-zero so that

$g(\hat{\theta}) = \dfrac{\hat{\theta}_1}{\hat{\theta}_2}$ is defined at θ.) We can also extend these results to the case of stochastic

matrices although great care must be taken as frequently the dimensions of the matrices in question are functions of T. However for the case where the dimensions are fixed and non-stochastic we can, by extensions of our theorem show that plim(CD) = plim(C)plim(D) and plim(C^{-1}) = plim (C)$^{-1}$ where C and D are stochastic matrices.

Example 4.3

In the case of the linear regression model $y_t = x_t\beta + \mu_t$

where
$$\begin{pmatrix} x_t \\ u_t \end{pmatrix} \sim \left[\begin{pmatrix} 0 \\ 0 \end{pmatrix}, \begin{pmatrix} \sigma_x^2 & p\sigma_x\sigma_u \\ p\sigma_x\sigma_u & \sigma_u^2 \end{pmatrix} \right]$$

$\text{plim}(\hat{B} - B) = \text{plim}\left(\dfrac{\sum x_t u_t}{\sum x_t^2}\right) = \text{plim}\left(\dfrac{\sum x_t u_t}{T}\right) \Big/ \text{plim}\left(\dfrac{\sum x_t^2}{T}\right)$. Now $\text{plim}\left(\dfrac{\sum x_t u_t}{T}\right) = p\sigma_x\sigma_u$

assuming that $V\left(\dfrac{\sum x_t u_t}{T}\right)$ tends to zero as T tends to infinity. This will be the case if the

fourth moments of the $\begin{pmatrix} x_t \\ u_t \end{pmatrix}$ distribution are bounded (see Exercise 1). $\text{plim}\left(\dfrac{\sum x_t^2}{T}\right) = \sigma_x^2$

under the same conditions, so that $\text{plim}(\hat{\beta} - \beta) = p\sigma_u/\sigma_x$, i.e. $\hat{\beta}$ is inconsistent in this

model. Note that if $\begin{pmatrix} x_t \\ u_t \end{pmatrix}$ are bivariate normal with the same mean and covariance as this example then the bias of $\hat{\beta}$ is equal to the asymptotic inconsistency. We now return to the problems of the single-equation estimation.

Inconsistency of OLS estimation

We re-write our equation as

$$y_t = Z_t\gamma_1 + u_{t1} \quad \text{where} \quad u_t' \sim (0, \sigma_{11}I_T)$$

$$\hat{\gamma}_1 - \gamma_1 = \left(\sum_{t=1}^{T} Z_t'Z_t\right)^{-1} \sum_{t=1}^{T} Z_t'u_{t1}$$

$$\text{plim}(\hat{\gamma}_1 - \gamma_1) = \text{plim}\left[\left(\sum_{t=1}^{T} \frac{Z_t'Z_t}{T}\right)\right]^{-1} \text{plim}\left(\sum_{t=1}^{T} \frac{Z_t'u_{t1}}{T}\right)$$

We can show that the first term is non-singular if the equation is identified (see Exercise 3). The second term is of the form $\text{plim}\left[\dfrac{\sum Y_{t1}' u_{t1}}{T}, \dfrac{\sum X_{t1}' u_{t1}}{T}\right]$. The second of these terms will have zero plim (see Exercise 4) but the first will not from the discussion in the example above, hence OLS is inconsistent as well as being biased and we need a different estimation procedure.

Two-stage least squares

We approach the problem of SEM estimation in two stages. We first consider the endogenous variables Y_{t1} on the right of the regression. Crudely what we shall do is the following:

We write $Y_{t1} = X_t\pi_1 + V_{t1}$ where X_t is the set of all exogenous variables. Then we replace Y_{t1} in our model by the term on the right so that we get

$$y_{t1} = E(X_t\pi_1)\alpha + X_{t1}\beta + u_{t1} + V_{t1}\alpha.$$

We notice that the regressors are now linear combinations of the exogenous variables and uncorrelated with the error term. In fact we do not know $E(X_t\pi_1)$ exactly so that we have to estimate it. There will be some correlation between the regressors and the error but it disappears as T tends to infinity so that we get asymptotically unbiased estimators. These in fact are consistent as well. We write the model in matrix notation,

$$Y_1 = X\pi_1 + V_1$$

and $\hat{Y} = X\hat{\pi}_1 = X(X'X)^{-1}X'Y_1$, also $Y_1 = \hat{Y}_1 + \hat{V}_1$. Then

$$y_1 = \hat{Y}_1\alpha + X_1\beta + \hat{V}_1\alpha + u_1.$$

Note that $X_1'\hat{V}_1 = \hat{Y}_1'\hat{V}_1 = 0$ since $X_1 \subset X$ and $X'\hat{V}_1 = 0$. This shows that our regressors are orthogonal to the extra term $\hat{V}_1$.

Let $\gamma = (\alpha, \beta)$ $\hat{Z}_1 = (\hat{Y}_1, X_1)$, then $\hat{\gamma}_{2SLS} = (\hat{Z}_1' \hat{Z}_1)^{-1} \hat{Z}_1' y_1$

$$\therefore \hat{\gamma}_{2SLS} = \begin{bmatrix} \hat{Y}_1' \hat{Y}_1 & \hat{Y}_1' X_1 \\ X_1' \hat{Y}_1 & X'X_1 \end{bmatrix}^{-1} \begin{bmatrix} \hat{Y}_1' y_1 \\ X_1' y_1 \end{bmatrix}$$

Firstly $\hat{Y}_1' X_1 = Y_1' X(X'X)^{-1} X' y_1$

but $X(X'X)^{-1} X' X_1 = X(X'X)^{-1} X' X(I_{k_1}, 0) = X(I_{k_1}, 0) = X_1$,

so that $\hat{Y}_1' X_1 = Y_1' X_1$.

Also $\hat{Y}_1' \hat{Y}_1 = Y_1' X(X'X)^{-1} X_1' Y_1$, $\hat{Y}_1' y_1 = Y_1' (X'X)^{-1} X' y_1$,

and $\hat{Z}_1' u_1 = (Y_1' X(X'X)^{-1} X' u_1, X' u_1)$

$\qquad = (Y_1' X(X'X)^{-1} X' u_1, X_1' X(X'X)^{-1} X' u_1)$

$\qquad = (Z_1' X(X'X)^{-1} X' u_1)$

Consistency of two stage least squares estimators

$$\text{plim}(\hat{\gamma}_{2SLS} - \gamma) = \text{plim}\left(\frac{Z_1' Z_1}{T}\right)^{-1} \text{plim}\left(\frac{Z_1' u_1}{T}\right)$$

Now $\text{plim}\left(\dfrac{\hat{Z}_1' \hat{Z}_1}{T}\right)$ will be non-singular if the equation is identified (see Exercise 7)

but

$$\text{plim}\left(\frac{Z_1' u_1}{T}\right) = \text{plim}\left(\frac{Z_1' X(X'X)^{-1}(X' u_1)}{T}\right)$$

$$= \text{plim}\left[\left(\frac{Z_1' X}{T}\right)\left(\frac{X'X}{T}\right)^{-1}\left(\frac{X' u_1}{T}\right)\right]$$

$$= \text{plim}\left(\frac{Z_1' X}{T}\right) \text{plim}\left(\frac{(X'X)}{T}\right)^{-1} \text{plim}\left(\frac{X' u_1}{T}\right)$$

$$= 0$$

therefore 2SLS is consistent.

Asymptotic covariance matrix of 2SLS

$$\text{plim}[T(\hat{\gamma}_{2SLS} - \gamma)(\hat{\gamma}_{2SLS} - \gamma)'] = \text{plim}\left(\frac{\hat{Z}_1' \hat{Z}_1}{T}\right)^{-1} \text{plim}\left(\frac{\hat{Z}_1' u_1 u_1' \hat{Z}_1}{T}\right) \text{plim}\left(\frac{\hat{Z}_1' \hat{Z}_1}{T}\right)^{-1}$$

and $\quad \text{plim}\left(\dfrac{\hat{Z}_1' u_1 u_1' \hat{Z}_1}{T}\right) = \text{plim}\left(\dfrac{Z_1' X}{T}\left(\dfrac{(X'X)}{T}\right)^{-1} \dfrac{X' u_1 u_1' X}{T} \left(\dfrac{(X'X)}{T}\right)^{-1} \dfrac{X' Z_1}{T}\right)$

$$\text{plim}\left(\frac{X' u_1 u_1' X}{T}\right) = \sigma_{11} \lim\left(\frac{X'X}{T}\right), \qquad \text{(See Exercise 5),}$$

so that
$$\text{plim}\left[\frac{Z_1'u_1u_1'Z_1}{T}\right] = \sigma_{11}\,\text{plim}\left[\frac{Z_1'X(X'X)^{-1}X'Z_1}{T}\right]$$

and since
$$\frac{Z_1'\hat{Z}_1}{T} = \frac{Z_1'X(X'X)^{-1}X'Z_1}{T}$$

we see that the asymptotic covariance matrix is $\sigma_{11}\,\text{plim}\left[\dfrac{Z_1'X(X'X)^{-1}X'Z_1}{T}\right]^{-1}$.

This would in practice be estimated by having σ_{11} replaced by $\hat{\sigma}_{11}$ the estimate of σ_{11} defined by $\hat{\sigma}_{11} = \hat{u}_1'\hat{u}_1/T$ where $\hat{u}_1 = y_1 - Z_1\hat{\gamma}_{SLS}$, the 2SLS residuals. It can be shown that $\hat{\sigma}_{11}$ is a consistent estimator of σ_{11} (see Exercise 6 to this section).

Therefore we have solved the problem of how to find consistent estimates of the parameters in a single equation from an SEM. We have not discussed inference and we give only the briefest of treatments. It can be shown that the 2SLS estimator is asymptotically normally distributed so that the 2SLS 't' statistic will have an approximate normal distribution. Thus we can test for the inclusion of variables by using our t-statistics and looking up our normal tables. Linear constraints on parameters can be tested using a Wald test based on the 2SLS estimators (see example below).

Example 4.4

In the model

$$y_{t1} = y_{t2}\alpha + X_t\beta + u_{t1}$$

we test that $\alpha + \beta = 1$ given

$$\hat{\gamma}_{2SLS} = \begin{pmatrix} \hat{\alpha}_{2SLS} \\ \hat{\beta}_{2SLS} \end{pmatrix} = \begin{pmatrix} 0.4 \\ 0.3 \end{pmatrix}$$

The estimated covariance matrix is $\begin{bmatrix} 2 & 0 \\ 0 & 2 \end{bmatrix}$, $\hat{\alpha} + \hat{\beta} = 0.7$, $\hat{\alpha} + \hat{\beta}$ is asymptotically

normal with mean equal to 1 (under H_0) and variance equal to $(1,1)\begin{pmatrix} 2 & 0 \\ 0 & 2 \end{pmatrix}\begin{pmatrix} 1 \\ 1 \end{pmatrix} = 4$.

Therefore $t = \dfrac{\hat{\alpha} + \hat{\beta} - 1}{2} \sim AN(0,1)$. (Here we use $\hat{\gamma} \sim AN(\gamma,V)$ to mean that $\hat{\gamma}$ is *asymptotically normal*, i.e., that $\sqrt{T}(\hat{\gamma} - \gamma)$ converges in distribution to $N(0,TV)$.) Now $t = -.15$ which is insignificant hence we do not reject $\alpha + \beta = 1$.

Testing multiple restrictions

We could test more than one restriction by a generalisation of this using the result that if $\hat{\gamma} \sim AN(\gamma,V)$ then $R\hat{\gamma} \sim AN(R\gamma, RVR')$ where R is an $r \times (k_1 + g_1)$ matrix of known constants. Then to test $R\gamma = 0$, under H_0

$$R\hat{\gamma} \sim AN(0, RVR')$$

and $(R\hat{\gamma})'(R\hat{V}R')^{-1}(R\hat{\gamma})$ is asymptotically chi-squared with r degrees of freedom. We note that r is the number of restrictions to test.

Exercises to section 4.6

1. Assuming that $\begin{pmatrix} x_t \\ u_t \end{pmatrix} \sim \left\{ \begin{pmatrix} 0 \\ 0 \end{pmatrix}, \begin{pmatrix} \sigma_x^2 & \rho\sigma_x\sigma_u \\ \rho\sigma_x\sigma_u & \sigma^2 \end{pmatrix} \right\}$

    show that $V\left(\dfrac{\sum_t^T x_t u_t}{T}\right)$ tends to zero if the fourth moments of the $\begin{pmatrix} x_t \\ u_t \end{pmatrix}$ distribution

    and bounded. Here $V(\ )$ means variance of the bracket.

2. Using the assumptions of Exercise 1, show that plim $\hat{\beta} = \dfrac{\rho\sigma_u}{\sigma_x}$ where $\hat{\beta}$ is the OLS

    estimator of β in the model $y_t = x_t\beta + u_t$.

3. In the equation (6.1), show that necessary conditions for plim $\dfrac{\sum Z_t' Z_t}{T}$ to be non-

    singular are that plim $\dfrac{X'X}{T}$ is non-singular and the equation is identified.

4. Under the usual assumptions of the model, show that plim $\dfrac{\sum X_{t1}' u_{t1}}{T} = 0$.

5. Under the normal assumptions of the model, show that plim $\dfrac{\sum X' u_1 u_1' X}{T} =$

    $\sigma_{11} \lim \dfrac{X'X}{T}$.

6. Show that the residual sum of squares of 2SLS residuals is a consistent estimator of

    σ_{11}.

7. Show that plim $\left\{ \dfrac{\hat{Z}_1' Z_1}{T} \right\}$ is non-singular if the equation is identified.

8. Justify the result on asymptotic chi-squares tests in the section on testing multiple restrictions above by using the result (proved in lemma 3.2, in section 3.2) that if $y \sim N_r(0,V)$ then $y'V^{-1}y \sim \chi^2(r)$.

Chapter 5

Applied Econometrics

We shall be concerned in this chapter with the application of the econometric concepts and methods developed earlier. In addition to making concrete these somewhat abstract ideas, it is also the intention to expose the reader to some of the problems and issues in applied econometric research. The applied econometrician needs to have a sound understanding of the economic theory underlying the study as well as of the relevant econometric techniques. In addition, knowledge of the availability and limitations of the data is essential. Our intention here is to show how the interplay of economic theory, econometric theory and the data, facilitates applied econometric research. The vehicle that we use for this purpose is a famous paper by Lucas and Rapping (1969) hereafter referred to as L–R. Not only does this paper pose and confront many of the issues facing applied econometricians but it is an important paper in its own right and has had a decisive influence on macro-economics. Our approach will be to provide a coherent summary of the paper and to draw out the implications both for the methodology and the details of applied econometric research. The main emphasis will be on the general relevance for the specification, estimation and testing of econometric models.

The first step in any applied econometrics exercise is the specification of the econometric model. As discussed in section 4.1 econometric models typically have both deterministic and stochastic elements. Usually economic theory provides the researcher with guidance in the construction of only the deterministic part of the econometric model. This is because most economic theory is usually specified as deterministic and causal relationships of the 'if...then' variety. Where the economics is itself couched in stochastic terms, then this can provide a guide to the stochastic specification of the econometric model as well. We shall not be discussing this possibility in any detail but rather will concentrate on the case where economic theory guides only the specification of the deterministic part of the econometric model.

Usually (though not always) the behavioural 'if...then' relationships of economic theory are derived from the optimising behaviour of economic agents. Specifying the

173

agents' objective function and constraint set are thus the first tasks in the construction of the economic model which is to provide the basis of the deterministic part of the econometric model. The first-order conditions of the static or dynamic constrained optimisation problem thus generated constitute the behavioural economic relations underlying the econometric model. Another source of deterministic relationships between economic variables which will sometimes be an input to an econometric model are definitions and/or identities which are simply definitionally true relationships. As discussed in section 4.2, identities cause no special econometric problems and we shall not discuss these further. These general and fairly abstract principles are aptly demonstrated by the L–R paper.

The L–R paper consists essentially of a labour market model which focuses on the problems of labour supply and unemployment. There are only two economic agents — a representative firm and a representative worker's household. Each of their decision processes is analysed in some detail by L–R. Only parameterised relationships can serve as an input to an econometric model since general functional forms cannot be estimated. This implies that the analyst faces two options. First the objective function (and the constraint set) can, at the outset, be specified in parametric terms so that the first-order conditions which yield the behavioural relations are also parametric and thus already in an estimable form. L–R use this approach when modelling the firm. Alternatively, one can solve the constrained optimisation problem using general functional forms for the objective function and constraint set and then write down a parametric relation which can be construed as an approximation to the first-order conditions. L–R use this method when modelling the worker household. The first method has the advantage of analytical tractability, whilst the second that of greater generality from the economic viewpoint. L–R use both methods as already noted.

The numbering of equations corresponds to the original paper. Additional equations we use will be numbered as 16(i), 16(ii) etc. In analysing the decision of the firm, L–R assume an aggregate production function given by:

$$y_t = [a(Q_t N_t)^{-b} + c(K_t)^{-b}]^{-1/b} \qquad \textbf{16}$$

where
y_t is real GNP (output)
K_t is real capital stock
N is employment
Q is a labour quality index

and all variables are measured at time t. The parameters a and c are both positive whilst $b > -1$.

The firm is assumed to maximise real profits subject to the constraint (16). Real profits are given by:

$$R_t = y_t - w_t N_t \qquad \textbf{16(i)}$$

where w_t is the real wage rate.
Substituting 16 into 16(i) yields

$$R_t = [a(Q_t N_t)^{-b} + c(K_t)^{-b}]^{-1/b} - W_t M_t \qquad \textbf{16(ii)}$$

Thus the firm chooses N_t to maximise R in 16(ii).

The first-order conditions are $\dfrac{\partial R_t}{\partial N_t} = w_t$. (Second order conditions are satisfied because of the parameter restrictions a, $c > 0$ and $b > -1$.) Differentiating and rearranging yields

$$w_t = aQ_t \frac{\{[a(Q_tN_t)^{-b} + c(K_t)^{-b}]^{-1/b}\}^{(1+b)}}{(Q_tN_t)^{1+b}} \qquad \textbf{16(iii)}$$

Several points should be noted about 16(iii). First, it is a deterministic behavioural parameterised relation which shows the firm's choice of N_t given Q_t, K_t and w_t, i.e. an 'if...then' statement. Second, the relationship is highly non-linear both in parameters and variables and there is no simple transformation which could linearise it. Thirdly, it explicitly contains K_t as an independent variable.

However, noting that the expression in curly parentheses on the right-hand side of 16(iii) is y_t, 16(iii) can be rewritten as

$$w_t = aQ_t \left(\frac{y_t}{Q_tN_t}\right)^{1+b} \qquad \textbf{17}$$

17 is clearly equivalent to 16(iii) but 17 contains y_t rather than K_t as an independent variable and, furthermore, can be easily converted into a linear form by the logarithmic transformation. These points will be of importance when deciding whether 16(iii) or 17 is the appropriate input into the econometric model.

On the other side of the labour market L–R assume that the representative household has a two-period utility function whose arguments are present and future consumption ($\bar{C}$ and $\bar{C}^*$ respectively) and present and future household labour supply ($\bar{N}$ and $\bar{N}^*$ respectively). The household is assumed to maximise utility subject to the constraint that the present value of (present and future) consumption equals the present value of future income with all present values being computed at the nominal interest rate r. Thus the household's constrained optimisation problem is to maximise

$$U(\bar{C}, \bar{C}^*, \bar{N}, \bar{N}^*) \qquad \textbf{5}$$

subject to

$$P\bar{C} + \frac{P^*\bar{C}^*}{1+r} = \bar{A} + W\bar{N} + \frac{W^*\bar{N}^*}{1+r} \qquad \textbf{6}$$

where p, W are the current price and nominal wage respectively, P^*, W^* are the corresponding future values and $\bar{A}$ is the household's current nominal assets. Equation 6 can be divided throughout by P to yield

$$\bar{C} + \frac{P^*}{P(1+r)}\bar{C}^* = \frac{\bar{A}}{P} + \frac{W}{P}\bar{N} + \frac{W^*}{P(+r)} \cdot \bar{N}^* \qquad \textbf{6(i)}$$

Maximising 5 subject to 6(i) yields four first-order conditions (one for each of $\bar{C}$, $\bar{C}^*$, $\bar{N}$, $\bar{N}^*$). Of these, only that for $\bar{N}$ is of real interest. From elementary demand theory the solution for $\bar{N}$ will clearly depend on real assets $\dfrac{\bar{A}}{P}$ and the three *relative* prices $\dfrac{W}{P}$, $\dfrac{W^*}{P(1+r)}$ and $\dfrac{P^*}{P(1+r)}$. (This is equivalent to stating that demand functions are homogenous of degree zero in prices and wealth.) Accordingly we may write

$$\bar{N} = F\left[\frac{\bar{W}}{P}, \frac{W^*}{P(1+r)}, \frac{P^*}{P(1+r)}, \frac{\bar{A}}{P}\right] \qquad \qquad 8$$

Several features of this result should be noted. First it is a deterministic relationship which has not been parameterised. Second, because of income and substitution effects, no *a priori* signs can be assigned to the partial derivatives of F without making further subsidiary assumptions about the relative magnitude of these effects. Had one started with a specific parameterised utility function instead of 5 we would have obtained a specific solution for $\bar{N}$ and could then have calculated the signs of the partial derivatives of F.

L–R parameterise 8 as follows (we shall use ℓn to refer to log (to base e) in this chapter).

$$\ell n\left(\frac{N_t}{M_t}\right) = \beta_0 + \beta_1 \ell n(W_t/P_t) - \beta_2 \ell n\left[\frac{W_t^*}{P_t(1+r)}\right] - \beta_3' \ell n\left(\frac{P_t^*}{P_t(1+r)}\right)$$

$$\qquad \qquad 10$$

$$- \beta_4 \ell n\left(\frac{A_t}{P_t M_t}\right)$$

where β_i is *assumed* > 0 (except β_0) and M_t is the number of households, A_t is aggregate assets and N_t is aggregate labour supply, i.e. $\dfrac{N_t}{M_t}$ and $\dfrac{A_t}{M_t}$ are the average amounts of labour supply and nominal assets of households. It is implicitly being assumed that the behaviour and assets of the representative household are reflected in national averages.

Letting $w_t = \dfrac{W_t}{P_t}$ and $w_t^* = \dfrac{W_t^*}{P_t^*}$, $a_t = A_t/P_t$ and $\beta_3 = \beta_2 + \beta_3' > 0$ and noting that $\ell n(1+r) \cong r$ implies that 10 can be rewritten (see Exercise 1) as:

$$\ell n\left(\frac{N_t}{M_t}\right) = \beta_0 + \beta_1 \ell n\, w_t - \beta_2 \ell n\, w_t^* + \beta_3 [r_t - \ell n(P_t^*/P_t)]$$

$$\qquad \qquad 11$$

$$- \beta_4 \ell n(a_t/M_t)$$

17 (or 16(iii)) and 11 constitute the current demand and supply functions of the labour market. Assuming market clearing, it is the intersection of these two which simultaneously determines w_t and N_t given the values of w_t^*, P_t^*, P_t, a_t, M_t, r_t, Q_t and y_t (or K_t).

In a model with market clearing the nature of unemployment is largely voluntary. In order to explain such unemployment, L–R introduce the concept of 'normal' supply. It is the difference between this and the market clearing level of employment which accounts for unemployment in this market. L–R define 'normal' labour supply at time $t(N_t^*)$ to be that labour supply which would have prevailed if current real wages and prices (w_t, P_t) were what they had been expected to be one period earlier. In period $t - 1$ the worker household had expectations of real wages and prices that would prevail in the future, i.e. in period t. These are obviously denoted by w^*_{t-1} and P^*_t. When the future, i.e. period t, arrives w_t and P_t are observable. If $w_t = w^*_{t-1}$ and $P_t = P^*_{t-1}$, the worker's previous expectations are realised and in this circumstance current labour supply in period $t(N_t)$ is the 'normal' labour supply in period t. In other words N^*_t is obtained by inserting $w_t = w^*_{t-1}$ and $P_t = P^*_{t-1}$ for w_t and P_t in 11 which yields:

$$\ell n\left(\frac{N^*_t}{M_t}\right) = \beta_0 + \beta_1(\ell n\, w^*_{t-1}) - \beta_2 \ell n\, w^*_t + \beta_3\left[r_t - \ell n\left(\frac{P^*_t}{P^*_{t-1}}\right)\right]$$

$$- \beta_4 \ell n(a_t/M_t) \tag{23}$$

Subtracting 11 from 23 yields:

$$\ell n\left(\frac{N^*_t}{N_t}\right) = \beta_1 \ell n\left(\frac{w_{t-1^*}}{w_t}\right) + \beta_3 \ell n\left(\frac{P^*_{t-1}}{P_t}\right) \tag{24}$$

See Exercise 2 of this chapter.

Since

$$\ell n\left(\frac{N^*_t}{N_t}\right) \doteq \left[\frac{N^*_t - N_t}{N_t}\right]$$

the left-hand side of 24 measures the unemployment rate (see Exercise 3 of this chapter) provided all unemployment is due only to unrealised expectations, i.e. $(w_t - w^*_{t-1})$ and $(P_t - P^*_{t-1}) \neq 0$. However, greater realism led L–R to include frictional unemployment as well even though it is not explicitly modelled. Noting that frictional unemployment rises with $\left(\frac{N^*_t - N_t}{N_t}\right)$, they assumed the *total* unemployment (frictional and non-frictional) rate U_t was given by:

$$U_t = g_0 + g_1 \ell n(N^*_t/N_t), g_0, g_1 > 0 \tag{25}$$

and substituting for (N^*_t/N_t) from 24 yields:

$$U_t = g_0 + g_1 \beta_1 \ell n\left(\frac{w^*_{t-1}}{w_t}\right) + g_1 \beta_3 \ell n\left(\frac{P^*_{t-1}}{P_t}\right) \tag{26}$$

17 (or 16(iii), 11, and 26) then constitute the economic model used by L–R. Employment and the real wage are jointly determined by 17 (or 16(iii)) and 11 whilst 26 determines unemployment.

Although the equations 17, 11 and 26 comprise a perfectly valid economic model, there are several questions which must be raised before one can regard these equations as an econometric model. These are:

1. Are all the equations parameterised so that they can be estimated?
2. Are all the variables observable and can data on them be obtained?
3. Are the dynamics of the equations sufficiently rich to be potentially useful in capturing reality?
4. Is the stochastic specification adequate?

The answer to 1. is clearly 'yes' and so need not detain us further. 2. is clearly much more problematic. Turning to 17 and its equivalent 16(iii), it has already been pointed out that data on K_t is not available whilst that on y_t is. Hence 17 contains observable variables and is preferred to 16(iii). Obviously 17 is also much easier to estimate being log-linear. However, both 11 and 26 contain unobservable variables, e.g. w_t^*, P_t^*, w_{t-1}^*, and P_{t-1}^*, these being workers' expectations of future real wages and prices at times t and $t-1$ respectively. Hence some hypothesis regarding expectation formation must be adduced in order for equations 11 and 26 to contain only observable variables.

L–R use the simple trend corrected adaptive expectations mechanism to generate expectations of the level of future wages and prices. This is of course equivalent to assuming adaptive expectations on the logarithm of future wages and prices and is given by:

$$\ell n w_t^* - \ell n w_{t-1}^* = \lambda' + \lambda[\ell n w_t - \ell n w_{t-1}^*]$$

or

$$\ell n w_t^* = \lambda' + \lambda \ell n w_t + (1-\lambda)\ell n w_{t-1}^* \qquad 13$$

and

$$\ell n(P_t^*) = \lambda'' + \lambda \ell n P_t + (1-\lambda)\ell n(P_{t-1}^*) \qquad 14$$

where λ' and λ'' are the trend rates of growth of real wages and prices respectively. In other words λ'' is the equilibrium inflation rate.

Combining 11, 13 and 14 and using the Koyck transformation (see Exercise 4 of this chapter) yields:

$$\ell n\left(\frac{N_t}{M_t}\right) = (\beta_0\lambda - \beta_2\lambda' - \beta_3\lambda'') + (\beta_1 - \beta_2\lambda)\ell n w_t$$
$$- \beta_1(1-\lambda)\ell n w_{t-1} + \beta_3(1-\lambda)\ell n(P_t/P_{t-1})$$
$$+ (1-\lambda)\ell n(N_t - 1/M_t - 1) \qquad 15$$

The reason why r_t and a_t/M_t have disappeared is that they were found to be of negligible importance.

Similarly using 26, 13 and 14 and using the Koyck transformation yields:

$$U_t = [\lambda g_0 + \lambda' g_1\beta_1 + \lambda'' g_1\beta_3] - g_1\beta_1\ell n\frac{w_t}{w_{t-1}}$$
$$- g_1\beta_3\ell n(P_t/P_{t-1}) + (1-\lambda)U_{t-1} \qquad 27$$

Equations 17, 15 and 27 now all contain only observable measurable variables.

With regard to 3. L–R take a somewhat odd position. They assume that firms cannot adjust their actual employment levels immediately to their optimum values as given by 17. However they do assume that workers can do so. This asymmetrical treatment is odd because if firms are bound by long-term contracts which make instantaneous adjustment impossible, then the same must be true for workers. 17 can be rewritten as

$$\ell n(N_t Q_t) = \ell n y_t - \sigma\ell n\left(\frac{w_t}{Q_t}\right) + \sigma\ell n a \qquad 17(i)$$

where $\sigma = \dfrac{1}{1+b}$ in the elasticity of substitution between labour and capital in the production function. Since Q_t is exogenous, 17(i) gives the firm's optional labour demand. L–R assume that 17(i) is true only in the steady state and that actual adjustment to 17(i) is not instantaneous but depends on the lagged values of y_{t-1} and $(Q_{t-1}N_{t-1})$. Thus actual labour demand is given by:

$$\ell n(Q_t N_t) = c_0 - c_1 \ell n(w_t/Q_t) + c_2 \ell n y_t + c_3 \ell n y_{t-1}$$
$$+ c_4 \ell n(Q_{t-1}N_{t-1})$$

19

Since in the long-run stationary state $Q_t N_t = Q_t N_{t-1} = QN$ and $y_t = y_{t-1} = y$, it follows from 19 that in the long run,

$$\ell n(QN) = c_0 - c_1 \ell n(W/Q) + c_2 \ell n y + c_3 \ell n y + c_4 \ell n(QN)$$

19(i)

$$\ell n\, QN = \frac{c_0}{1-c_4} - \frac{c_1}{1-c_4}\ell n(W/Q) + \frac{(c_2 + c_3)}{1-c_4}\ell n y$$

and comparing the parameters of 19(i) with 17(i) which is also the stationary state labour demand equation yields:

$$c_0 = \sigma \ell n\, a(1-c_4),\ c_1 = (1-c_4)\sigma,\ c_2 + c_3 = 1 - c_4$$

20

Substituting $c_3 = 1 - c_4 - c_2$ in 19 and rearranging yields:

$$\ell n\!\left(\frac{Q_t N_t}{y_t}\right) = c_0 - c_1 \ell_n\!\left(\frac{w_t}{Q_t}\right) + c_4 \ell n\!\left(\frac{Q_{t-1}N_{t-1}}{y_{t-1}}\right)$$

$$+ (c_2 - 1)\ell n\!\left(\frac{y_t}{y_{t-1}}\right)$$

22

L–R use 22, 27 and 15 as the dynamic economic model which apart from the stochastic specification (discussed below) is the basis of the econometric model. Convergence of 22 to its steady state 17(i) requires $0 < c_4 < 1$.

The final step in the discussion of the econometric model concerns the stochastic specification of the model. This issue can be more easily discussed if the model is written in the conventional matrix notation. The three equations 22, 27 and 15 jointly 'explain' the behaviour of the three endogenous variables $\ell n w_t$, $\ell n(N_t/M_t)$ and U_t. These will be labelled y_{1t}, y_{2t}, and y_{3t}. The exogenous variables are unity (for the constants), $\ell n Q_t M_t$, $\ell n y_t$, $\ell n M_t$, and $\Delta \ell n P_t$. These are labelled x_{1t}, x_{2t}, x_{3t}, x_{4t} and x_{5t}. The lagged endogenous variables $\ell n w_{t-1}$ and $\ell n\!\left(\dfrac{N_{t-1}}{M_{t-1}}\right)$ and U_{t-1} are written as $y_{1t-1} \equiv x_{6t}$, $y_{2t-1} \equiv x_{7t}$ and $y_{3t-1} \equiv x_{8t}$ respectively. The lagged exogenous variables $\ell n(Q_{t-1}M_{t-1})$ and $\ell n y_{t-1}$, are labelled x_{9t} and x_{10t}, respectively. Dropping the time subscripts, the vector of endogenous variables is $y = (y_1, y_2, y_3)'$ and the vector of predetermined variables is $x = (x_1, x_2 \ldots x_{10})'$. Let A be a 3×3 matrix of coefficients (A_{ij}) and let B be a 3×10 matrix of coefficients (b_{ij}). Then the three equation econometric model corresponding to 22, 15 and 27 can be written in its most general form as

$$Ay + Bx = u \qquad\qquad 27(i)$$

where $u = (u_1, u_2, u_3)'$ is the error vector. The stochastic specification consists of making various assumptions about the distribution of u. Typically it is assumed $E(u) = 0$ (the means are zero), each component of the error vector is serially independent $[E(u_{it}, u_{is}) = 0$ for all $i, t \neq s)]$ and the (contemporaneous) covariance matrix of u is finite, i.e.

$$E(u'u) = V = \begin{bmatrix} \sigma_{11} & \sigma_{12} & \sigma_{13} \\ \sigma_{21} & \sigma_{22} & \sigma_{23} \\ \sigma_{31} & \sigma_{32} & \sigma_{33} \end{bmatrix}$$

With this the specification of the econometric model as represented by 27(i) is complete. The elements of A and B are nothing but the parameters of 22, 15 and 27 with several restrictions imposed. To see this we shall derive explicitly what the 39 elements of A and B are in terms of the original parameters of 22, 15 and 27. 22, 15 and 27 can be rewritten in terms of our new notation as:

$$y_{1t} + \left(\frac{1}{c_1}\right)y_{2t} + 0.y_{3t} + \left(-\frac{c_0}{c_1}\right)x_{1t} + \left(\frac{1}{c_1} - 1\right)x_{2t} + \left(-\frac{c_2}{c_1}\right)x_{3t}$$

$$+ 1x_{4t} + 0x_{5t} + 0x_{6t} + \left(-\frac{c_4}{c_1}\right)x_{7t} + 0x_{8t} + \left(-\frac{c_4}{c_1}\right)x_{9t} \qquad 22'$$

$$+ \left(\frac{c_2 + c_4 - 1}{c_1}\right)x_{10t} = u_{1t}$$

$$\{-(\beta_1 - \beta_2)\}y_{1t} + y_{2t} + 0y_{3t} + \{-(\beta_0 - \lambda'\beta_2 + \lambda''\beta_3\}x_{1t} + 0x_{2t}$$

$$+ 0x_{3t} + 0x_{4t} + \{-\beta_3(1 - \lambda)\}x_{5t} + \{(1 - \lambda)\beta_1\}x_{6t} + \{-(1 - \lambda)\}x_{7t} \qquad 15'$$

$$+ 0x_{8t} + 0x_{9t} + 0x_{10t} = u_{2t}$$

$$g_1\beta_1 y_{1t} + 0y_{2t} + 1y_{3t} + \{-(\lambda g_0 + \lambda' g_1\beta_1 + \lambda'' g_1\beta_3)\} + 0x_{2t} + 0x_{3t}$$

$$+ 0x_{4t} + \{-g_1\beta_3\}x_{5t} + \{-g_1\beta_1\}x_{6t} + 0x_{7t} + \{-(1 - \lambda)\}x_{8t} + 0x_{9t} \qquad 27'$$

$$+ 0x_{10t} = u_{3t}$$

Using Exercise 5 of this chapter we can see that

$$A = \begin{bmatrix} 1 & \dfrac{1}{c_1} & 0 \\ \{-(\beta_1 - \lambda\beta_2) & 1 & 0 \\ g_{1\,1} & 0 & 1 \end{bmatrix}$$

and

$$
B = \begin{bmatrix}
\left(\dfrac{-c_0}{c_1}\right) & \left(\dfrac{1}{c_1}-1\right) & \left(\dfrac{-c_2}{c_1}\right) & 1 & 0 & 0 \\[2ex]
\{-(\beta_0 \lambda' \beta_2 + \lambda'' \beta_3)\} & 0 & 0 & 0 & \{-(\beta_3(1-\lambda))\} & \beta_1(1-\lambda) \\[2ex]
\{-(\lambda g_0 + \lambda' g_1 \beta_1 + \lambda'' g_1 \beta_3)\} & 0 & 0 & 0 & \{-g_1 \beta_3\} & \{-g_1 \beta_1\}
\end{bmatrix}
$$

$$
\begin{bmatrix}
\left(\dfrac{-c_4}{c_1}\right) & 0 & \left(\dfrac{-c_4}{c_1}\right) & \dfrac{c_2 + c_4 - 1}{c_1} \\[2ex]
\{-(1-\lambda)\} & 0 & 0 & 0 \\[2ex]
0 & \{-(1-\lambda)\} & 0 & 0
\end{bmatrix}
$$

These elements of A and B are the structural parameters of the econometric model. Note that there are several restrictions on these parameters which reflect the underlying economic theory from which we started. First there are several zero restrictions. These simply state that the economic theory suggests that not all of the variables appear in every equation. As an example consider the first row of B which corresponds to 22'. The elements b_{15}, b_{16} and b_{18} are zero. This states that the variables x_5, x_6 and $x_8 (\Delta \ell n P_t, \ell n w_{t-1}$ and $U_{t-1})$ play no part in determining labour demand. The other zeros have a similar interpretation.

Secondly there are restrictions which constrain a particular parameter to take a prespecified numerical value other than zero. For example, all the elements on the main diagonal of A are unity. These are simply 'normalisation' (see section 4.2) restrictions which are of no economic significance. On the other hand the restriction that $b_{14} = 1$ reflects the economic theory.

Thirdly these are within equation restrictions. These reflect the fact that in any given equation some of the parameters are functionally related to others in the same equation. In terms of A and B, the implication is that some elements in any row of the matrix [A, B] are related functionally to other elements in the same row of [A, B]. As an example consider the first row of [A, B]. From inspection it is clear that $b_{17} = b_{19}$. This is a within-equation restriction in the first equation of the econometric model. (See Exercise 6 of this chapter.)

Fourthly there are cross-equation restrictions which imply a functional relationship between some of the parameters in one equation and those in other equations. For example it is obvious that for the econometric model 22', 15' and 27', the following cross-equation restrictions hold:

$$b_{27} = b_{38}, \text{ and } \frac{b_{35}}{b_{36}} = \frac{-b_{25}}{b_{26}}.$$

These restrictions provide a link between the second and third equations.

All the restrictions we have been discussing above relate to the structural parameters in $[A, B]$. Sometimes restrictions are also placed on the covariance matrix V. Up to now we have placed no restrictions on V other than the obvious symmetry restrictions $\sigma_{ji} = \sigma_{ij}$ for all i, j.

The complete econometric model then consists of the three-equation system

$$Ay + Bx = u$$

with A and B as defined and the full set of restrictions discussed above. The issue that now arises is the appropriate estimation technique to obtain reliable estimates of the structural parameters. It should be noted that the econometric model is fully simultaneous because (i) the matrix A has some non-zero off-diagonal elements (ii) there are cross-equation restrictions and (iii) V has non-zero off-diagonal elements. Further all three equations are over-identified. Hence a full systems estimator like 3SLS or F1ML (see Chapter 4) which takes into account all of these three features must be used in order to obtain asymptotically efficient estimates of the structural parameters. However great simplification could have been achieved if (ii) and (iii) above were not true. Both 3SLS and F1ML are computationally awkward procedures and this was certainly the case in the 1960s when L–R were writing. They used a much simpler computational procedure by assuming that the off-diagonal elements of V were all zero (i.e. $\text{cov}(u_i, u_j) = 0 i \neq j$) and ignoring the two cross-equation restrictions In this case the only source of simultaneity which remains is the fact that A still contains non-zero off-diagonal elements so that an endogenous variable appears in more than one equation. Furthermore, since a_{13} and a_{23} are zero this reduces the extent of simultaneity even more. The implication of $a_{13} = a_{23} = 0$ is that only the first two equations are simultaneous and that once these two have been jointly estimated, the predicted values of y_{1t} can be used as instruments to estimate the third equation by OLS. In effect ignoring the cross-equation restrictions and assuming zero covariances means that there is no 'feedback' from the third equation to either of the first two. This was in essence the approach followed by L–R.

As a further aid to computation, L–R 'substituted out' all the within-equation restrictions. This is often a convenient way of incorporating within-equation restrictions. Consider, for example, the first equation (equation 22'). Expanding the terms in parentheses and writing $(-c_2/c_1)x_3$ as $-\dfrac{1 x_3}{c_1} + \left(\dfrac{1 - c_2}{c_1}\right)x_3$ yields:

$$y_1 + \frac{1}{c_1}y_2 + (-c_0/c_1)x_1 + \frac{1}{c_1}x_2 - \frac{1 x_3}{c_1} + \left(\frac{1 - c_2}{c_1}\right)x_3$$

$$+ 1 \cdot x_4 + (-c_4/c_1)x_7 + (-c_4/c_1)x_9 + \left(\frac{c_2^{-1}}{c_1}\right)x_{10} + \left(\frac{c_4}{c_1}\right)x_{10} = u_1$$

Multiplying throughout by c_1 and collecting terms with the same coefficients yields:

$$(x_2 + y_2 - x_3) = c_0 x_1 - c_1\{y_1 + x_4 - x_2\} + c_4\{x_9 + x_7 - x_{10}\}$$
$$- (1 - c_2)\{x_3 - x_{10}\}$$

Substituting back the original variables for $x_1, x_2 \ldots, y_1, y_2$ etc. yields:

$$\ell n\left(\frac{Q_t N_t}{y_t}\right) = \beta_{10} - \beta_{11} \ell n\left(\frac{\omega_t}{Q_t}\right) + \beta_{12} \ell n\left(\frac{Q_{t-1} N_{t-1}}{y_{t-1}}\right)$$
$$+ \beta_{13} \ell n(y_t / y_{t-1}) + u_{1t} \tag{28}$$

where $\beta_{10} = c_0$ etc.

Similarly equations 15' and 27' can be written as:

$$\ell n(N_t / M_t) = \beta_{20} + \beta_{21} \ell n(\omega_t) - \beta_{22} \ell n(\omega_{t-1})$$
$$+ \beta_{23} \ell n(P_t / P_{t-1}) + \beta_{24} \ell n\left(\frac{N_{t-1}}{M_{t-1}}\right) + u_{2t} \tag{30}$$

and

$$U_t = \beta_{30} - \beta_{31} \ell n\left(\frac{\omega_t}{\omega_{t-1}}\right) - \beta_{32} \ell n(P_t / P_{t-1})$$
$$+ \beta_{33} U_{t-1} + u_{3t} \tag{32}$$

Equations 28, 30 and 32 comprise the econometric model L-R estimated assuming that cov $(u_{it}, u_{jt}) = 0$ for all $i \neq j$ and ignoring the two cross-equation restrictions

$$\beta_{31}/\beta_{32} = \beta_{21}/\beta_{23} \text{ and } \beta_{33} = \beta_{24} \tag{34}$$

Further inequality type restrictions on the parameters are

$$\beta_{11} > 0, 0 < \beta_{12} < 1, 0 < \beta_{21} < \frac{\beta_{22}}{\beta_{24}}, \beta_{22} > 0, 0 < \beta_{24} < 1, \beta_{31} > 0, \beta_{32} > 0, \tag{32'}$$
$$0 < \beta_{33} < 1$$

(See Exercise 7 of this chapter.)

Unlike the equality-type restrictions of 34 these inequality-type restrictions cannot be incorporated into the estimation procedure. They are, however, hypotheses which can and should be tested when the estimation is carried out.

Note that the normalisation used by L–R is unusual. Conventional normalisation (as we did earlier) would have had w_t as the LHS variable in 28. As a consequence L—R used only the reduced form equation for w_t (which was not restricted by 34 as it properly should have been) to generate the predictions $\hat{w}_t$. These were then used in the second stage of the 2SLS procedure in equations 28, 30 and 32 to obtain estimates of the structural parameters β_{ij} in the L–R model for US data in the period 1929–65. US data from 1929–1965.

Before discussing the estimates it is essential to check whether the econometric model is stable. Stability means convergence of the dynamic econometric model to its long-run equilibrium. This is an important issue not only because unstable models are hard to interpret but also because most of the conventional hypothesis testing methods (t tests etc.) are valid only for convergent models. In this model, for example, 'explosion' implies that in finite time the unemployment rate would exceed unity. This is clearly absurd. Hence if this model failed a stability test, it could almost be rejected as implausible on those grounds alone.

Stability analysis for difference equations is a mathematical subject well treated in Goldberg (1958) and Glaister (1972). Here we offer only a summary statement.

In dynamic econometric models, stability is analysed by examining the final form. Under the usual assumptions about exogenous variables, only the lagged endogenous variables are relevant in stability analysis. In this particular model, stability of the unemployment equation can be analysed separately from the rest of the model since unemployment does not feed back onto the other two equations. L–R show that the model is stable given their estimates. The reader is referred to the original paper for a fuller discussion.

All the parameter estimates conform to the inequality restrictions 32'. Several of the coefficients are significantly different from zero at the 5 per cent level. Failure to impose the cross-equation restriction $\beta_{33} = \beta_{24}$ is confirmed by the fact that their estimates are different (0.80 and 0.64) respectively. No formal test of the hypothesis $\beta_{33} = \beta_{24}$ was carried out by L–R. Similarly L–R's test of the other cross-equation restrictions $\beta_{31}/\beta_{32} = \beta_{21}/\beta_{23}$ was inadequate. These are both serious shortcomings.

Another informal step in assessing the plausibility of the econometric model is checking that the estimates of the various parameters are of 'sensible orders of magnitude'. Deciding what constitutes sensible orders of magnitude is of course a judgemental affair which requires some experience. Naturally it is a grey area where disagreement is likely.

Usually it is desirable to examine the magnitudes of those parameters which are of economic interest. Common examples are elasticities of supply, demand, substitution between factors, etc. In a dynamic econometric model such as this, it is also necessary to distinguish between long and short-run elasticities (or multipliers).

L–R concentrate on the short- and long-run elasticity of labour supply with respect to the real wage, the elasticity of substitution between labour and capital in the production function and the short- and long-run elasticity of employment with respect to output. A serious omission by L–R is the long-run unemployment rate — the so-called natural rate of unemployment.

The short-run elasticities are easy to compute. They are obtained directly from the estimated structural equations. Thus the short-run labour supply elasticity is $\hat{\beta}_{21} = 1.40$ whilst the short-run employment elasticity is $1 + \hat{\beta}_{13} = 0.79$. The substitution elasticity (see Exercise 8 of this chapter) σ is given by $\dfrac{c_1}{1 - c_4}$ (see equation 22) = $\dfrac{\hat{\beta}_{11}}{1 - \hat{\beta}_{12}} = 1.09$. L–R do not test the hypothesis $\sigma = 1$ even though this is a hypothesis of considerable economic interest. (The test (which is suggested because $\hat{\sigma} = 1.09$) is complicated though standard. We do not discuss it here.) The implication of $\sigma = 1$ is that the CES production function assumed by L–R can be replaced by the much simpler Cobb–Douglas production function.

In order to compute long-run elasticities (or multipliers) it is first necessary to define what is meant by long-run equilibrium. There are two long-run concepts one might use. One is the stationary equilibrium and the other is the steady state or growth equilibrium. In the stationary equilibrium all economic variables are constant. Thus a stationary equilibrium is calculated by the simple procedure of letting $y_t = y_{t-1} = \bar{y}$ for all economic variables y_t. The steady state equilibrium is one where the growth rate of economic variables is a constant. It is obtained by setting $y_t = (1 + g)y_{t-1}$ or $\Delta \ell n y_t = g$ for all economic variables y_t. It should be noted that the stationary state is a special case of a steady state with $g = 0$. In both equilibria economic variables which are ratios will be a constant (e.g. the unemployment rate).

L–R used the steady state concept to evaluate long-run elasticities. This is consistent with their earlier assumption that there is a trend in real wages of λ'. To see how these calculations are done consider the labour supply equation 30. In steady state equilibrium

$$\Delta \ell n w_t = \lambda' \text{ or } \ell n w_t = \ell n w_{t-1} + \lambda'$$

Assuming that the constant growth rates of N_t and M_t are equal in the equilibrium $\ell n(N_t/M_t) = \ell n\left(\dfrac{N_{t-1}}{M_{t-1}}\right)$, then 30 can be rewritten as:

$$\ell n\left(\frac{N_{t-1}}{M_{t-1}}\right) = \beta_{20} + \beta_{21}\lambda' + (\beta_{21} - \beta_{22})\ell n w_{t-1}$$

$$+ \beta_{23}\lambda'' + \beta_{24}\ell n(N_{t-1}/M_{t-1})$$

$$\ell n\frac{N_{t-1}}{M_{t-1}} = \frac{\beta_{20} + \beta_{21}\lambda'}{1 - \beta_{24}} + \frac{\beta_{21} - \beta_{22}}{1 - \beta_{24}}\ell n w_{t-1} \qquad \textbf{30(i)}$$

$$+ \frac{\beta_{23}}{1 - \beta_{24}}\lambda''$$

where λ'' is the equilibrium inflation rate $= \ell n(P_t/P_{t-1})$ in equilibrium. Hence the long-run labour supply elasticity is $\dfrac{\beta_{21} - \beta_{22}}{1 - \beta_{24}}$. Note that this does *not* depend on the value of λ' (growth rate of real wages) and hence the elasticity of long-run labour supply would be unaltered if $\lambda' = 0$ (which corresponds to a stationary state). From their estimates L–R calculate this elasticity to be 0.03 which is close to zero.

The calculation of the long-run unemployment rate does, however, depend crucially on whether we assume $\lambda' = 0$ (stationary state) or $\lambda' > 0$ (steady state).

To see this consider equation 22 and let $\Delta \ell n w_t = \lambda'$ as before. In the steady state $U_t = U_{t-1} = U^*$ (since it is an unemployment *rate* which lies in the interval $(0, 1)$). Therefore 32 can be rewritten (it is not being implied that U^* depends on λ''; see Exercise 9) as

$$U^* = \beta_{30} - \beta_{31}' - \beta_{32}\lambda'' + \beta_{33}U^*$$

$$U^* = \left[\frac{\beta_{30} - \beta_{32}}{1 - \beta_{33}}\right]\lambda'' - \left[\frac{\beta_{31}}{1 - \beta_{33}}\right]\lambda'' \qquad \textbf{32(1)}$$

where U^* is the long-run unemployment rate. Clearly whether $\lambda' = 0$ or not makes a crucial difference. Given the estimates of β_{30}, β_{32}, β_{33} and β_{31} and assuming $\lambda'' = 0.04$ (4 per cent per annum) then $U^* = 0.02$ if $\lambda' = 0.04$ but $U^* = 0.10$ if $\lambda' = 0$. The difference between 2 per cent and 10 per cent is of course considerable.

Conclusions

We have used the L–R study to illustrate the main issues in applied econometric research. These are:

1. The specification of the econometric model, including dynamic and stochastic specification. The role of economic theory and the data in the specification was discussed.
2. The estimation of the model. The role of the assumptions about stochastic behaviour and the various restrictions on the parameters generated by the economic theory was emphasised.
3. In discussing the estimates, stability analysis, hypothesis testing and the evaluation of long-run values of economically meaningful parameters was emphasised.

This is by no means a complete catalogue. There are several other features important in applied econometrics which we have not discussed, e.g. testing for structural breaks, post-sample forecasting etc. Considerations of space and complexity have forced these choices. Applied econometrics is a doing person's subject. Only by doing it and making mistakes can one actually learn about the subject and improve one's judgement. It is hoped that our effort will be both a help and a stimulus for students to embark in that direction.

EXERCISES

1. Show that 10 can be rewritten as 11.
   Hint: First rewrite 10 as

   $$ln(N_t/M_t) = \beta_0 + \beta_1 ln(W_t/P_t) - \beta_2 ln\left[\left(\frac{W_t^*}{P_t^*}\right)\left(\frac{P_t^*}{P_t}\right)\frac{1}{(1+r)}\right]$$

   $$- \beta_3' ln\left[\left(\frac{P_t^*}{P_t}\right)\frac{1}{1+r}\right] - \beta_4 ln\left[\left(\frac{A_t}{P_t}\right)/M_t\right]$$

   and then expand the terms in β_2 and β_3' and regroup.
2. Derive equation 24 from 11 and 23.
   Hint: Expand the term in β_3 and the LHS of both 11 and 23. Then subtract 11 from 23 and regroup.
3. Show that $ln\left(\dfrac{N_t^*}{N_t}\right) \doteq \left(\dfrac{N_t^* - N_t}{N_t}\right)$

Hint: Write $\ln\left(\dfrac{N_t^*}{N_t}\right) = \ln\left[1 + \left(\dfrac{N_t^* - N_t}{N_t}\right)\right]$

Then use $\ln(1 + x) \simeq x$ for small x.

4. Derive equation 15 using the Koyck transformation.

   Hint: Consider the model $y_t = \beta\hat{x}_t$ **1**

   where x_t is the expected value of some variable x_t. Suppose expectations are generated adaptively so that

$$\hat{x}_t = \hat{x}_{t-1} + \lambda(x_{t-1} - \hat{x}_{t-1})$$ **2**

   It is required to obtain an equation which relates y_t to observable variables only. The Koyck transformation achieves this as follows.

   Rewrite 2 as

$$\hat{x}_t = \lambda x_{t-1} + (1 - \lambda)\hat{x}_{t-1}$$ **3**

   Mag 1 by one period and then multiply through by $(1 - \lambda)$

$$(1 - \lambda)y_{t-1} = \beta(1 - \lambda)\hat{x}_{t-1}$$ **4**

   Subtract 4 from 1

$$y_t - (1 - \lambda)y_{t-1} = \beta\hat{x}_t - \beta(1 - \lambda)\hat{x}_{t-1}$$
$$= \beta(\hat{x}_t - (1 - \lambda)\hat{x}_{t-1})$$
$$= \beta\lambda x_{t-1} \text{ from 3}$$

   \# $y_t = \beta x_{t-1} + (1 - \gamma)y_{t-1}$ which contains observables only. Apply this technique to 11, 13 and 14. Can you see why the adjustment parameter λ must be the same in both 13 and 14?

5. Show that the model comprising 22, 15 and 27 can be rewritten as 22′, 15′ and 27′.

   Hint: Rewrite 22 as

$$\ln\left\{\frac{(Q_t M_t)\left(\dfrac{N_t}{M_t}\right)}{y_t}\right\} = c_0 - c_1\ln\left\{\frac{(w_t)(M_t)}{(Q_t M_t)}\right\} + c_4\ln\left\{\frac{(Q_{t-1} M_{t-1})\left(\dfrac{N_{t-1}}{M_{t-1}}\right)}{y_{t-1}}\right\}$$
$$+ (c_2 - 1)\ln(y_t/y_{t-1}) \text{ and expand.}$$

   Then regroup all the terms making the coefficient of w_t unity. In equations 15 and 27 note that $\ln P_t/P_{t-1} = \Delta\ln P_t$. In equation 27 note that $-g_1\beta_1\ln(w_t/w_{t-1}) \equiv -g_1\beta_1\ln(w_t) + g_1\beta_1\ln(w_{t-1})$.

6. What are the other within-equation restrictions in the first equation of the econometric model?

7. Show that the various restrictions in 32′ follow directly from the assumptions $c_1 > 0$, $0 < c_4 < 1$ in 22, $\beta_1 > 0$, $\beta_2 > 0$, $\beta_3 > 0$ and $\beta_1 > \lambda\beta_2$ in 15, $g_1 > 0$ in 27 and $0 < \lambda < 1$ in 13.

   Hint: Evaluate each of the β_{ij}'s in terms of the original parameters of 22, 15 and 27.

8. Show that the short-run elasticity of employment with respect to output is $1 + \hat{\beta}_{13}$.

Hint: The elasticity of y with x is defined as

$$e_{y_1 x} = \frac{dy}{dx} \frac{x}{y} = \frac{d\ell n y}{d\ell n x}$$

$$\ldots e_{N_t, y_t} = \frac{d\ell n N_t}{d\ell n y_t}$$

9. Show that U^* does not depend on the inflation rate in 32(1).
   Hint: Rewrite $\hat{\beta}_{30}$ β_{31}, β_{32}, and β_{33} in terms of the original parameters of the model. From 32 and 27,

$$\beta_{30} = \lambda g_0 + \lambda' g_1 \beta_1 + \lambda'' g_1 \beta_3$$
$$\beta_{31} = g_1 \beta_1$$
$$\beta_{32} = g_1 \beta_3$$
$$\beta_{33} = 1 - \lambda$$

Substituting the above in 32(1) yields

$$U^* = g_0 \text{ which is independent of the inflation rate.}$$

Note that g_0 cannot be identified and hence an assumption about λ'' is crucial in determining U^*.

REFERENCES FOR PART II

Cagan, P. (1956) 'The Monetary Dynamics of Hyperinflation', in M. Friedman (ed.) *Studies in the Quantity of Theory of Money*. Chicago: University of Chicago Press.

Glaister, S. (1972) *Mathematical Methods for Economists*, Oxford: Basil Blackwell.

Goldberg, S. (1958) *Introduction to Difference Equations*, New York: Wiley.

Lucas, R. E., and Rapping, L. A. (1969) 'Real Wages, Employment and Inflation,' *Chicago Journal of Political Economy*, pp. 720, 721–51.

Stewart, M., and Wallis, K. (1980) *Introductory Econometrics*, Oxford: Basil Blackwell.

Theil, H. (1971) *Principles of Econometrics*, New York: Wiley.

Part III

Applications in Political Economy

Chapter 6

Time Series Analysis: The Box–Jenkins Approach

Macro-economic modelling using econometric methods began with relatively simple Keynesian specifications (Klein et al. 1961) and has become more and more complex and sophisticated over time. There are now macro-models which include many hundreds of equations as well as complex interactions between different subsectors of the economy, and the international economy (Gordon 1977, Ormerod 1979).

However, just at a time when economic modelling appears to be more successful than ever before, serious doubts have been expressed about the reliability and validity of large-scale macro-economic models. These doubts were perhaps first articulated by writers in the monetarist tradition who advocated relatively small-scale models to test their ideas (Sargent 1976, Laidler 1976). But more generally, some writers have argued that large-scale econometric models involve too many implausible assumptions and require incredible constraints on relationships in order to estimate parameters (Sims 1980). It has also been suggested that many traditional approaches to econometric modelling, which purport to be based on economic theory, are so constrained by arbitrary assumptions as to be inadequate tests of such theory (Sargent and Sims 1977). Jenkins has gone even further and set out a comprehensive critique of some traditional econometric methods which implies that they are almost useless for empirically testing macro-economic relationships (Jenkins 1979, pp. 88–93).

These developments have encouraged some researchers to pursue a more open-minded approach to modelling which emphasises exploratory data analysis, rather than the pretence of confirmatory analysis. However, the exploratory approach has achieved mixed results, since it has shown that a number of relationships apparently sanctified by economic theory are non-existent or even perverse (Feige and Pierce 1976, 1979, Pierce 1977). Undoubtedly, this is partly because traditional theory is deficient and needs to be rethought. But another reason may well be that the exploratory analytical procedures used have very often been rather *ad hoc* and unsystematic in character (Haugh 19/6, Sims 1972).

By contrast Box and Jenkins (1976) have introduced a comprehensive model-building strategy for identifying, estimating and forecasting time series models. They adopt an integrated approach rather than *ad hoc* methods for the causal modelling of time series variables. It emphasises the importance of developing models from the information embedded in the data, and thus is much more concerned with exploratory data analysis than traditional econometric methods. It provides the best systematic strategy for the multivariate causal modelling of time series data in the social sciences.

The purpose of this chapter is to introduce the Box–Jenkins approach to the univariate and multivariate analysis of time series data. The discussion is divided into three broad parts: firstly there is an introductory section which outlines the nature of the models, secondly a section which discusses the strategies involved in univariate and multivariate model building, and finally we examine a couple of examples of the model-building strategy applied to substantive problems in political science and economics.

6.1 THE BOX–JENKINS APPROACH TO TIME SERIES MODELLING

As we have already suggested, the Box–Jenkins approach emphasises the importance of exploring the data in order to capture the information within it. The model-building strategy is summarised in Figure 6.1. From a combination of theoretical knowledge

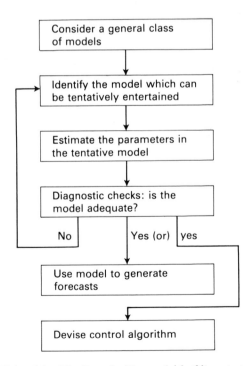

Figure 6.1 *The Box–Jenkins model-building strategy*

and exploration of the data we define a tentative model for the data. In building multivariate models we begin by developing univariate models for each of the series involved. This process of identifying an initial model can also provide preliminary estimates of parameters. The initial model is then fitted to the data and provides starting values for an iterative maximum likelihood estimation procedure which is required for these models, most of which are non-linear. After the estimates are obtained various diagnostic checks are carried out which are designed to uncover possible inadequacies. If there are problems with a model then modifications are made and the iterative cycle of estimation and diagnostic checking is repeated until a suitable representation is found. A final stage is to use the model for purposes of forecasting or controlling the behaviour of a series. In econometric and social science applications forecasting is rather more important than controlling time series, largely because of the difficulties involved in the latter. However, attempts have been made to use optimal control techniques in macroeconomics (Bray 1971, Renton 1975).

Univariate models of time series

Univariate Box–Jenkins models are developed from the idea that in a time series consisting of closely associated observations, a model of the series can be derived from a set of random uncorrelated shocks $\{a_t\}$ known as 'white noise'. These shocks are random observations from a normal distribution with mean zero and constant variance. The term 'white noise' originates from radio engineering since it provides a statistical representation of static noise. The process can be expressed in the form:

$$z_t = \mu + a_t + \varphi_1 a_{t-1} + \varphi_2 a_{t-2} + \cdots$$
$$= \mu + \varphi(\mathrm{B})a_t$$

6.1

Here z_t is the observed time series, and μ is a constant term

while

$$\mathrm{E}(a_t a_{t-k}) = \sigma_a^2 \text{ if } k = 0,$$

$$0 \text{ otherwise}$$

B is the 'backshift' operator, or generalisation of the lag operator L (see Chapter 3) given by $(\mathrm{B})a_t = a_t + a_{t-1} + a_{t-2}\ldots, \varphi(\mathrm{B})$ is a polynomial in the lag operator, a linear operation on B. Since $\varphi(\mathrm{B})$ transforms the white noise into the observations, it is referred to as a transfer function. The idea that a series with highly related successive observations is a product of white noise is initially rather counter-intuitive. But it can be seen that if 6.1 were not influenced by the noise shocks then z_t would have a constant value μ. The observations differ over time because they are buffeted by these random shocks.

A key assumption is that 6.1 is a stationary process which fluctuates around μ but does not depart from it over a long period. More formally stationarity implies that the joint probability distribution of the observations is invariant over time, that is

$$p(z_1, z_2, \ldots, z_k) = p(z_{1+t}, z_{2+t} \cdots z_{k+t})$$

6.2

This implies that the series behaves in a similar way, and therefore the joint probability distribution of the z values is the same at any point of time.

To see why the stationarity assumption is important we can consider the problem of estimating the variance–covariance matrix of the observations. This is a symmetric matrix containing n^2 elements.

$$
\begin{bmatrix}
v(z_1) & c(z_1 z_2) & \cdots & c(z_1 z_n) \\
 & v(z_2) & & \cdot \\
\cdot & \cdot & \cdots & \cdot \\
\cdot & \cdot & & \cdot \\
c(z_n z_1) & \cdot & \cdots & v(z_n)
\end{bmatrix}
$$

Where $v(z_i), c(z_i z_j)$ is the variance and the covariance of z_i and $z_i z_j$ respectively. Since this matrix is symmetric there are $\frac{1}{2}(n^2 + n)$ distinct variances and covariances to estimate. It is obviously impossible to estimate these from the original set of observations without simplifying assumptions. However, expression 6.2 implies that the marginal probability distributions for any two observations are the same. Thus:

$$ p(z_1, z_2) = p(z_{t+1}, z_{t+2}) \ t = \pm 1, \pm 2 $$

so that

$$ c(z_1, z_2) = c(z_{t+1}, z_{t+2}) = \gamma $$

and more generally for any pair of observations separated by, say, k periods

$$ p(z_t, z_{t+k}) = p(z_{t+m}, z_{t+m+k}) $$
$$ c(z_t, z_{t+k}) = c(z_{t+m}, z_{t+m+k}) = \gamma_k $$

Here γ_k is the autocovariance at lag k. In this case the variance–covariance matrix becomes:

$$
\begin{bmatrix}
\gamma_0 & \gamma_1 & \cdots & \gamma_{n-1} \\
\cdot & \gamma_0 & & \cdot \\
\cdot & \cdot & \cdots & \cdot \\
\cdot & \cdot & & \cdot \\
\gamma_{n-1} & \cdot & \cdots & \gamma_0
\end{bmatrix}
$$

where $v(z_t) = \gamma_0$.

This now involves only $n - 1$ distinct terms. It is also the case that in most empirical series of interest the autocovariances at large lags are likely to approximate zero, and so in practice we are estimating fewer than $n - 1$ terms.

To ensure that the process is stationary the mean and the variance–covariance matrix of the process must exist and be invariant over time. In the case of the mean this implies

$$ E(z_t) = \mu + E(a_t + \varphi_1 a_{t-1} + \cdots + \varphi_q a_{t-q}) $$
$$ = \mu $$

6.3

In the case of the variance

$$\gamma_0 = E(z_t - E(z_t))^2$$
$$= E(a_t + \varphi_1 a_{t-1} + \cdots)^2$$
$$= E(a_t^2 + \varphi_1^2 a_{t-2}^2 + \cdots) +$$
$$E(\varphi_1^2 a_t a_{t-1} + \cdots)$$

where for convenience we assume $\mu = 0$. As we saw in 6.1 the cross-product terms in this expression are zero, and so it reduces to

$$\gamma_0 = \gamma_a^2 \sum_{i=1}^{\infty} \varphi_i^2 \qquad \qquad 6.4$$

Clearly 6.4 is only finite if $\sum_{i=1}^{\infty} \varphi_i^2$ converges. The covariance between z_t and say z_{t-j} is given by

$$\gamma_i = E(z_t - E(z_t))(z_{t-j} - E(z_{t-j}))$$
$$= E((a_t + \varphi_1 a_{t-1} + \cdots)(a_{t-j} + \varphi_1 a_{t-j-1} + \cdots))$$
$$= E(((\varphi_i a_{t-j}^2) + (\varphi_1 \varphi_{j+1} a_{t-j-1}^2) + \cdots)$$
$$+ E(a_t a_{t-j}) + (\varphi_1 a_{t-1} a_{t-j}) + \cdots)) \qquad \qquad 6.5$$
$$= \gamma_a^2(\varphi_i + \varphi_1 \varphi_{j+1} + \cdots)$$
$$= \gamma_a^2 \sum_{i=1}^{\infty} \varphi_i \varphi_{i+j}$$

Again 6.5 is only finite if $\sum_{i=1}^{\infty} \varphi_i \varphi_{i+j}$ converges.

In empirical estimation of the process the φ_i weights will approximate zero after a given period of time. In this case we write 6.1 as follows:

$$z_t = \mu + a_t - \theta_1 a_{t-1} - \cdots - \theta_q a_{t-q} \qquad \qquad 6.6$$

This is known as a qth order moving-average process, because the z_t observations are a moving average of disturbances reaching back for q periods. We distinguish between the moving-average model and the general model 6.1 by using different notation for the parameters in the former. Minus signs are used in expression 6.6 by convention. The moving average model may also be written as

$$\tilde{z}_t = \theta(B)a_t \quad \text{where} \quad \tilde{z}_t = z_t - \mu$$

It contains $q + 2$ unknown parameters $\mu, \theta_1, \ldots, \theta_2, \gamma_a^2$ which have to be estimated. This is also referred to as an MA(q) model.

Another model which can be derived from the general form 6.1 is the autoregressive model. From 6.1

$$a_t = z_t - \mu - \varphi_1 a_{t-1} - \varphi_2 a_{t-2} - \cdots \qquad \qquad 6.7$$

Assuming stationarity 6.6 applies to any time period, so that

$$a_{t-1} = z_{t-1} - \mu - \varphi_1 a_{t-2} - \varphi_2 a_{t-2} \cdots \qquad \qquad 6.8$$

and substituting 6.8 into 6.7

$$z_t = \mu(1 - \varphi_1) + \varphi_1 z_{t-1} + a_t + (\varphi_2 - \varphi_1^2)a_{t-2}$$
$$+ (\varphi_3 - \varphi_1\varphi_2)a_{t-3} + \cdots$$

This eliminates a_{t-1}, and by successive substitution a_{t-2}, a_{t-3} and so on are also eliminated giving

$$z_t = \pi_1 z_{t-1} + \pi_2 z_{t-2} + \cdots + \delta + a_t$$

Here π_i is a function of the φ_i weights and δ is a function of μ and the φ_i weights.

When written as an autoregressive model it is expressed in different notation to distinguish it from the general form:

$$z_t = \phi_1 z_{t-1} + \phi_2 z_{t-2} + \cdots + \phi_p z_{t-p} + \delta + a_t \qquad \textbf{6.9}$$

which is known as a pth order autoregressive process since it is essentially a regression model relating z_t to its own past values. It may be written

$$\phi(B)\tilde{z}_t = a_t + \delta$$

where

$$\tilde{z}_t = z_t - \mu$$

The model contains $p + 2$ unknown parameters $\mu, \phi_1 \cdots \phi_p, \gamma_a^2$ which are estimated from the data. It is referred to as an $AR(p)$ model.

A natural extension of the autoregressive and moving average models is a combined autoregressive–moving-average model which can be written:

$$z_t = \phi_1 z_{t-1} + \cdots + \phi_p z_{t-p} + \delta + a_t - \phi_1 a_{t-1} - \cdots - \theta_q a_{t-q} \qquad \textbf{6.10}$$

which is also expressed as

$$\phi(B)\tilde{z}_t = \theta(B)a_t + \delta$$

employing $p + q + 2$ unknown parameters $\mu, \phi_1 \cdots \phi_p, \theta_1 \cdots \theta_a, \gamma_a^2$ to be estimated from the data. This is referred to as an $ARMA$ (p,q) model. There are constraints placed upon the model parameters to ensure that it is stable. The major constraint is that the parameters ϕ and θ of the autoregressive and moving-average operators $\phi(B)$ and $\theta(B)$ should lie inside the unit circle. To illustrate the meaning of this we can examine the illustrative example of a first-order autoregressive process:

$$z_t = \phi_1 z_{t-1} + a_t$$

the parameter ϕ_1 must be constrained to the interval

$$-1 < \phi_1 < +1$$

If this condition is not met then it is easy to see that z_t would be dominated by observations further and further back in time, since

$$z_0 = a_0$$
$$z_1 = \phi_1 z_0 + a_1$$
$$= \phi_1(a_0) + a_1$$
$$z_2 = \phi_1^2(a_0) + \phi_1 a_1 + a_2$$

and so on.

If $\phi_1 > 1.0$ then a_0 would have a bigger impact than a_1 which in turn would be more important than a_2 in influencing z_2. Without this requirement the model is explosively unstable. With higher-order models the parameter constraints are more complex involving constraints on the cross-products of parameters.

Models for non-stationary series

Many time series in the social sciences are not stationary but contain distinct trends over time. For example, there has been a trend rise in unemployment in advanced industrial countries in the seventies and eighties. In some countries there has been a trend increase in inflation, with several experiencing accelerated rates of inflation, particularly in the 1970s.

However, many non-stationary series are stationary in differenced form:

$$w_t = z_t - z_{t-1} = (1 - B)z_t = \nabla z_t$$

where ∇ is the difference operator. The general ARMA (p, d, q) model in differenced form is written

$$\phi(B)w_t = \theta(B)a_t \qquad \qquad \textbf{6.11}$$

The parameter d is the order of differencing required to induce stationarity. In most applications d is equal to one, and it is rarely greater than two. In the case where $d = 2$

$$y_t = w_t - w_{t-1} = (z_t - z_{t-1}) - (z_{t-1} - z_{t-2})$$
$$= z_t - 2z_{t-1} + z_{t-2}$$

Thus

$$y_t = \nabla w_t = \nabla^2 z_t$$

Stationarity implies homogeneity so that a series behaves in a similar way regardless of the time period. If a non-stationary series is homogeneous apart from a long-run trend then differencing the series should induce stationarity. However, a series might fluctuate with increasing amplitude over time. In this case since the absolute magnitude of changes increases over time, differencing will not induce stationarity. On the other hand the relative percentage change in the series may be constant even though the absolute magnitude of the change is not. Thus we can induce stationarity in such a series by differencing and transforming the series into logarithms. Since changes in logarithms are the same as percentage changes, logarithms ensure that a series is homogeneous with respect to its rate of change.

In differenced form the mean of the original series μ disappears. However, as we have seen, it is possible to have an ARMA model containing a constant term, δ. This has the effect of adding or subtracting a constant amount from the differenced and transformed series. A model with such a term drifts upwards or downwards during the estimation period, even though the transformed series is assumed to be stationary. This is not a paradox since stationarity can only be rigorously defined in the limit, and since we are always dealing with sample data, a theoretically stationary series might drift to a certain extent during the estimation period.

Models for series with seasonal components

Some series contain seasonal components or other regular cycles. For example, unemployment tends to fall in the summer months because there are extra jobs available at that time. A cycle of regular periodicity in the data makes a series non-stationary with respect to this component, and this must be corrected if the model is to be estimated properly.

To deal with seasonal non-stationarity we difference the series over the amplitude of the cycle:

$$w_t = z_t - z_{t-12} = (1 - B)^{12} z_t = \nabla^{12} z_t$$

assuming the cycle lasts twelve months.

If a series is non-stationary in its level and over a twelve-month cycle we would difference it twice:

$$w_t = (z_t - z_{t-1})(z_{t-12} - z_{t-13}) = (1 - B)(1 - B)^{12} z_t = \nabla \nabla^{12} z_t$$

In general:

$$\phi(B)^d (B)^D w_t = \theta(B) a_t \qquad\qquad 6.12$$

where D is the seasonal difference operator.

Multivariate models of time series

Multivariate models are of two distinct types. Firstly, there are intervention models which involved a quantitative output variable and one or more dummy input variables (Box and Tiao 1958).

$$z_t = f(I_t) + N_t \qquad\qquad 6.13$$

Thus z_t depends on an intervention dummy variable which takes on the value 1 when an event or succession of events perturbs the series, and 0 otherwise. The term N_t represents an ARMA model of the univariate residuals.

Secondly, there is the transfer function model with a quantitative input variable which dynamically influences the dependent variable.

$$z_t = f(x_t) + N_t \qquad\qquad 6.14$$

Of course the intervention model is merely a special case of the transfer function model, and in practice a model might contain a mixture of quantitative and dummy input variables.

If we examine the general case to begin with, a transfer function is a discrete linear difference equation of the following type:

$$(1 - \delta_1 B^1 - \cdots - \delta_r B^r) z_t = (w_0 - w_1 B - \cdots - w_s B^s) x_{t-b} + N_t \qquad 6.15$$

or in more compact notation

$$\delta(B) z_t = w(B) x_{t-b} + N_t$$

$$z_t = \frac{w(B)}{\delta(B)} x_{t-b} + N_t$$

Estimation of this model involves identifying the lag structures, the w and δ weights where they exist, and the delay parameter b which measures the time lag between the change in the input variable and the effect of this on the output variable. It can be seen that $w(B)$ is a moving average operator, with a quantitative rather than a stochastic input as in the univariate model; and $\delta(B)$ is an autoregressive operator. In this expression we are assuming that both input and output variables are stationary, although obviously transformations may be necessary to ensure this.

If several input variables $x_{1t}, x_{2t} \cdots x_{lt}$ are to be related to the output then expression 6.15 may be generalised to:

$$z_t = \sum_{j=1}^{l} \frac{w_j(B)}{\delta_j(B)} x_{j, t - b_j} + N_t \qquad \textbf{6.16}$$

Each x variable has its own autoregressive and moving average operators and delay parameters; seasonal components can be included as well.

Intervention models may involve a 'pulse' variable, which takes on the value '1' when the specific event being modelled occurs, and '0' otherwise. Alternatively, they may involve a 'step' variable which takes on the value '0' before a change, and '1' after such a change.

To get a feel for the nature of transfer function models it is useful to consider some examples. Perhaps the simplest case is the step intervention model

$$z_t = w_0 I_t + N_t \qquad \textbf{6.17}$$

An example of this is discussed by McSweeney (1978) who used the model to evaluate the impact of directory assistance charges on the average call rates for assistance in Cincinnati, Ohio. The w_0 parameter estimated the impact of such changes from the time they were introduced.

Another fairly simple transfer function model is of the following type:

$$z_t = (w_0 - w_1 B)B^3 x_t + N_t \qquad \textbf{6.18}$$

or

$$z_t = w_0 x_{t-3} - w_1 x_{t-4} + N_t$$

Thus z_t is influenced by changes in x_t lagged three periods. If x_{t-3} is the first observation in the series then the model is the same as 6.17 (except x_t is a quantitative variable). The full impact of the input variable is felt when the first observation in the series is x_{t-4}.

A rather different model which also involves changes over two periods is given by

$$z_t(1 - \delta_1 B) = w_0 I_t + N_t \qquad \textbf{6.19}$$

or

$$z_t = \delta_1 z_{t-1} + w_0 I_t + N_t$$

Since the input term I_t has an impact on changes in z_t the final impact of the

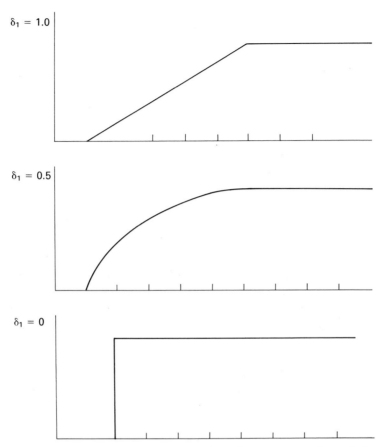

$\delta_1 = 1.0$

$\delta_1 = 0.5$

$\delta_1 = 0$

Figure 6.2 *Impacts on the output variable resulting from various values of the adjustment coefficient in model 6.19*

intervention term depends on δ_1. If $\delta_1 = 1.0$ then the final output is attained by a 'ramp' adjustment process; if $\delta_1 = 0$ then the output is achieved by a 'step' process. Intermediate values of δ_1 give adjustment processes of various rates of change. These are illustrated in Figure 6.2.

More elaborate transfer functions exist, for example

$$z_t(1 - \delta_1 B - \delta_2 B^2) = (w_0 + w_1 B)B^3 x_t + N_t \qquad \textbf{6.20}$$

or

$$z_t = \frac{w_0 x_{t-3} + w_1 x_{t-4}}{1 - \delta_1 B - \delta_2 B^2} + N_t$$

In this model there is an initial peak in the output series resulting from changes in the input series, and then the output settles down to a lower level after the full effects of x have worked through. Such models are very rare in the social sciences though more common in science and engineering applications.

To summarise the discussion so far, a time series z_t, after suitable transformation to induce stationarity can be regarded as a product of an input variable plus a stochastic noise term. The input variable may be a dummy variable or, more commonly, a quantitative variable. If the input variable is a white noise process then the model is a univariate ARMA model. In transfer function models input and output variables are dynamically related, and the parameters and lags are determined by reference to the data.

6.2   MODEL IDENTIFICATION, ESTIMATION AND DIAGNOSTIC CHECKING

The identification of models

Identification is concerned with tentatively defining the most suitable model for a time series. The first step is to ensure that the series is stationary, for reasons we have already discussed. The main aids to model identification are the autocorrelation and partial autocorrelation functions. The autocorrelation function measures the relationship between successive observations of a series up to k periods apart. It is calculated from the following expression:

$$r_j = \frac{\sum\limits_{t=j}^{T} (z_t - \bar{z})(z_{t+j} - \bar{z})}{\sum (z_t - \bar{z})^2} \qquad \textbf{6.21}$$

where r_j is the autocorrelation between observations up to time t and observations up to time $t+j$. T is the total number of observations. The partial autocorrelation function measures the correlation between current and past values of the series, controlling for intermediate values. The formula for the partial autocorrelation function depends on the model under consideration. But it can be illustrated in the case of a first-order autoregressive process as follows:

$$z_t = \phi_{11} z_{t-1} + a_t$$
$$z_t = \phi_{21} z_{t-1} + \phi_{22} z_{t-2} + a_t$$
$$z_t = \phi_{p1} z_{t-1} + \phi_{p2} z_{t-2} + \cdots + \phi_{pp} z_t + a_t$$

The partial autocorrelation functions at lags $1, 2, 3$ and so on are the regression coefficients $\phi_{11}, \phi_{22}, \phi_{33}$. It is possible to determine the theoretical behavior of the autocorrelation and partial autocorrelation functions for different kinds of model. This provides a means of identifying the actual model underlying the data.

In Figure 6.3 we illustrate the theoretical shape of the autocorrelation and partial autocorrelation functions for first- and second-order autoregressive processes. The first-order autoregressive process is expression 6.10 which can also be written

$$(1 - \phi B)z_t = a_t$$

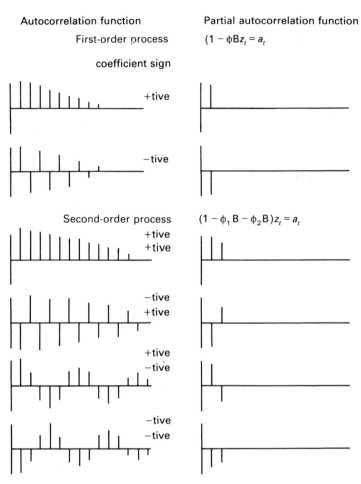

Autocorrelation function   Partial autocorrelation function

First-order process $(1 - \phi B z_t = a_t$

coefficient sign

+tive

−tive

Second-order process $(1 - \phi_1 B - \phi_2 B)z_t = a_t$

+tive
+tive

−tive
+tive

+tive
−tive

−tive
−tive

Figure 6.3 *Theoretical autocorrelation and partial autocorrelation functions for first- and second-order autoregressive processes (coefficient signs refer to ϕ_1 and ϕ_2)*

and the second-order process is written

$$(1 - \phi_1 B - \phi_2 B^2)z_t = a_t$$

In the theoretical relationships of Figure 6.2 the autocorrelation functions all have significant values for several time periods. The pattern formed depends on whether or not the roots of the operator are real or complex. Positive real roots give damped exponentials in the autocorrelation functions, whereas negative real roots give damped exponentials which change signs; complex roots give damped sine waves.

The partial autocorrelation functions in Figure 6.3 help to distinguish between first- and second-order models. The second order coefficient in this function is statistically significant in the second-order model. In most practical applications models will involve first- or second-order processes, and any higher-order autoregressive process can often be a combination of first and/or second order processes. The autocorrelation

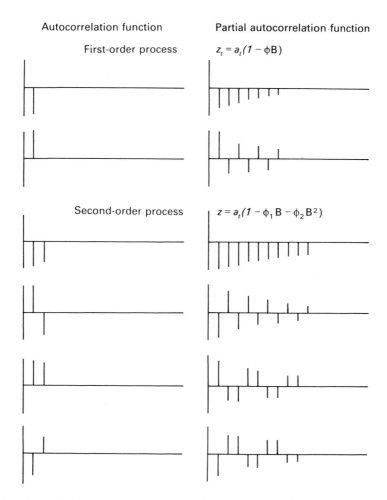

Figure 6.4 *Theoretical autocorrelation and partial autocorrelation functions for first- and second-order moving-average processes*

function of higher-order processes involves a mixture of damped exponentials and sine waves of considerable complexity. For this reason the autocorrelation function is rather less useful in identifying such models.

In Figure 6.4 we illustrate the theoretical autocorrelation and partial autocorrelation functions for first- and second-order moving-average processes. The first-order moving-average process is represented by

$$z_t = a_t(1 - \phi B)$$

and the second-order process by

$$z_t = a_t(1 - \phi_1 B - \phi_2 B^2)$$

It can be seen that Figure 6.4 is really the 'mirror image' of Figure 6.3, in that the autocorrelation functions for a moving-average model behave very much like the partial autocorrelation function for an autoregressive model, and vice versa.

A third class of models are mixed autoregressive moving-average models. In this case both functions exhibit damped exponential and/or damped sine wave behaviour. In such models it is usually the case that the autoregressive or the moving-average component will be dominant, and thus a tentative model which reflects this fact should be chosen.

Since in practice we do not know the theoretical correlations, it is important to assess how far the estimated values of these correlations will differ from the theoretical value. Specifically, it is necessary to know whether the autocorrelation or partial autocorrelation functions are effectively zero after a given lag. The standard error of the estimated autocorrelation function can be computed from the following expression:

$$\hat{\sigma}(r_k) = \left[(1/T)\left(1 + 2 \sum_{j=1}^{k} r_i^2 \right) \right]^{1/2} \qquad \textbf{6.22}$$

In the case of the partial autocorrelation function the standard error can be computed from

$$\hat{\sigma}(\phi_{kk}) = 1/(T)^{1/2} \qquad \textbf{6.23}$$

The distribution of an estimated autocorrelation coefficient for a reasonable sized sample of observations is approximately normal. Thus on the hypothesis that the theoretical autocorrelation coefficient is zero, the estimate r_k divided by the standard error $\hat{\sigma}(r_k)$ will be approximately distributed as a normal deviate. This is also true for the partial autocorrelation function. Thus we have a test of significance for the estimated functions which can be used to determine whether or not their theoretical values differ significantly from zero.

The identification of multivariate models proceeds by identifying and estimating univariate models as a preliminary to examining bivariate relationships. Multivariate model-building with several input variables is rather more difficult than univariate model-building since the different input variables can interact in complex ways to produce the output. But we proceed by examining the bivariate relationship between each of the inputs and the output variable in turn, before specifying and estimating a full model. A key to the identification of multivariate models is the cross-correlation function which is calculated from the following expression

$$\hat{r}_k^{xz} = \frac{\displaystyle\sum_{t=1}^{T-k} (x_t - \bar{x})(z_{t+k} - \bar{z})}{\left[\displaystyle\sum_{t=1}^{T} (x_t - \bar{x})^2 \sum_{t=1}^{T} (z_{t+k} - \bar{z})^2 \right]^{1/2}} \qquad \textbf{6.24}$$

Just as the autocorrelation function measures the within-series correlation, the cross-correlation function measures the between-series correlation. However, the relationship between the two series is influenced by the relationship within each series. To illustrate this we can represent the relationship between the two time series by the impulse response function:

$$z_t = v_0 x_t + v_1 x_{t-1} + \cdots + v_k x_{t-k} + N_t \qquad \textbf{6.25}$$

In this model the output deviation z_t is a linear aggregate of the input deviations at times $t, t - 1$ and so on, where the deviations are from the mean values.

To derive the cross-correlation function 6.25 is multiplied by $x_t, x_{t-1}, \ldots, x_{t-k}$. The result is a set of equations

$$x_t z_t = v_0 x_t x_t + \cdots + v_k x_t x_{t-k} + x_t N_t$$
$$x_{t-1} z_t = v_0 x_{t-1} x_t + \cdots + v_k x_{t-1} x_{t-k} + x_{t-1} N_t$$

$$\begin{matrix} \cdot & & \cdot \\ \cdot & & \cdot \\ \cdot & & \cdot \end{matrix}$$

$$x_{t-k} z_t = v_0 x_{t-k} x_t + \cdots + v_k x_{t-k} x_{t-k} + x_{t-k} N_t$$

Taking the expected values of this equation system and standardising by dividing by σ_x and σ_z, the standard deviations, gives:

$$CCF(0) = v_0 \frac{\sigma_x}{\sigma_z} + \cdots + v_k \frac{\sigma_x}{\sigma_z} ACF(k)$$

$$CCF(1) = v_0 \frac{\sigma_x}{\sigma_z} ACF(1) + \cdots + v_k \frac{\sigma_x}{\sigma_z} ACF(k-1)$$

$$CCF(k) = v_0 \frac{\sigma_x}{\sigma_z} ACF(k) + \cdots + v_k \frac{\sigma_x}{\sigma_z}$$

Thus the cross-correlation function ($CCF(k)$) at any lag depends on the v weight relationship between the two series, and on the autocorrelation function ($ACF(k)$) of the input series x.

However, suppose that both input and output series are white noise, after having been suitably filtered. Since the autocorrelation function of a white noise process is expected to be zero, then the cross-correlation function becomes:

$$CCF(0) = v_0 \frac{\sigma_x}{\sigma_z}$$

$$CCF(1) = v_1 \frac{\sigma_x}{\sigma_z}$$

$$\begin{matrix} \cdot \\ \cdot \\ \cdot \end{matrix}$$

$$CCF(k) = v_k \frac{\sigma_x}{\sigma_z}$$

In this case the cross-correlation function is not influenced by within-series correlation. This highlights a fundamentally important point: in order to assess the true relationship between the input and output variables uncontaminated by within-series variations we have to filter or pre-whiten the two series. This issue has been relatively neglected in empirical econometric analysis in the past. It arises because in time-series analysis variables which are theoretically unrelated can very often be highly correlated merely because they happen to grow in a similar way. Hendry (1980) illustrates the problem in an amusing article in which he demonstrates a highly significant relationship which meets all the conventional statistical criteria between cumulative rainfall and the rate of inflation in Britain! Thus it is essential to control for spurious relationships between variables in order to get a true picture.

Prewhitening involves estimating a univariate model for the input series, and then using this to transform or filter the output series. The residuals of the input model are then cross-correlated with the residuals of the filtered output variable in order to calculate the true relationship between the series. Take the ARMA model for x_t:

$$\phi(B)x_t = \theta(B)a_t$$
$$\phi(B)\theta(B)^{-1}x_t = a_t$$

We then use the same model with the same parameter estimates to prewhiten z_t

$$\phi(B)\theta(B)^{-1}z_t = u_t$$

The cross-correlation function $\hat{r}_j^{au}$ will then give an accurate picture of the relationship between x_t and z_t. Prewhitening places the onus on the data to demonstrate a relationship between the variables, but it has been criticised as being too stringent (Freeman 1983).

Once the prewhitened cross-correlation function has been calculated then knowledge of the theoretical behaviour of this function provides a guide to the relationship between x_t and z_t. For example, a significant pulse in the CCF at a given lag is evidence of a model of the following type:

$$z_t = w_0 x_{t-b} + N_t$$

Other examples of the CCF in relation to specific transfer function models are given in Figure 6.5. Broadly speaking, moving-average components show up as single pulses in the cross-correlation function, whereas autoregressive components show up as damped exponentials or damped sine waves depending on the signs of the coefficients. If the damped exponential or sine wave behaviour does not start from the first significant coefficient this implies that the model contains both autoregressive and moving-average components, as in the last example of Figure 6.5.

When there are several input variables the picture is more complex since the interrelationship between independent variables can produce a misleading picture when looked at in purely bivariate terms. In this case we have to rely more on the diagnostic tests after the tentative model has been estimated.

The estimation of models

Assuming that the model has been identified accurately the next stage of the procedure involves obtaining efficient parameter estimates. In this section we will discuss the

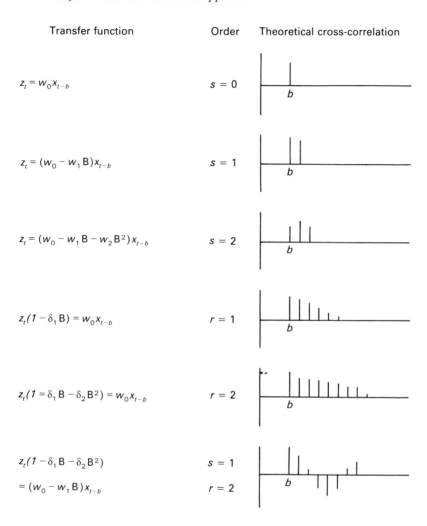

Transfer function	Order	Theoretical cross-correlation

$z_t = w_0 x_{t-b}$ — $s = 0$

$z_t = (w_0 - w_1 B) x_{t-b}$ — $s = 1$

$z_t = (w_0 - w_1 B - w_2 B^2) x_{t-b}$ — $s = 2$

$z_t(1 - \delta_1 B) = w_0 x_{t-b}$ — $r = 1$

$z_t(1 = \delta_1 B - \delta_2 B^2) = w_0 x_{t-b}$ — $r = 2$

$z_t(1 - \delta_1 B - \delta_2 B^2) = (w_0 - w_1 B) x_{t-b}$ — $s = 1$, $r = 2$

Figure 6.5 *Theoretical pre-whitened cross-correlation functions for various transfer functions*

conceptual issues involved in doing this, rather than examining in detail the maximum likelihood estimation of particular models.

We use maximum likelihood estimation since it provides the most efficient estimates when the sample is reasonably large. The rationale behind this procedure is easy to understand. Given a set of observations of a series $z_1, z_2, \ldots, z_k$ we know that these observations have been generated by a particular ARMA model. In the univariate case the model would have the parameters $\phi_1, \ldots, \phi_p, \theta_1, \ldots, \theta_2$ and σ_a^2.

The joint probability distribution of the series can be written as follows:

$$p(z_1, z_2, \ldots, z_k | \phi_1, \ldots, \phi_p, \theta_1, \ldots, \theta_q, \sigma_a^2)$$

This can also be conceptualised in reverse, as a joint probability of model parameters given the observations:

$$\ell(\phi_1, \ldots, \phi_p, \theta_1, \ldots, \theta_q, \sigma_a^2 | z_1, z_2, \ldots, z_k) \qquad \textbf{6.26}$$

This is known as a likelihood function, since it describes the likelihood of the parameters given the observations. Maximum likelihood estimation involves finding those parameters which are most likely to have been generated by the observations. It can be shown that the maximum likelihood estimates of the model are equivalently obtained by minimising the sum of squares of the disturbance terms, that is

$$s(\phi, \theta) = \sum_{t=1}^{T} a_t^2 \qquad \textbf{6.27}$$

in the ARMA (p, q) model:

$$a_t = z_t + \phi_1 z_{t-1} + \cdots + \phi_p z_{t-p} + \theta_1 a_{t-1} + \cdots + \theta_q a_{t-q}$$

Obviously in order to obtain the disturbance terms so that 6.27 can be defined it is necessary to know $a_0, a_1, \ldots, a_{t-1}$ in addition to the z_t observations. But the lagged disturbance terms are not known until the model is defined. Thus in order to be able to proceed we give the disturbance terms initial starting values and then estimate a value for a_t given values of the parameters. This is repeated for different parameter values and the likelihood surface relating the residual sum of squares to parameter values is mapped out. It only remains subsequently to find the maximum likelihood estimates.

For example, if the model was identified as an MA(1) process:

$$z_t = (1 - \theta B)a_t$$

then

$$a_t = z_t + \theta a_{t-1}$$

If we define

$$a_0 = 0$$

then

$$a_1 = z_t$$
$$a_2 = z_1 + \theta a_1 \text{ for a given value of } \theta$$

and so on.

The disturbance term a_t can then be calculated by iterative means, and the residual sum of squares determined. The exercise is then repeated for a different value of θ. If the series is reasonably long then the assumption that $a_0 = 0$ will not influence the resulting estimate much. Alternatively, it is possible to backcast, or forecast the series in negative time $t = 1, -1, -2$ and, so on, the iterative calculation is then started at a point in negative time so that the distortion of a_0 is negligible.

It will be appreciated that this iterative procedure is ideally suited to computer processing. Some of the models, notably purely autoregressive models, can be adequately estimated by linear regression methods. But models containing moving-average components are inherently non-linear, and this involves iterative 'grid-search' procedures in order to explore the likelihood surface.

The estimation of transfer functions is merely a rather more complex version of the exercise of estimating univariate models. The transfer function and ARIMA noise models are estimated simultaneously, and consequently the likelihood function contains many parameters and takes longer to estimate for this reason.

Diagnostic checking of models

Diagnostic checking is concerned with assessing the adequacy of a model once it has been estimated. This raises three types of issues. Firstly, there is the question of the adequacy of model parameters, which are assessed with the aid of the standard errors of the parameters; in this regard the correlation matrix of the parameter estimates is also important since it provides information about the nature of the likelihood surface. Secondly, there are diagnostics which are concerned with the likely forecasting performance of the model, notably the residual variance, and the histogram of the residuals. Thirdly, there are the autocorrelation and partial autocorrelation functions of the model residuals which are useful for detecting whether or not the model has picked up all the significant information in the data.

In looking at the standard errors of the parameters it is obviously desirable only to include parameters which are statistically significant. One common strategy in assessing model adequacy is to over-fit a model, that is, to include extra parameters in the model. If the extra parameters are statistically significant at the usual levels this suggests that the original model is inadequate. It is also clearly important to have model parameters which are independently estimated. The correlation matrix of parameter estimates provides information on the independence of estimates. A high correlation between two parameters indicates that one of them is redundant and should be deleted.

One important point relating to higher-order autoregressive or moving-average models is that they might be more parsimoniously specified with fewer parameters. A general theme running through the Box–Jenkins approach is the principle of parsimony: that simpler models with fewer parameters are preferable to more complex models with many parameters.

To illustrate this point, suppose we had fitted a third-order autoregressive model which gave the following estimates (standard errors in parenthesis)

$$(1 + 0.85\,\text{B} + 0.72\,\text{B}^2 + 0.62\,\text{B}^3)z_t = a_t$$
$$(0.05) \qquad (0.05) \qquad (0.05)$$

It can be seen that the model parameters decline approximately in the proportions 0.85, $(0.85)^2$, $(0.85)^3$ which is equivalent to a first-order moving-average model:

$$z_t = (1 - 0.85\,\text{B})a_t$$
$$(0.05)$$

The equivalence can be seen as follows. The moving-average model can be written:

$$(1 - 0.85\,\text{B})^{-1}z_t = a_t$$

which is the same as

$$(1 + 0.85\,\text{B} + 0.72\,\text{B}^2 + 0.61\,\text{B}^3 + \cdots)z_t = a_t$$

Since the moving-average version is considerably more parsimonious than the autoregressive version we should choose that in preference as the best model.

Diagnostics which are concerned with the forecasting performance of a model are particularly important. One of the most useful measures which can be used to assess this is the residual mean square statistic (RMS) which is computed from the following expression.

$$\text{RMS} = \frac{1}{T}\sqrt{\sum_{t=1}^{T} a_t^2}$$

This is used in time series analyses as a measure of the goodness of fit of a model rather than the more familiar coefficient of determination or r^2 statistic. Unlike r^2 the RMS statistic is not standardised, and so cannot be compared across different variables. It is used instead of the r^2 statistic, partly through tradition and partly because the latter measure can be misleading in some cases, two models can have the same r^2 when the residuals of the first are very much more variable than the residuals of the second. The RMS statistic distinguishes between these cases when the r^2 does not (see Arestis and Hadjimatheou 1982, pp. 26–27). The histogram of the residuals is also a useful device for locating systematic patterns in the residuals, or significant outliers which might coincide with some important event which perturbs the series. The model residuals should be a white noise process with a mean of zero and a constant variance. They should exhibit no anomalous behaviour at any stage, and so if these features are not present it indicates an inadequate model.

The autocorrelation and partial autocorrelation functions of the residuals are perhaps the strongest tests of model inadequacy. A comparison of the coefficients of these two functions with their standard errors provides evidence of the information content of the residuals. It is possible that the odd coefficient in the autocorrelation function of the residuals is statistically significant, but there should be no evidence of several significant coefficients. In addition to examining individual coefficients it is possible to test the residual autocorrelation function as a whole. The Ljung–Box statistic (1978) is distributed approximately as a chi-square distribution, and is computed from the residual autocorrelation function by the following formula

$$Q(k) = T(T + 2) \sum_{i=1}^{k} (T - i)^{-1} \text{r}_i^a \qquad\qquad \textbf{6.28}$$

Here r_i^a is the residual autocorrelation coefficient at lag i. The statistic is approximately χ_{k-p}^2 where p is the number of model parameters. Rejection of the null hypothesis in this case indicates model inadequacy, since it implies that the residuals contain systematic information not picked up by the model.

The diagnostic testing of multivariate transfer functions is similar to that of univariate models: we examine individual model parameters and the forecasting performance of the model. One of the most useful exercises is to compare the RMS statistic of the multivariate model with that of the univariate model. If the input variables are significant causal influences on the output variable then the RMS should be reduced in magnitude in the multivariate model in comparison with the univariate model. However, this does not apply to intervention variables to the same extent as to quantitative variables, since the intervention variables may only influence the series for short periods of time.

Another useful diagnostic in the multivariate model is the cross-correlation function between the model residuals and the prewhitened input series. This should pick up any significant relationships between the input and output series which have been missed in the model specification. Just as the prewhitened cross-correlation function is an important aid to model identification, the residual cross-correlation function is an important diagnostic tool.

To summarise the discussion so far, the Box–Jenkins model-building strategy provides a comprehensive approach to the identification and estimation of multivariate and univariate time series models. It is more concerned with correctly modelling the information within the data than traditional econometric methods, and unlike many of these it involves systematically exploring the model and the residuals for evidence of inadequacy. This means that transfer function estimates are considerably more reliable, given the correct model specification, than many of the equations in large-scale econometric models.

In the next two sections of this chapter we examine the Box–Jenkins model-building approach applied to two important substantive questions in political science and economics.

6.3 APPLICATIONS

The estimation of a popularity function in Britain

A popularity function measures the influence of changes in the economy, notably inflation and unemployment, on government and opposition popularity in the opinion polls (Frey and Schneider 1975). There has been a great deal of work in political science on this question, and there are now many papers relating to a variety of countries on this topic. The research relating to Britain has been characterised by controversy, with some writers finding strong and significant relationships (Frey and Schneider 1978, 1981) and others finding weak or non-existent relationships (Chrystal and Alt 1981). The present writer has argued that this confusion arises from a failure to specify and estimate models properly (Whiteley 1984). The Box–Jenkins model building strategy provides the best means of assessing the links between the popularity of the government and the state of the economy.

We specify the popularity function as follows:

$$(B)POP_t = f[(B)\underset{\sim}{z}_t, (B)P\underset{\sim}{D}_t] \qquad\qquad \textbf{6.29}$$

where POP_t is the lead of the governing party over the opposition party at time t

1. $\underset{\sim}{z}_t$ is a vector of short-term issue variables

2. $\underset{\sim}{PD_t}$ is a vector of long-term predisposition variables
3. B is the generalised back shift operator

In this specification government popularity depends on a set of short-term issues which includes the state of the economy, as well as various political shocks which are described below. It also depends on long-term predisposition, notably party identification, or the individual's psychological attachment to one or other of the major parties (Butler and Stokes 1974), the region of the country in which the voter lives, consumption and production sector locations, and local constituency characteristics.

Data on long-term predispositions are not generally available in the polls, but we can employ a simple transformation of equation 6.29:

$$\nabla(B)POP_t = f(\nabla(B)\underset{\sim}{z_t}) \qquad\qquad \textbf{6.30}$$

where ∇ is the difference operator.

In effect we are assuming that long-term predispositions do not change between successive poll observations, and therefore can be omitted from the specification.

From the theoretical model 6.30 we develop the following estimation equation, which is a multivariate transfer function:

$$\begin{aligned} \nabla\delta(B)POP_t = \nabla(B)[w_1 z_{1t-b} + w_2 z_{2t-c} + \cdots \\ + w_j z_{jt-k}] + (B)\theta_q a_t \end{aligned} \qquad \textbf{6.31}$$

where $\delta, w_1, \ldots, w_j$ are weights to be estimated when they exist, $b, e, \ldots, k$ are delay parameters, $z_1, z_2, \ldots, z_j$ are the short-term issue variables, and $(B)\theta_q a_t$ is a univariate ARMA model of the error structure.

The major criteria for including variables in the model are whether or not they exhibited significant short-term variation, which excluded economic indicators such as the growth of real incomes, and secondly whether or not prior evidence existed that such indicators had prominently featured in news stories in the media. This is because the communications medium (newspapers, TV) is one of the two important channels for transmitting changes in the economy to the public. The other channel is the direct experience of voters of unemployment and inflation.

Given these criteria we included a total of six variables in the popularity function for Britain. The function was estimated using monthly Gallup data from January 1947 to December 1980, giving a total of 407 observations. The details of the data and sources appear in the Appendix. The variables were unemployment and inflation, both quantitative scales, and four dummy variables. There were two 'economic' dummy variables: firstly a devaluation variable scoring one when the pound was devalued against the dollar or floated as in 1971, and zero otherwise. Secondly, there was an 'economic shock' variable which scored one at times of economic crisis, such as a balance of payments crisis or the OPEC oil price rise of 1973, and zero otherwise. The remaining dummy variables measured political shocks; the first scored one during the month of a general election campaign, and zero otherwise. General elections represent large shocks to public opinion, and this is captured by a dummy variable. Secondly, a dummy variable was included to measure the effect of the Labour Party being in office as opposed to the Conservatives. This was designed to assess if voters reacted differently to changes in the economy under different incumbent parties.

Univariate ARMA models of government lead, unemployment and inflation for Great Britain 1947–1980 (N = 406)

Government Lead

$$\nabla POP_t = a_t(1 - 0.28\,B^1 - 0.15\,B^3)$$
$$(5.9) \qquad (3.2)$$

RMS = 21.06   Q = 18, 24 d.f.

Inflation

$$\begin{array}{cccc} (2.8) & (2.6) & (16.9) & (2.4) \end{array}$$
$$\nabla I_t = a_t \frac{(1 + 0.11\,B^2 + 0.10\,B^4 - 0.62\,B^{12} - 0.09\,B^{26})}{(1 - 0.13\,B^1)}$$
$$(2.7)$$

RMS = 0.69   Q = 33, 24 d.f.

Unemployment

$$\begin{array}{ccc} (6.7) & (2.5) & (3.5) \end{array}$$
$$\nabla U_t = a_t \frac{(1 - 0.38\,B^1 - 0.13\,B^2 - 0.16\,B^{15})}{(1 - 0.95\,B^1)}$$
$$(32.2)$$

RMS = 218.27   Q = 27, 24 d.f.

(Note: The critical value of χ^2, 24 degrees of freedom $p < 0.05 = 36.4$, t values in parenthesis.)

In the models shown above we include the estimates of the univariate models of the continuous variables, government lead in the polls, inflation and unemployment. It can be seen that the univariate model of the government's lead is fairly straightforward. It is a moving-average model with significant coefficients at lags 1 and 3. The RMS statistic is included for purposes of comparison with the multivariate model. The Ljung–Box statistics, Q, are all non-significant indicating that the model residuals are white noise.

The inflation model shown contains significant moving average components up to 26 months, and it also has an autoregressive component. Thus the relationship between successive observations of inflation is considerably stronger than the relationship between successive observations of the poll series. The same is true of the unemployment series. This has such a large autoregressive coefficient that it is close to being non-stationary, which implies an accelerating rate of increase of unemployment. However, the autocorrelation function of the differenced unemployment series damped down to

Table 6.1 Pre-whitened cross-correlations between unemployment, inflation and government lead

	Government lead and inflation	Government lead and unemployment
1	−0.02	0.01
2	−0.01	0.04
3	0.01	<u>0.12</u>
4	0.01	−0.01
5	0.03	−0.05
6	−0.01	−0.01
7	0.01	0.04
8	0.01	−<u>0.12</u>
9	−0.01	<u>0.11</u>
10	0.06	−0.05
11	0.06	<u>0.10</u>
12	−0.09	−0.07
13	0.05	−0.03
14	0.02	0.05
15	0.01	−0.06
16	−0.01	0.01
17	0.0	−0.02
18	−0.02	0.01
19	0.03	−0.02
20	−0.02	−0.03

(Note: Statistically significant coefficients are under-
lined)

non-significant levels after about six months which tends to refute the possibility that the series is non-stationary. It is very important to avoid unnecessary differencing of a series since this can create statistically significant effects which are purely an artifact of the differencing process (McLeod 1983, pp. 11–32). So we modelled the unemployment series in single differenced form.

The univariate inflation and unemployment models were used to pre-whiten the popularity series and the filtered economic series appear in Table 6.1. It appears from this table that unemployment significantly influenced popularity at several lags, whereas inflation did not influence popularity at all. However, bivariate cross-correlations can be a poor guide to multivariate relationships, just as bivariate correlations can be a poor guide to partial correlations in survey analysis. The information in the cross-correlation function is used to specify the initial model, but the various diagnostic tests are used subsequently to improve the model.

The diagnostics suggested that the relationship between popularity and the economic series was heteroscedastic over the thirty-three year period. In other words the variances of these series were a function of time. Accordingly, we transformed the two series by taking their natural logarithms. The initial model included inflation with a zero lag, and unemployment with lagged values of three, eight, nine and eleven months. In this specification inflation proved to be statistically significant as did unemployment lagged eight months, but the other unemployment coefficients were not significant. Accordingly, we respecified and re-estimated the transfer function. The results of this appear as follows.

Transfer function models of government lead 1947–1980

1. $\nabla POP_t = -2.44 \, \nabla \ln I_t + a_t(1 - 0.28 \, \mathrm{B} - 0.15 \, \mathrm{B}^3)$

(0.99)   (6.0)   (3.2)

   $\mathrm{RMS} = 21.09$ $Q = 19$, 24 d.f.

2. $\nabla POP_t = -8.94 \, \nabla \ln I_t - 16.43 \, \nabla \ln U_{t-8} + a_t(1 - 0.32 \, \mathrm{B} - 0.19 \, \mathrm{B}^3)$

(2.4)   (3.5)   (6.8)   (4.0)

   $\mathrm{RMS} = 20.83$ $Q = 21$, 24 d.f.

3. $\nabla POP_t = -8.45 \, \nabla \ln I_t - 14.80 \ln U_{t-8} - 0.06 \text{ shock}$

(2.2)   (3.1)   (0.09)

   $+ 1.74 \text{ election} - 6.13 \text{ devaluation} + 0.11 \text{ Labour}$

(1.15)   (2.5)   (0.72)

   $+ \alpha_t(1 - 0.32 \, \mathrm{B}^1 - 0.20 \, \mathrm{B}^3)$

(6.7)   (4.0)

   $\mathrm{RMS} = 20.6$ $F^{(m)}_{(n-k)} = 3.17$ $Q = 24$, 24 d.f.

There are three models: the first includes inflation alone, the second includes unemployment and inflation as predictors of popularity, and the third includes the four intervention dummy variables. In the last two models unemployment and inflation are significant predictors of popularity. The lag on the unemployment variable suggests that the transmission mechanism linking changes in the economy and public opinion operates directly as well as via the mass media. If the transmission operated via the media alone we would not expect to see any lags at all. A shock rise in unemployment when highlighted by the press should influence public opinion as quickly as a rise in inflation. The existence of a lag suggests that the process must be operating on the direct experience of voters. Unemployment affects only a relatively small percentage of the electorate directly even when it is quite high, and the effects take longer to diffuse throughout the economy than inflation. In the case of inflation, anyone who buys, sells, borrows or lends is influenced by rising prices so the direct effects of inflation should be felt immediately. For this reason we might expect to see a lag in the influence of unemployment in comparison with inflation when it is mediated through the direct experience of voters. (See Whiteley 1986.)

The diagnostics in these models indicate that the model residuals are white noise. An important feature of the transfer function models in comparison with the univariate models is that the RMS statistic is only marginally smaller. Moreover, the error structure of the univariate model has not been significantly changed by incorporating the predictor variables; our ability to forecast the behaviour of government popularity is not significantly improved by including unemployment and inflation or the four intervention variables in the model. Essentially, this means that the error structure dominates the model. This summarises all the other influences on government popularity, many of them unique, one-off phenomena such as a political scandal or some domestic policy shock. The error structure also incorporates measurement error and unreliability, as well as the inherent noise generated by voters' responses to questions which may not be very salient to them when an election is years away.

The second model includes the intervention terms discussed earlier. Of these the devaluation dummy variable is statistically significant, and there is some weak evidence that an election gives a short-term boost to the popularity of an incumbent party. The economic shock and the Labour incumbency variables are not remotely significant. Thus this particular set of economic shocks did not influence opinion over and above the extent to which they influenced the other economic variables. Finally the electorate did not appear to distinguish between Labour and Conservative governments when they reacted to economic events, since the Labour incumbency variable was not significant.

The second model contains an additional diagnostic, a *Chow* test of the stability of the model parameters. It is defined as follows

$$F^m_{n-k} = \frac{(ss - ss_1)/m}{ss_1/n - k}$$ 6.32

where ss is the residual sum of squares for the entire series
ss_1 is the residual sum of squares for the first half of the series.
m is the number of observations excluded in calculating ss_1
n is the number of observations included in calculating ss_1
k is the number of parameters in the model.

This is distributed as an F-distribution, and indicates whether or not a significant shift in the model parameters has occurred in the second half of the series compared with the first half. The statistic in the transfer function models is significant at the 0.01 level which indicates that the model parameters shifted in value over time.

Overall, this evidence suggests that there is a weak, but statistically significant, relationship between unemployment, inflation and a devaluation of the currency in Britain and government popularity over this thirty-three year period. However, the relationships are not stable and tend to shift over time.

To investigate this instability we divided up the sample into three ten-year sub-periods: 1950 to 1959; 1960 to 1969; and 1970 to 1979, each subperiod containing 120 observations. The model-building strategy was then repeated for each subperiod and the results of this appear below. Initially the full model with six predictor variables was estimated for each period and then non-significant variables were deleted and the lags adjusted in the light of the diagnostics.

Transfer function estimates 1950–1980

1950 to 1959

$$\nabla POP_t = 4.64 \nabla \ln I_{t-2} - 9.07 \nabla \ln U_{t-8} + a_t(1 - 0.18 B^3 - 0.33 B^{10} - 0.43 B^{24})$$
$$(1.4) \qquad (1.7) \qquad\qquad (3.4) \quad (4.9) \quad (6.1)$$

RMS = 8.83 $\qquad\qquad Q = 32, N = 120$

1960 to 1969

$$\nabla POP_t = -15.33 \, \nabla \ln I_{t-2} - 34.60 \, \nabla \ln U_{t-8} + a_t (1 - 0.28 \, \mathrm{B}^1 - 0.25 \, \mathrm{B}^3 - 0.41 \, \mathrm{B}^{24})$$

$$\qquad\qquad (1.4) \qquad\qquad\qquad (3.7) \qquad\qquad\qquad\qquad\qquad (3.6) \qquad (3.2) \qquad (5.5)$$

RMS = 22.11 $\qquad\qquad\qquad\qquad\qquad\qquad\qquad\qquad\qquad\qquad\qquad Q = 22, \ N = 120$

1970 to 1979

$$\nabla POP_t = -22.31 \, \nabla \ln I_t - 28.57 \, \nabla \ln U_{t-13} + 0.53 \text{ labour}$$

$$\qquad\qquad (3.8) \qquad\qquad (7.4) \qquad\qquad\qquad (3.6)$$

$$+ \, a_t (1 - 0.71 \, \mathrm{B}^1 - 0.26 \, \mathrm{B}^4)$$

$$\qquad\quad (13.5) \qquad\quad (4.2)$$

RMS = 27.70 $\qquad\qquad\qquad\qquad\qquad\qquad\qquad\qquad\qquad\qquad\qquad Q = 21, \ N = 120$

It is fairly clear from the above estimates that significant shifts in parameter values and lags occurred over time. In the first subperiod both unemployment and inflation had a weaker influence on popularity than later. This was partly due to the great strength of partisanship in British politics in the fifties which reduced the importance of short-term issue variables: for example, in the general election of 1955 the Labour and Conservative parties combined obtained 96 per cent of the popular vote; in the 1983 election they obtained 72 per cent. But it was also due to the fact that unemployment and inflation were at historically low levels in the fifties and for this reason were less influential than later.

During the sixties the relationships were much stronger than earlier. The inflation coefficient more than doubled and the unemployment coefficient more than tripled in comparison with the fifties. This was partly because of greater media coverage of these issues than earlier, but also because economic performance in relation to both variables deteriorated in comparison with the fifties. This continued to be the case in the seventies when the key problem was stagflation or a combination of unemployment and inflation. The inflation coefficient particularly increased in magnitude in the seventies compared with earlier. As inflation grew worse, reaching record levels in 1975, it grew more salient in the eyes of the public. Furthermore, the lag on the inflation variable which had existed up to 1969 disappeared in the seventies, which is also consistent with inflation having a more salient and more immediate influence on public opinion. Clearly throughout the postwar period voter reactions to economic conditions adjusted in the light of their experiences of those conditions; hence the shifting parameters.

The evidence suggests that the state of the economy does influence voting behaviour in the short run, but the influences are not particularly strong or stable.

Estimating the relationship between the money supply and national income

There is a vast and growing literature on the economic determinants of inflation

(Laidler and Parkin 1975). Much of this debate has centred on the theoretical and empirical validity of the monetarist assertion that inflation is always and everywhere a monetary phenomenon. The central point of the monetarist case is that changes in the money supply are the most important determinants of aggregate economic activity as represented by nominal national income or the gross national product (Friedman 1956, Friedman and Schwartz 1963, Desai 1981). It is argued that changes in the real economy such as the growth of productivity and employment are independent of changes in the money supply except for temporary disturbances due to imperfect foresight. This means that increases in the money supply in excess of that required to maintain the growth of real income will automatically produce inflation. One of the key, empirical questions then in assessing the monetarists' case is whether or not changes in the supply of money directly influence changes in nominal income, and hence inflation.

Following the pioneering work of Granger (1969) on testing causal relationships between time series variables a number of writers have examined the relationship between nominal income and the money supply. In Granger's terms one series x_t can be said to cause another series y_t, if after extracting all the information from past values of y_t the use of x_t as a predictor reduces the error variance of y_t. In this sense a variable is causal if it explains the residuals of another variable which cannot be explained by the past history of that variable. It will be immediately apparent to the reader that information of this kind is provided by the pre-whitened cross-correlation function of the two variables. However, empirical work on the relationship between money and income has not used the full Box–Jenkins strategy.

Granger causality in the present context can be explained in terms of the following model:

$$\beta_{11}(B)M_t + \beta_{12}(B)y_t = a_{1t}$$
$$\beta_{21}(B)M_t + \beta_{22}(B)y_t = a_{2t}$$

where

M_t is the money supply

y_t is nominal income

a_{1t} and a_{2t} are white noise processes.

In this model M_t causes y_t if $\beta_{11}(B) \neq 0$ and $\beta_{12}(B) = 0$. In addition the money supply has an instantaneous causal influence on income if β_{21} at lag zero is non-zero. By contrast if $\beta_{11}(B) \neq 0$ and $\beta_{12} = 0$ at lag zero but all the other coefficients of $\beta_{12}(B) \neq 0$ then there is feedback from income to money. This particular model was examined by Sims (1972) using quarterly data for the US from 1947 to 1969. His findings supported the proposition that money caused income, and there were no significant influences running from income to money. Thus Sims appeared to confirm the monetarists' theoretical expectations. However, his approach used conventional regression methods which faced the problem that the model residuals were autocorrelated. He was aware of this problem but applied an essentially arbitrary filter to the series to correct it. In subsequent work Feige and Pearce (1979) showed that this arbitrary filter produced misleading estimates, and they called into question the validity of Sim's conclusions.

Feige and Pearce (1976) had themselves explored the relationship between money and income using a partial Box–Jenkins approach. They constructed univariate ARMA models for the two series, and then calculated the cross-correlation function of the residuals of the two filtered series. This approach was originally suggested by Pierce and Haugh (1977) and they found no evidence of a causal relationship between money and income, which tends to refute the monetarist case.

However, Feige and Pearce did not carry out the Box–Jenkins model-building strategy properly. In particular they did not pre-whiten the income series with the univariate model of the money supply series, as Box and Jenkins suggest. Instead they prefiltered both input and output variables with the separate ARMA models and cross-correlated the residuals. This is a significant departure from the Box–Jenkins approach and could produce misleading results.

In the light of this we applied the strategy to the question of examining the causal influence of the money supply on nominal income in Britain using quarterly data from 1963 (2) to 1983 (2). Money supply was measured using M_3, the broadly based definition of money which includes cash and time deposits in banks, nominal income was measured using total personal disposable income in current prices. Both series were unadjusted. Data sources are cited in the Appendix.

Obviously both national income in current prices and the money supply are highly non-stationary series and so we began the analysis by differencing both series. It was also apparent from a plot of the differenced series that both variables had variances which were a function of time. Thus logarithmic transformations were called for to deal with this problem.

The autocorrelation and partial autocorrelation functions of changes in the money supply and in national income appear in Figures 6.6 and 6.7. The functions include 95 per cent confidence intervals for the various coefficients. It is readily apparent in both figures that the series are affected by seasonal components which generate annual cycles; this can be seen from the significant pulses in the functions which appear at lags 4, 8, 12 and 16. Accordingly we differenced each series over the four quarter periods of the cycle.

When the seasonal differencing was carried out and the functions recalculated there remained a significant pulse in the autocorrelation function of the money supply series at lag 4. This suggests a fourth-order moving-average process. By contrast the seasonally differenced autocorrelation function of the national income model showed evidence of a damped exponential starting at lag 4. This suggests a fourth-order autoregressive model. Thus both models were defined in these terms.

The estimation and diagnostic checking of the money supply model showed that the fourth-order moving-average model was adequate. However, in the case of the national income series there was a significant pulse in the residual autocorrelation function at lag 8, and the fourth-order autoregressive coefficient was highly significant. The national income model was re-estimated with a moving average component at lag 8 included, and this proved to be diagnostically satisfactory.

Plot of autocorrelations

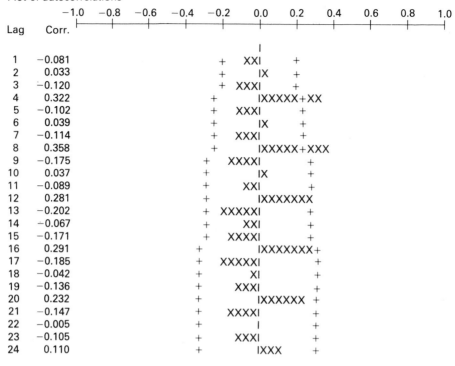

```
             -1.0   -0.8   -0.6   -0.4   -0.2    0.0    0.2    0.4    0.6    0.8    1.0
             |------+------+------+------+------+------+------+------+------+------|
Lag   Corr.
                                                   I
 1   -0.081                                   +   XXI      +
 2    0.033                                   +    IX      +
 3   -0.120                                   +   XXXI     +
 4    0.322                               +        IXXXXX+XX
 5   -0.102                               +   XXXI         +
 6    0.039                               +    IX          +
 7   -0.114                               +   XXXI         +
 8    0.358                               +        IXXXXX+XXX
 9   -0.175                           +   XXXXI             +
10    0.037                           +    IX               +
11   -0.089                           +   XXI               +
12    0.281                           +        IXXXXXXX
13   -0.202                           +  XXXXXI             +
14   -0.067                           +   XXI               +
15   -0.171                           +   XXXXI             +
16    0.291                       +            IXXXXXXX+
17   -0.185                       +  XXXXXI                  +
18   -0.042                       +   XI                     +
19   -0.136                       +   XXXI                   +
20    0.232                       +            IXXXXXX  +
21   -0.147                       +  XXXXI                    +
22   -0.005                       +    I                      +
23   -0.105                       +  XXXI                      +
24    0.110                       +    IXXX                    +
```

Plot of partial autocorrelations

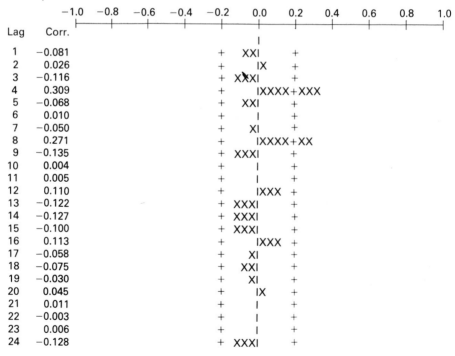

```
             -1.0   -0.8   -0.6   -0.4   -0.2    0.0    0.2    0.4    0.6    0.8    1.0
             |------+------+------+------+------+------+------+------+------+------|
Lag   Corr.
                                                   I
 1   -0.081                                   +   XXI      +
 2    0.026                                   +    IX      +
 3   -0.116                                   +  XXXI      +
 4    0.309                                   +    IXXXX+XXX
 5   -0.068                                   +   XXI       +
 6    0.010                                   +    I        +
 7   -0.050                                   +   XI        +
 8    0.271                                   +    IXXXX+XX
 9   -0.135                                   +  XXXI       +
10    0.004                                   +    I        +
11    0.005                                   +    I        +
12    0.110                                   +    IXXX  +
13   -0.122                                   +  XXXI     +
14   -0.127                                   +  XXXI     +
15   -0.100                                   +  XXXI     +
16    0.113                                   +    IXXX  +
17   -0.058                                   +   XI      +
18   -0.075                                   +  XXI      +
19   -0.030                                   +   XI      +
20    0.045                                   +    IX     +
21    0.011                                   +    I      +
22   -0.003                                   +    I      +
23    0.006                                   +    I      +
24   -0.128                                   +  XXXI     +
```

Figure 6.6 *The autocorrelation and partial autocorrelation functions of changes in the money supply M_3 1963 to 1983*

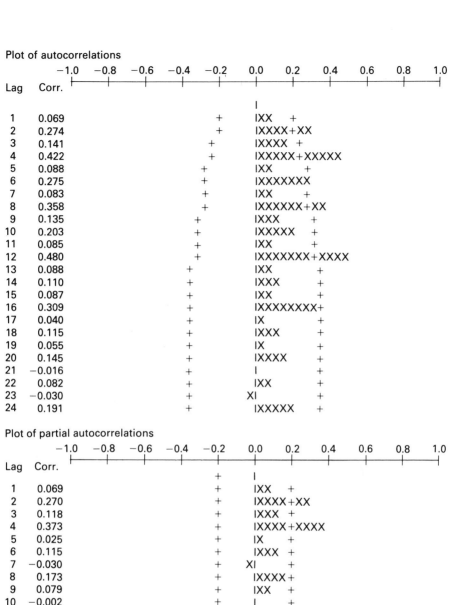

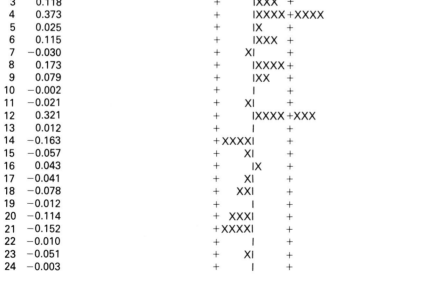

Figure 6.7 *The autocorrelation and partial autocorrelation function of changes in national income 1963 to 1983*

Univariate ARMA models of money supply and national income 1963 to 1983

Money supply

$$\nabla^4 \ln \nabla^1 M_t = (1 - 0.86\, B^4)\alpha_t$$
$$(15.4)$$

RMS $= 0.83$ $\qquad\qquad\qquad\qquad\qquad\qquad Q = 7.0, 20\ \text{d.f.}$

National income

$$(4.1)$$
$$\nabla^4 \ln \nabla^1 Y_t = \frac{(1 - 0.44\, B^8)}{1 + 0.65\, B^4}\, \alpha_t$$
$$(6.6)$$

RMS $= 1.02$ $\qquad\qquad\qquad\qquad\qquad\qquad Q = 20, 20\,\text{d.f.}$

Correlation of AR and MA parameters $= -0.66$.

The estimates of the univariate models appear above. It is apparent from these results and from the Q statistics that the model residuals are white noise in both cases. The parameter estimates in both models were highly significant according to the t statistics. Moreover, the correlation of the autoregressive and moving average coefficients in the national income model indicates that neither parameter was redundant. The autocorrelation functions of the two residual series appear in Figure 6.8, and it can be seen that no statistically significant relationships existed in these functions up to a lag of six years.

Having identified and estimated the univariate models the next stage involved pre-whitening the output series, national income, with the ARIMA model of the input series, M_3, and cross-correlating this with the filtered input series. The cross-correlation function from this procedure appears in Figure 6.9, in which the money supply leads and lags national income for up to six years.

Figure 6.9 provides the clearest evidence that the money supply did not Granger-cause national income in Britain over this twenty-year period. None of the coefficients in which income leads the money supply were remotely statistically significant. However, there was evidence of a weak relationship in reverse, since there is a pulse, which is on the margins of statistical significance, when the money supply led income by one period. This is an intriguing finding, but one which has a perfectly respectable theoretical explanation. Thurow (1983, p. 69) for example points out that if the velocity of circulation of money is highly unstable and rises as the money supply falls, then the latter will not influence national income. Moreover, if changes in national income significantly influence changes in the velocity of circulation of money then the direction of causation between money and income will be the reverse of that postulated by the monetarists. Kaldor (1982) has made a similar point, and presented evidence to show

Plot of autocorrelations of money supply model residuals

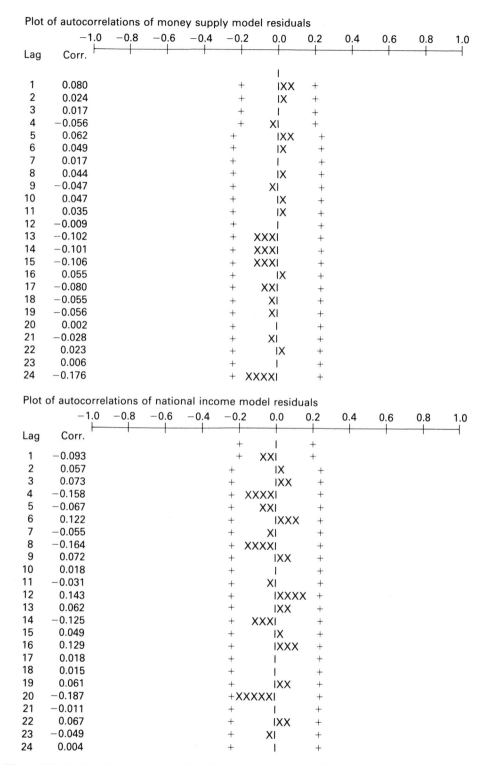

Lag	Corr.	
		−1.0 −0.8 −0.6 −0.4 −0.2 0.0 0.2 0.4 0.6 0.8 1.0
1	0.080	+ IXX +
2	0.024	+ IX +
3	0.017	+ I +
4	−0.056	+ XI +
5	0.062	+ IXX +
6	0.049	+ IX +
7	0.017	+ I +
8	0.044	+ IX +
9	−0.047	+ XI +
10	0.047	+ IX +
11	0.035	+ IX +
12	−0.009	+ I +
13	−0.102	+ XXXI +
14	−0.101	+ XXXI +
15	−0.106	+ XXXI +
16	0.055	+ IX +
17	−0.080	+ XXI +
18	−0.055	+ XI +
19	−0.056	+ XI +
20	0.002	+ I +
21	−0.028	+ XI +
22	0.023	+ IX +
23	0.006	+ I +
24	−0.176	+ XXXXI +

Plot of autocorrelations of national income model residuals

Lag	Corr.	
		−1.0 −0.8 −0.6 −0.4 −0.2 0.0 0.2 0.4 0.6 0.8 1.0
		+ I +
1	−0.093	+ XXI +
2	0.057	+ IX +
3	0.073	+ IXX +
4	−0.158	+ XXXXI +
5	−0.067	+ XXI +
6	0.122	+ IXXX +
7	−0.055	+ XI +
8	−0.164	+ XXXXI +
9	0.072	+ IXX +
10	0.018	+ I +
11	−0.031	+ XI +
12	0.143	+ IXXXX +
13	0.062	+ IXX +
14	−0.125	+ XXXI +
15	0.049	+ IX +
16	0.129	+ IXXX +
17	0.018	+ I +
18	0.015	+ I +
19	0.061	+ IXX +
20	−0.187	+XXXXXI +
21	−0.011	+ I +
22	0.067	+ IXX +
23	−0.049	+ XI +
24	0.004	+ I +

Figure 6.8 *Residual autocorrelation functions for the money supply and national income univariate ARIMA models*

Plot of cross-correlations

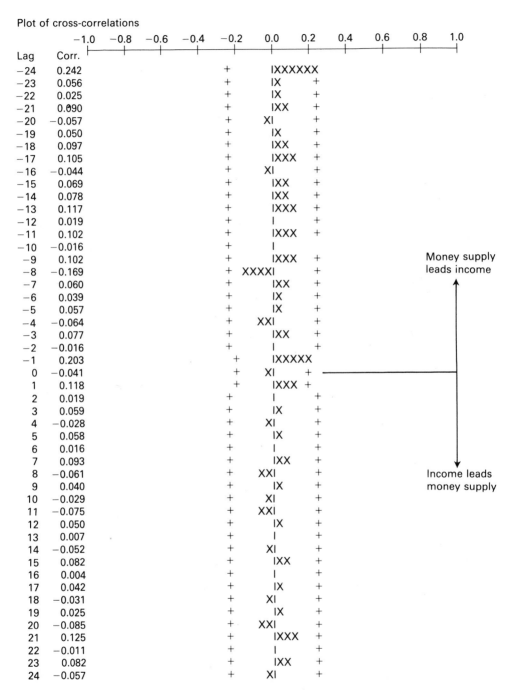

Lag	Corr.
−24	0.242
−23	0.056
−22	0.025
−21	0.090
−20	−0.057
−19	0.050
−18	0.097
−17	0.105
−16	−0.044
−15	0.069
−14	0.078
−13	0.117
−12	0.019
−11	0.102
−10	−0.016
−9	0.102
−8	−0.169
−7	0.060
−6	0.039
−5	0.057
−4	−0.064
−3	0.077
−2	−0.016
−1	0.203
0	−0.041
1	0.118
2	0.019
3	0.059
4	−0.028
5	0.058
6	0.016
7	0.093
8	−0.061
9	0.040
10	−0.029
11	−0.075
12	0.050
13	0.007
14	−0.052
15	0.082
16	0.004
17	0.042
18	−0.031
19	0.025
20	−0.085
21	0.125
22	−0.011
23	0.082
24	−0.057

Figure 6.9 *Cross-correlation function of filtered money supply and pre-whitened national income series 1963 to 1983*

Plot of cross-correlations

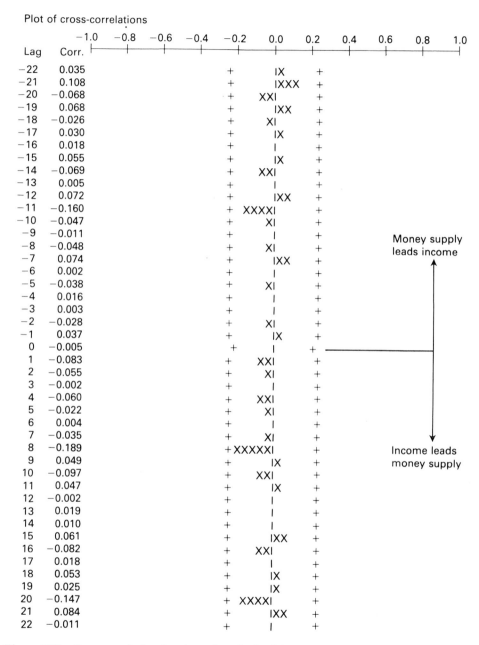

Lag	Corr.
−22	0.035
−21	0.108
−20	−0.068
−19	0.068
−18	−0.026
−17	0.030
−16	0.018
−15	0.055
−14	−0.069
−13	0.005
−12	0.072
−11	−0.160
−10	−0.047
−9	−0.011
−8	−0.048
−7	0.074
−6	0.002
−5	−0.038
−4	0.016
−3	0.003
−2	−0.028
−1	0.037
0	−0.005
1	−0.083
2	−0.055
3	−0.002
4	−0.060
5	−0.022
6	0.004
7	−0.035
8	−0.189
9	0.049
10	−0.097
11	0.047
12	−0.002
13	0.019
14	0.010
15	0.061
16	−0.082
17	0.018
18	0.053
19	0.025
20	−0.147
21	0.084
22	−0.011

Figure 6.10 *Cross-correlation functions of residuals of the transfer function model and the filtered predictor variable*

that the velocity of circulation of money appears to be very unstable in a number of
countries over time. The evidence in Figure 6.9 suggests this is indeed what happened
in Britain over this twenty-year period. The transfer function estimates appear as
follows.

Transfer function model of national income as a predictor
of the money supply 1963 to 1983

$$\nabla^4 \ln \nabla^1 M_t = 0.21 \nabla^4 \ln (B^1) \nabla^1 Y_t + (1 - 0.91\, B^4) a_t$$
$$\qquad\qquad (2.4) \qquad\qquad\qquad\qquad (24.9)$$

RMS $= 0.80$ $Q = 20,20\,\text{d.f.}$

Correlation of parameter estimates $= -0.05$.

A further diagnostic test of the transfer function model was carried out by cross-
correlating the model residuals with the filtered national income series. This was
designed to show up any significant relationships between the input and output
variables which might have been missed. This cross-correlation function appears in
Figure 6.10, and there is a slight suggestion of a significant relationship between the
two series lagged eight periods. The model was re-estimated incorporating this lagged
relationship, but it proved to be non-significant which indicates that the original model
was representationally adequate. Thus national income appears to weakly Granger-
cause the money supply in Britain.

This concludes our review of the Box–Jenkins model-building procedure. It provides
the most comprehensive approach to the estimation of relationships between time
series variables. As we have seen it can produce results which are markedly different
from those postulated by conventional theoretical analysis. Clearly this is a problem
for conventional theory, particularly in economics, which has neglected the question of
exploratory analysis in theory building and all too often has relied on questionable a
priori theoretical analysis. As the Box–Jenkins approach becomes more well-known
this will undoubtedly change.

6.4 APPENDIX: DATA AND SOURCES

The popularity function model

POP_t: government lead is the percentage of respondents supporting the incumbent
party minus the percentage supporting the opposition in response to the question 'If
there was a general election tomorrow, which party would you support?' Don't knows
were excluded, but incliners were included in these percentages. The data are series c
of the voting intentions responses in the Gallup Political Index (London: Gallup
Polls Ltd) various issues.

Unemployment is the wholly unemployed in thousands, seasonally adjusted from various issues of the *Department of Employment Gazette* (London: HMSO).

Inflation is the percentage annual increases in the index of retail prices from various issues of *Economic Trends* (London: HMSO).

The economic shock variable was defined from the list of economic crisis events in Butler and Sloman (1980, pp. 343–345).

The money supply and national income model

The money supply is unadjusted changes in M_3, pp. 146–147. National income is total personal disposable income in current prices, pp. 19–20.

From *Economic Trends* Annual Supplement 1984 (London: HMSO).

REFERENCES FOR PART III

Arestis, P. and Hadjimatheou, G. (1982) *Introducing Macroeconomic Modelling.* London: Macmillan.

Box, G. E. P. and Jenkins, G. M. (1975) *Time Series Analysis: Forecasting and Control* (revised edition). San Francisco: Holden-Day.

Box, G. E. P. and Tiao, G. C. (1975) 'Intervention analysis with application to economic and environmental problems,' *Journal of the American Statistical Association,* **70**, 70–92.

Bray, J. (1971) 'Dynamic Equations for Economic Forecasting with the GDP–Unemployment Relation and the Growth of GDP in the United Kingdom as an Example,' *Journal of the Royal Statistical Society, Series A,* **134**, 167–227.

Butler, D. and Stokes, D. E. (1974) *Political Change in Britain.* London: Macmillan.

Butler, D. and Sloman, A. (1980) *British Political Facts 1900–1979.* London: Macmillan.

Chrystal, K. P. and Alt, J. E. (1981) 'Some problems in formulating and testing a politico–economic model of the United Kingdom,' *Economic Journal,* **91**, 730–736.

Desai, H. (1981) *Testing Monetarism.* London: Frances Pinter.

Feige, E. L. and Pearce, D. K. (1976) 'Economically rational expectations: are innovations in the rate of inflation independent of innovations in measures of monetary and fiscal policy?' *Journal of Political Economy,* **84**, 499–522.

Applications in Political Economy

Feige, E. L. and Pearce, D. K. (1979) 'The casual causal relationship between money and income: some caveats for time series analysis,' *Review of Economics and Statistics*, **61**, 521–533.

Freeman, J. (1983) 'Granger causality and time series analysis of political relationships,' *American Journal of Political Science*, **27**, 327–358.

Frey, B. S. and Schneider, F. (1975) 'On the modelling of politico–economic interdependence,' *European Journal of Political Research*, **3**, 339–360.

Frey, B. S. and Schneider, F. (1978) 'A politico–economic model of the UK,' *Economic Journal*, **88**, 243–253.

Frey, B. S. and Schneider, F. (1981) 'A politico–economic model of the UK: new estimates and predictions,' *Economic Journal*, **91**, 737–740.

Friedman, M. (1956) 'The quantity theory of money: a restatement,' M. Friedman (ed.) *Studies in the Quantity Theory of Money*. Chicago and London: University of Chicago Press (especially pp. 3–24).

Friedman, M. and Schwartz, A. (1963) *A Monetary History of the United States 1867–1960*. Princeton, NJ: Princeton University Press.

Gordon, R. J. (1977) 'World inflation and monetary accommodation in eight countries,' Washington, DC: Brookings Institute, Brookings Papers on Economic Activity.

Granger, C. W. J. (1969) 'Investigating causal relations by econometric models and cross spectral methods,' *Econometrica*, **37**, 424–435.

Haugh, L. D. (1976) 'Checking the independence of two covariance-stationary time series: a univariate residual cross correlation approach,' *Journal of the American Statistical Association*, **71**, 378–385.

Hendry, D. F. (1980) 'Econometrics — Alchemy or Science?' *Economica*, **47**, 387–406.

Jenkins, G. M. (1979) *Practical Experiences with Modelling and Forecasting Time Series*. St. Helier, Jersey: Gwelyn Jenkins and Partners.

Kaldor, N. (1982) *The Scourge of Monetarism*. Oxford: Oxford University Press.

Klein, L. R., Ball, R. J., Hazelwood, R. J. and Vandome, P. (1961) *An Econometric Model of the United Kingdom*. Oxford: Basil Blackwell.

Laidler, D. (1976) 'Inflation in Britain: a monetarist perspective,' *American Economic Review*, **66**, 485–500.

Laidler, D. and Parkin, M. (1975) 'Inflation: a survey,' *Economic Journal*, **85**, 741–809.

Ljung, G. and Box, G. E. P. (1978) 'On a measure of lack of fit in time series models,' *Biometrika*, **65**, 297–304.

McLeod, G. (1983) *Box–Jenkins in Practice*. Lancaster: Gwelyn Jenkins and Partners Ltd.

McSweeney, A. J. (1978) 'The effects of response cost on the behaviour of a million persons: charging for directory assistance in Cincinnati', *Journal of Applied Behavioural Analysis*, **11**, 47–51.

Ormerod, P. A. (1979) *Economic Modelling*. London: Heinemann.

Pierce, D. A. (1977) 'Relationships — and the lack thereof — between economic time series with special reference to money and interest rates,' *Journal of the American Statistical Association*, **72**, 11–22.

Pierce, D. A. and Haugh, L. D. (1977) 'Causality in temporal systems: characterizations and a survey,' *Journal of Econometrics*, **5**, 265–293.

Renton, C. A. (1975) *Modelling the Economy*. London: Heinemann.

Sargent, T. J. (1976) 'A classical macroeconometric model for the United States,' *Journal of Political Economy*, **84**, 207–37.

Sargent, T. J. and Sims, C. A. (1977) 'Business cycle modelling without pretending to have too much a priori economic theory,' in C. A. Sims (ed.) *New Methods in Business Cycle Research*. Minneapolis: Federal Reserve Bank.

Sims, C. A. (1972) 'Money, Income and Causality,' *American Economic Review*, **62**, 540–552.

Sims, C. A. (1980) 'Macroeconomics and Reality,' *Econometrica*, **48**, 1–48.

Thurow, L. (1983) *Dangerous Currents: The State of Economics*. Oxford: Oxford University Press.

Whiteley, P. (1984) 'Inflation, Unemployment and Government Popularity — Dynamic Models for the United States, Britain and West Germany,' *Electoral Studies*, **3**, 3–24.

Whiteley, P. (1986) 'Macroeconomic performance and government popularity in Britain — the short run dynamics', *European Journal of Political Research* (forthcoming).

Index